FOR YOUR EYES ONLY

Published by ECW PRESS
2120 Queen Street East, Suite 200, Toronto, Ontario, Canada M4E 1E2

NATIONAL LIBRARY OF CANADA CATALOGUING IN PUBLICATION DATA

Giammarco, David
For your eyes only : behind the scenes of the Bond films

ISBN 1-55022-499-9

1. James Bond films. 2. Bond, James (Fictitious character)
I. Title.

PN1995.9.J3G42 2002   791.43´75   C2001-904083-0

Developing Editor: Jen Hale
Cover and text design: Tania Craan
Typesetting: Tannice Goddard
Production: Mary Bowness
Printing: Transcontinental

All film stills in this book are from the author's media archives and private collection, unless otherwise noted. The James Bond films are Copyright © Danjaq LLC and United Artists Corporation, licensed by Eon Productions Limited 1962-2002. Ian Fleming's James Bond novels are Copyright © Gildrose Publications Limited. Additional photos come courtesy of Roger Moore, Jerry Pam, George Lazenby, Ken Adam, Tom Mankiewicz, Jane Seymour, Island Outpost, Graham Rye, and Warner Bros/MGM Home Video Canada.

This book is set in Minion, Imago, and Ink Pad

The publication of *For Your Eyes Only* has been generously supported by the Government of Canada through the Book Publishing Industry Development Program. Canadä

DISTRIBUTION

CANADA: Jaguar Book Group, 100 Armstrong Avenue, Georgetown, ON L7G 5S4

UNITED STATES: Independent Publishers Group, 814 North Franklin Street, Chicago, Illinois 60610

PRINTED AND BOUND IN CANADA

ECW PRESS
ecwpress.com

FOR YOUR EYES ONLY

Behind the Scenes of the James Bond Films

David Giammarco

ECW PRESS

For my father, Michael R. Giammarco,
for inspiring my sense of adventure at a very early age

Table of Contents

ACKNOWLEDGMENTS

For their time, consideration, and enormous contributions, I am indebted to the following five men for navigating me firsthand through their world of James Bond: Sean Connery, George Lazenby, Roger Moore, Timothy Dalton, and Pierce Brosnan.

I wish to express my sincere gratitude for the insightful and entertaining interviews with the following talents, both before and behind the cameras, from across the United States and Canada to the United Kingdom, Australia, Spain, Scotland, and France: Guy Hamilton, Ken Adam, Peter Hunt, John Glen, Peter Lamont, Derek Meddings, Tom Mankiewicz, Michael Wilson, Barbara Broccoli, Vic Armstrong, Chris Corbould, Monty Norman, Martin Campbell, Roger Spottiswoode, Michael Apted, Lee Tamahori, Lois Maxwell, Desmond Llewelyn, Honor Blackman, Maud Adams, Jane Seymour, Maryam d'Abo, John Rhys-Davies, Christopher Walken, Grace Jones, Izabella Scorupco, Famke Janssen, Robbie Coltrane, Michelle Yeoh, Judi Dench, Jonathan Pryce, Teri Hatcher, Sean Bean, Götz Otto, Allan Cameron, Dickey Beer, John Richardson, Joe Don Baker, Denise Richards, Sophie Marceau, Robert Carlyle, John Cleese, Bruce Feirstein, Jeffrey Caine, Michael France, Neal Purvis, Robert Wade, John Amiel, Halle Berry, Toby Stephens, Rosamund Pike, Dolph Lundgren, Bo Derek, Michael Bay, Raquel Welch, Sheryl Crow, Kevin Costner, Harrison Ford, and Hugh M. Hefner.

For their valuable behind-the-scenes contributions, I must thank Jerry Pam, Dick Guttman, Guttman & Associates, Hervey/Grimes, Natasha Stevenson, Rona Menashe, Tom Carlile, Charles Juroe, Eric Kops and Amanda Marishinsky of MGM/UA, Barbara Sloan of UNICEF, and Bill Farley at *Playboy*.

Immeasurable appreciation goes out to the entire staff at Eon Productions for their warm hospitality over the years, including Gordon Arnell, Anne Bennett, Amanda Schofield, Patricia O'Reilly, Keith Hamshere, Geraldine Moloney, and the incomparable Geoff Freeman, who all made my numerous trips across the pond such memorable experiences.

Grateful recognition goes out to the CIA's E. Howard Hunt for educating me on Cold War politics and the real world of international espionage.

Special thanks to Hugh Hefner and Bill Farley for all the great times over the years at The Playboy Mansion.

For their valuable cooperation in this endeavor, I wish to thank the following participants: David Haslam and Alexandra Lenhoff, Ron Base, Michelle Revuelta, the Fontainebleau Hotel (Miami Beach), Lisa Cole, Blue Moon Hotel (South Beach), Simon Willis, the Great Eastern Hotel (London), the Landmark Hotel (London), the Caledonian Hotel (Edinburgh), the Monte Carlo Casino (Monaco), Brad Packer of Island Outpost (Jamaica), Rob Lee, Tanya Hvilivitzky, Greg Medulun, and Shane Cawley of Warner Brothers.

Special thanks also to James Adams, George Anthony, Julia Perry, Heather MacGillivray, Natalie Amaral, Greg Ferris, Anne Davidson Muru, Angela Asher, Phillip MacKenzie, Alfred Tonna, Christine Diakos, Rebecca Kollias, Jeff Martin, Chris Mavridis, Noreen Flanagan, Rita Silvan, Beth Waldman, Howard Glassman, Fred Patterson, Jeff Domet, Kimberly Wells, Michael Rechtshaffen, Andria Valentini, and the Honorable William R. McMurtry, Q.C.

Artistic contributions from the immensely talented Jeremy Benning and Melanie Marden are greatly appreciated, as is the fine work of Jen Hale and Jack David at ECW, and editors Richard Bowness and Dallas Harrison.

My sincere appreciation to Kevin Costner for his friendship and support over the years. Thank you, Pierce, for a great friendship of laughs and memorable times. And the encouragement from Sheryl Crow, Alanis Morissette, Raquel Welch, and Bo Derek was very kind — thank you ladies.

My city or mountains . . . Cathy McNeil, thank you for indulging my globe-trotting endeavors and regrettable absences. "The things we do for England."

To Michael Wilson and Barbara Broccoli, thank you for continuing on the legacy with unwavering dedication.

FOREWORD
by E. Howard Hunt

Around the world, the James Bond films have continually been enormously amusing fantasies. To those of us who served in covert operations overseas with the Central Intelligence Agency and before that the Office of Strategic Services, the Bond films often occasioned chuckles. If only our missions were as consistently exciting as those of 007!

Probably less than five percent of any Bond film was rooted in reality; the rest was inspired filmmaking fiction. Sure, we utilized protective gadgets and ingeniously disguised weapons, and, yes, I often found myself engaged in precarious and menacing situations, but more regularly I fought paperwork and internal bureaucracy rather than giant steel-toothed assassins. Furthermore, the presumption was that any exotic beauties encountered on foreign soil were likely to be enemy agents.

An Intelligence agent must have anonymity as his goal; he spends his entire professional life developing a cover identity. If a maître d'or bartender in town knows who you really are, chances are that the enemy does as well. You wouldn't survive long enough to sip your first vodka martini.

Intelligence work offers the enticement of being "in the know." In the CIA, we approached our work with deadly seriousness; there was little time for frivolity as not only our lives but also those of many more around the world were at risk. The stakes were too high to fool around.

It takes years to train an agent. I matured professionally during the Cold War, although nowadays many young people don't want to put that kind of time into sharpening their capabilities. They are required to have certain language skills, but now the demand is away from the Romance languages. It's the exotic tongues, like Korean, Arabic, Swahili, Urdu, and Farsi, that are needed. And in reality, few are willing to go through that learning ordeal for a government salary unless the person is unusually dedicated. Qualified people would like to join but often can't afford to because they can start out at massive corporations with a much better entry level.

The mind-set required for a life of covert operations is rare indeed. Ian Fleming probed that psychological makeup in the James Bond novels and consequently won many fans within Intelligence services, including JFK and my boss Allen Dulles, CIA director from 1953 to 1961. Dulles was intrigued by Fleming's grasp of espionage methods and operations and felt that the Bond films cast a favorable light on the Intelligence services of the Western world.

Although several actors have depicted James Bond, his persona has remained essentially the same. The Bond character brings with it a sense of style and a casual attitude that blend into continental glamor. Even the beauties he beds add to his charisma by becoming "the Bond girls." This fictional character is not troubled with kitchen cares or any activity that could make Bond seem at all commonplace, although the Bond stories do give the reader a basic education in the kingdom of wines and distinctive culinary tastes.

Very quickly, James Bond became a role model for young men intrigued by this upper-class English clubman. His fans return repeatedly to escape the reality of ordinary, routine lives. No matter how vicious the hand-to-hand combat between Bond and the killer-of-the moment, he never fails to win so that good may prevail over evil. Bond has never appealed to hard-core feminists, who would prefer a less masculine hero. Since James Bond embodies so many masculine elements, his character is not about to change.

David Giammarco has produced a unique examination of the Bond legend. He enjoyed unparalleled behind-the-scenes access to the Bond principals, as reflected in this book, making it much more than a rote listing of 007 films.

So here's a toast to James Bond on his 40th anniversary: we'll always need men like him.

E. Howard Hunt
Brown University (1936-40)
United States Navy (1940-45)
OSS (1943-49)
CIA (1949-70)
The White House (1970-72)

INTRODUCTION

As a print and broadcast journalist for over 15 years, I've traveled around the globe many times over, covering leading entertainment and political figures. From legendary actors, directors, and all of Hollywood's A-Listers to prominent leaders from the White House, Senate, Pentagon, FBI, and CIA, I've interviewed and rubbed shoulders with many significant world figures. But some of the greatest thrills of my career have been on the sets of the James Bond films. I've been on countless high-profile movie sets over the years, but nothing compares to the sheer spectacle and excitement of being behind the scenes of 007. No matter how jaded or cynical a person may be, he or she will become the proverbial kid in a candy store walking into the world of a James Bond film. I've witnessed many respected and high-profile visitors turn into giggling school kids on the Bond sets. It's an amusing reaction that is testament to the enduring fascination with Bond, a connection that taps directly into our childhood fantasies, when James Bond became our first awe-inspiring cinema experience.

The first interviews I ever did as a young reporter were with Roger Moore and Sean Connery, and I have spoken with most of the Bond filmmakers and actors from the past four decades. So it seems somehow fitting that I should write this book: not only to share the fascinating stories, anecdotes, and incomparable experiences of being behind the scenes on the 007 films, but also to document the ingenuity and dedication of the many artists who helped craft the indelible world of James Bond.

Ian Fleming's literary creation proved inspired source material, and his spirit has continued to be honored throughout the film series. The same applies to Albert "Cubby" Broccoli and Harry Saltzman, the formidable and tenacious producers who shepherded Bond to the silver screen and never relented in their goal to dazzle moviegoers. Broccoli was instrumental in creating a "Bond family," and that has held true to this day — not only are there many original crew members still working on Bond, but so are their second- and third-generation off-spring. The Bond crew are some of the industry's hardest-working people, and their loyalty to the Bond family is unwavering. They consider it an honor to be part of the Bond legacy and go far beyond the call of duty to uphold those enormous standards. Broccoli's daughter Barbara and his stepson Michael Wilson rose through the ranks and are now at the helm of the Bond series. They have adhered strongly to Cubby's traditions while also smoothly and seamlessly updating Bond for a whole new century of moviegoers. The results have been stellar, as Pierce Brosnan's Bonds have taken the series to all-time box office heights. With this book, I have aimed to connect the past with the present while focusing on this new era of James Bond.

Over the past 40 years, a plethora of 007 imitators have come and gone, each hoping to duplicate the Bond success. Even recent films like Vin Diesel's xxx have tried to blatantly steal the Bond thunder, and Mike Myers' Austin Powers movies have banked on an unabashed spoofing of the series. But in the end, there is only one James Bond. Worldwide audiences are quite discerning when it comes to the genuine article, and they hold a deep-rooted affection for the iconic screen hero. The box office might is unsurpassed, and the record-breaking video and DVD sales of the back catalogue show that the demand for Bond is stronger than ever. So it seems Broccoli and Saltzman displayed remarkable prescience back in 1962 when they named their company Eon, for James Bond has truly stood the test of time.

With the 20th 007 adventure, *Die Another Day*, the phenomenon has reached another milestone in its distinction as the longest-running and most successful film franchise of all time. This year's 40th anniversary of the James Bond films has proven that, indeed, nobody does it better.

David M. Giammarco
September 2002

The Man with the Golden Pen

In 1945, Ian Fleming was asked by a friend what he intended to do after the war. "Why, write the spy novel to end all spy novels" was his rather pithy reply.

Although it would take another eight years before *Casino Royale* was published, the then 37-year-old Naval Intelligence officer had no idea just how prophetic his playful boast would prove. The literary introduction of licensed-to-kill British Secret Service agent James Bond amid the baroque splendor of the Royale-les-Eaux casino was a sly juxtaposition of the dirty business of espionage with the gleaming polish of society's elite. James Bond became as much cloak-and-dagger adventure as a style guide of mannered taste and worldly sophistication. James Bond was also a probe into the darker recesses of the human psyche and a navigational tool of post- World War II geopolitics as polarities shifted and Cold War paranoia ushered in a new era of global war games.

"History is moving pretty quickly these days and the heroes and villains keep on changing places," wrote Fleming in *Casino Royale*. Bond was seen, however, as an incorruptible constant in that murky battle of good versus

The Spymaster: Ian Fleming poses for the camera in 1963.

evil, a reassurance that Britain — and by extension the Western world — were still in good hands. But the literary Bond was also a reluctant hero, his pessimism mastered only by his fierce loyalty to the British Empire. He was a highly skilled and patriotic civil servant willing to die in service to Her Majesty the Queen. Cold, ruthless, and emotionally scarred, Bond was a loner haunted by demons he could never quite vanquish, as hard as he might try through innumerable vices and indulgences.

But at their core, the Bond novels were good old-fashioned adventure stories — plain and simple. They were thrilling excursions that captured the imaginations of readers, providing vicarious sex, violence, and exotic locales for those of more routine lives. Fleming would pen 16 Bond novels in total, and by the time of his death in August 1964 of a heart attack at age 56 there were more than 10 million Bond paperbacks in print in America alone. At the dawn of the 21st century — nearly 50 years since *Casino Royale* first appeared — the figure had risen to over 60 million copies sold. Fleming would enjoy only a brief taste of the worldwide film phenomenon his writing would inspire — he passed away having seen only the first two screen adaptations — which soon became the most successful film franchise in motion picture history. It's been estimated that over half the Earth's population has seen at least one Bond movie, with total box office receipts well past the $3 billion mark so far. As one of the biggest pop culture icons of the 20th century, James Bond has attained a mythological status, an immortality that even his creator's wild imagination would have summarily dismissed as completely implausible.

Born into privilege on May 28, 1908, in Mayfair, Ian Lancaster Fleming was the second of four sons of Major Valentine Fleming, a Conservative Member of Parliament who was killed at the Battle of the Somme in 1916, when Ian was only eight years old. Winston Churchill was one of the notables among the Fleming family's circle of friends and, in fact, wrote the major's obituary for the London *Times*. Ian's mother, Evelyn, was a talented violinist who often gave recitals at Pitt House, the Flemings' Georgian mansion on the brow of Hampstead Heath. Ian's paternal grandfather, Robert Fleming, was a private banker and an associate of J.P. Morgan, who had backed the Anglo-Persian Oil Company. But young Ian would soon rebel against the staid traditions and grand expectations that distinguished his affluent and influential lineage.

Entering Eton at age 13, Fleming excelled at athletics but was often a troublemaker and his obstinacy frequently invoked the ire of the headmaster. An apt student who was easily bored, Fleming had to drop out of Eton (like Bond) and was sent by his mother to various private schools in England and Austria. Fleming had already gained a reputation for girls, cars, and mischief when he entered Sandhurst, England's military academy, in 1926. He proved himself a fine marksman — he shot for Sandhurst against West Point — but Fleming's apathy towards army life led him to drop out after only one term. With an eye on a diplomatic career, Fleming then moved on to the Munich and Geneva universities, where he cultivated his writing skills, learned French and German, and indulged in his favorite pastimes of skiing, climbing mountains, and chasing women. But after failing to make the grade on the Foreign Office examination (he came in 25th out of the 62 applicants), Fleming abandoned the hope of becoming a diplomat and returned to London, where a family friend offered him a job at the Reuters news agency.

Fleming would soon make his name as a reporter in March 1933 at the age of 25, when he was sent to Moscow to cover the famous trials of six British Metro-Vickers engineers accused by the Stalin regime of spying and sabotage. Inexperienced, but with his imaginative flair, Fleming impressed his superiors with a knack for details and a keen grasp of international espionage. Fleming even devised an elaborate scheme to outsmart his fellow reporters by disabling their telephones, thereby beating them to the punch once the verdict was read.

But Fleming left Reuters less than a year later — turning down a posting in Shanghai — to make himself some money. He went to work for a London stock brokerage firm, and throughout the rest of the '30s Fleming dedicated himself to the world of high finance. But it seemed Fleming was far more concerned with his swinging bachelor lifestyle, reveling in fine food, liquor, gambling, and a string of female beauties. However, in March 1939, Fleming returned to Moscow at the behest of British trade minister Robert Hudson for a Russian trade mission. Ostensibly, Fleming's duties were as a reporter for the *Times* of London, but actually he was secretly working for the Foreign Office, helping prepare an estimate of potential Soviet military strength and morale. With war nearing, the Secret Service had begun quietly enlisting perceptive young men, and it turned out Fleming's older brother Peter — who had scored great success with two travel books, *Brazilian Adventure* and *News from Tartary* in the 1930s — had already been working part time for Military Intelligence in the British SOE (Special Operations Executive).

By all accounts, Ian Fleming's spycraft skills were sufficient enough to impress Rear Admiral John Godfrey — Director of Naval Intelligence — who invited the 31-year-old Fleming to lunch at London's Carlton Grill in May 1939. The meeting was a success, and for the next two months Fleming was a frequent visitor to the Admiralty, immersing himself in the procedure and protocol of Naval Intelligence. By August that year, Fleming was named personal assistant to the Director of Naval Intelligence (DNI), assuming the rank of lieutenant. By the time war was declared on September 3, Fleming was promoted to commander (as Bond would be too), and the distinction of his rank would be forever commemorated by the three gold bands adorning his (and Bond's) custom-made Morland cigarettes he purchased from a small tobacconist's shop on Grosvenor Street in London.

Headquartered in Room 39 — his office in the nerve center of Intelligence at the Admiralty — Fleming enthusiastically embraced his new job.

22 Ebury Street: Ian Fleming's stately London home — located a mere stone's throw away from Buckingham Palace — until his death in 1964. Note the Latin inscription above his door (right).

It seemed the restless playboy had finally found something other than girls, gambling, and exotic cars to hold his interest. Fleming's thirst for adventure and vivid imagination dovetailed nicely with his new position in covert mission planning, as his tasks of propaganda and deception schemes evolved into full-scale military operations.

"He [Fleming] always tended to be presented with the unusual jobs that no ordinary department would take responsibility for," recalled Admiral Sir Norman Denning, a postwar Director of Naval Intelligence who crossed paths with Fleming frequently during the war. "A lot of Ian's ideas were just plain crazy . . . but a lot of them had just that glimmer of possibility in them. Ian was the combination of an ideas man and a 'fixer'!" Fleming would soon segue from his administrative position into the field, participating in numerous covert operations — many of which still remain cloaked in mystery. Decades later, it would be revealed that Fleming worked closely with Canadian-born millionaire and British spymaster Sir William Stephenson, whose Ultra network had broken the German diplomatic code in 1939. On one such mission, Stephenson — who represented British Intelligence in the U.S. as Director of British Security Coordination (BSC) during World War II — participated with Fleming in the surreptitious microfilming of a Japanese codebook, which they secretly removed from a locked safe located in the Rockefeller Center offices of the Japanese consul general. Stephenson was perhaps better known by his code name: Intrepid. His daring exploits — which earned him a knighthood after the war — would be chronicled later in such books as *The Quiet Canadian* and *A Man Called Intrepid*.

On another transatlantic visit later in the war, Fleming ended up in Canada on the outskirts of Toronto, where Bill Stephenson had converted an old farmhouse into a secret training base for British agents. Code-named "Camp X," the facility specialized in the art of sabotage and subversion, and Fleming participated in exercises ranging from infiltrating the main Toronto power station and placing a dummy bomb to nautical missions involving a moored tanker in Lake Ontario. The latter exercise was the Canadian spy camp's final test, which involved a long underwater swim in the dark of night to affix limpet mines to the hull of the ship. Fleming was one of the few who actually succeeded in attaching the explosives firmly in place and escaping back to shore undetected. It was a stunt that would later surface in the plot of *Live and Let Die*, as would a number of other Camp X activities in later Bond novels.

In Washington, Fleming also forged a friendship with General "Wild Bill" Donovan, whom President Roosevelt had appointed "Coordinator of Information." Fleming spent a few days in Donovan's Washington home, helping write the original charter of the Office of Strategic Services — forerunner of the Central Intelligence Agency. Donovan presented Fleming with a gift of a .38 Colt revolver bearing the inscription "For Special Services." Though most of Fleming's espionage activity was primarily cerebral, he always carried with him a commando-fighting knife — engraved with his name and rank — and a fountain pen which he claimed contained tear gas. Fleming had a particular affinity for guns, knives, and gadgets, and he maintained regular contact with technical specialists like Charles Fraser-Smith, a "Q"-like figure who crafted such gadgets as saw-edged shoelaces and hollowed-out golf balls that were used to send messages to prisoners of war.

Years later, it would also be revealed that Fleming was responsible for creating the No. 30 Assault Unit, an intelligence-gathering commando team he affectionately dubbed "my Red Indians." Fleming's elite corps of Royal Marines — or "Fleming's Private Navy," as they were nicknamed within Intelligence circles — accompanied attack troops for the purpose of seizing enemy codes and equipment. Fleming personally trained them in safe-blowing, lock-picking, and plastic explosives, but more vital was his expertise in recognizing and capturing ciphers, codebooks, secret directives, and new weapons. The No. 30 Assault Unit succeeded in a number of key raids, retrieving the order of battle of the enemy fleets. After the war, Admiral Godfrey — later serving as a model for Bond's boss "M" — would remark of Fleming's stellar service, "Ian should have been director [of Naval Intelligence] and I his adviser."

When the war ended in 1945, Commander Fleming joined the Kemsley Newspapers as foreign manager, charged with keeping track of foreign correspondents and advising at editorial conferences at the *London Sunday Times* — a position he would hold until 1959.

Fleming's contract stipulated that he receive a two-month vacation each winter, which he faithfully spent in Jamaica every year from 1946 until his death. He had fallen in love with the island after visiting during an Anglo-American naval conference in 1944 and shortly thereafter asked his good friend, American millionaire Ivar Bryce, to purchase a plot of beachfront property on his behalf. Fleming's vacation home was soon built above a private cove near the tiny banana port of Oracabessa on Jamaica's beautiful north coast. He christened the property "Goldeneye," a nod to the code name of one of his secret World War II operations, which involved overseeing stay-behind allied agents in Spanish ports in the event the Iberian Peninsula was overrun by the Germans, and also the title of the Carson McCullers novel *Reflections in a Goldeneye.*

It would be here, in the sun-drenched sojourns of Fleming's annual retreat, that a legend would be born. Fleming appropriated the name of his fictional hero from a favorite book that graced his coffee table — *Birds of*

Bond's Birthplace: Ian Fleming's three-bedroom house Goldeneye on Jamaica's north shore, offering sweeping vistas of the nearby reef and Caribbean ocean.

the West Indies — by American ornithologist James Bond. "I wanted the simplest, dullest, plainest-sounding name I could find — James Bond seemed perfect," Fleming would later explain. "I was determined that my secret agent should be as anonymous a personality as possible. It struck me that his name — brief, unromantic, and yet very masculine — was just what I needed." Inspired by his idyllic Caribbean paradise and fueled by a need to "take my mind off the shock of getting married at the age of 43" after years of much-cherished bachelorhood, Fleming pounded out *Casino Royale* on his portable 20-year-old Royal typewriter in less than 10 weeks. On March 24, 1952 — six days after completing the manuscript — Fleming married Lady Anne Rothermere in a civil ceremony in Port Maria, Jamaica, witnessed by Fleming pal and neighbor Noel Coward. At the time, Anne was already pregnant with the couple's son Caspar.

Anne Rothermere was a beautiful, strong-willed, and cultured socialite who had gained notoriety for her marriage to newspaper magnate Lord

Rothermere as well as her infamous luncheons and dinners that boasted the literary world's biggest names. The morning after exchanging their vows, Ian and Anne Fleming flew back to London and with them the manuscript of *Casino Royale*. Over lunch with friend and author William Plomer, Fleming mentioned that he had written a novel. Plomer — who had worked with Fleming in Intelligence during the war — was now associated with British publisher Jonathan Cape and, with his curiosity piqued, offered to give Fleming's manuscript a read.

Plomer suggested some minor revisions, but overall he found it a compelling thriller and recommended its publication to Jonathan Cape. Fleming celebrated by buying himself a new typewriter — but no ordinary model by any means. It was a rare gold-plated version of the Royal Quiet de Luxe, which cost $174. Perhaps the rather extravagant indulgence foreshadowed Fleming's soon-to-be Midas touch. (Forty-two years later, the infamous typewriter sold for £50,000 at a Christie's auction in London. The anonymous buyer was rumored to be Pierce Brosnan, although the actor has since denied it.) And so it was, on April 13, 1953, that James Bond made his debut in England to mostly positive reviews, although in its first year *Casino Royale* sold a mere 7,000 copies. American reaction was even less enthusiastic, as three prominent U.S. publishers turned down the book for its lack of "believability."

But Macmillan Publishing finally took a chance on Bond and published *Casino Royale* in 1954. It sold fewer than 4,000 copies in the U.S. that year, yet Fleming had already written a follow-up entitled *Live and Let Die*, which took Bond to Harlem, Florida, and Jamaica. All the while, Fleming continued to indulge in journalism as a columnist for the *Sunday Times*, where his various foreign assignments would further inspire and shape the burgeoning world of 007. Despite mediocre sales in the U.S., Fleming consistently churned out a new Bond thriller every winter escape. Remarked Fleming: "Would these books have been born if I had not been living in the gorgeous vacuum of a Jamaican holiday? I doubt it."

Intrigued by the possibilities of a fresh television hero, the CBS network optioned *Casino Royale* from Fleming for its weekly live telecast *Climax Mystery Theater*. American Barry Nelson — not Sean Connery — would be the first actor to portray 007, and Peter Lorre — as Soviet master spy Le Chiffre — became the first Bond villain. But the hour-long pilot failed miserably. Hampered by an embarrassingly minuscule budget and ridiculous Americanization of the British agent, the October 1954 broadcast barely registered with critics or in the ratings. CBS quickly pulled the plug on plans for a weekly series.

Disappointed, and anxious for some extra income, Fleming ended up selling the movie rights for *Casino Royale* to film director Gregory Ratoff for a mere $6,000. Hopes for a big-screen treatment, however, soon evaporated as Bond failed to garner much interest in Hollywood. This was the case again in 1956, when actor Ian Hunter's purchase of a six-month option on Fleming's third novel, *Moonraker*, also came up snake eyes. Further stabs at film and TV productions followed throughout the rest of the '50s, but all seemed to stall in the early planning stages. Spurred on somewhat by the cursory interest, Fleming continued penning new 007 escapades, confidant Bond would bring him the commercial success he longed for. In a letter to his New York agent, Fleming wrote: "I have an idea that one of these days the film and television rights to James Bond and his adventures may be worth quite a lot of money." He never fathomed, however, just how lucrative those rights would become.

With the publication of his sixth novel, *Dr. No,* in 1958, Fleming started sensing an increasing literary respect for his spy thrillers. The fan base was slowly expanding across cultural and ideological divides as the groundswell of interest grew for the exploits of James Bond. Notables from Somerset Maugham and Raymond Chandler to Prince Phillip and CIA Director Allen Dulles all became vocal champions of Fleming's work.

John F. Kennedy was another Bond devotee, and a chance Washington encounter between Fleming and Senator Kennedy on March 13, 1960, resulted in an invitation to Kennedy's Georgetown residence that evening. Over dinner, talk ranged from American politics to Fleming's unique theories on dealing with Cuba and the Soviet Union. Their lively exchange that night left a lasting impact on Kennedy, who was at once charmed by Fleming and puzzled by some of his more fanciful ideas. Fleming went on to develop a relationship with the Kennedy family, sending inscribed copies of

Just another day at the office for Hugh M. Hefner, one of James Bond's original proponents in the early 1960s. (right) Author David Giammarco with Hugh Hefner at the Playboy Mansion

his books to JFK and Robert Kennedy as well as to their sister Eunice. The bond between JFK and Fleming would prove most fortuitous for Fleming when, in the spring of 1961, President Kennedy released to *Life Magazine* a list of his top 10 favorite books. Right up there with the biographies of world leaders and intellectual nonfiction was Ian Fleming's *From Russia with Love*. It was a big boost to Fleming's career, and almost overnight James Bond became an American sensation. Fleming would return the favor later in *The Man with the Golden Gun* by having Bond read Kennedy's *Profiles in Courage*.

The nudging of Bond into the cultural zeitgeist had begun, fueled in no small way by Hugh Hefner's enthusiastic embrace of the stylish secret agent, whose sophisticated taste, sexual freedom, and wolfish charm was the archetype of the *Playboy* philosophy. "Two of the major cultural phenomena to come out of the 1960s were *Playboy* and James Bond, and they were very closely related," explained Hefner during an early evening chat at the Playboy Mansion West. Dressed in his de rigueur smoking jacket and silk pajamas, Hefner recalled the early alliance formed between them. "In the late '50s, Ian Fleming came to Chicago, and one of our editors took him on a tour around

Framed reminder of Ian Fleming displayed inside Goldeneye's main house.

the city because he was doing research for his book *The Wicked Cities* and wanted to see some of the major gang-land crime sites, like the site of the St. Valentine's Day Massacre." Fleming stayed for dinner that night at the mansion, and Hefner remembered Fleming telling him that, "'if James Bond was a real person, he would definitely be a *Playboy* subscriber.'"

The two titans of titillation struck up a friendship, and, when Hefner expressed plans for acquiring a resort hotel in Jamaica and building a Playboy club, Fleming wrote him a letter, alerting Hefner to the destructive force of Jamaica's hurricane season. *Playboy* would end up becoming the first American magazine to publish James Bond when Fleming's short story "The Hildebrand Rarity" debuted in the March 1960 issue. The tradition continued as *Playboy* began serializing the novels prepublication, starting with *On Her Majesty's Secret Service* in April, May, and June of 1963. "It's funny, I remember my editorial director wasn't happy with the title of *On Her Majesty's Secret Service* and wanted to change the name," chuckled Hefner. "And I said, 'No, you can't change the title — that's what they're going to be using on the book!'" Later, *The Property of a Lady, You Only Live Twice, The Man with the Golden Gun,* and *Octopussy* would all appear first in the pages of *Playboy* magazine. It was a symbiotic swinging '60s relationship made in 007th heaven that has continued to this day.

Fleming reveled in the attention his mythical alter ego was receiving, knowing full well the payoff of big-film money — something which had eluded him for so long — was finally close at hand. And he was right. But perhaps Fleming sensed the reward would arrive too late in the game, for he once wrote that "Gamblers, just before they die, are often given a great golden streak of luck."

Fleming's Bond Books:

Year indicates U.K. First Edition

1953 *Casino Royale*
1954 *Live and Let Die*
1955 *Moonraker*
1956 *Diamonds Are Forever*
1957 *From Russia with Love*
1958 *Dr. No*
1959 *Goldfinger*
1960 *For Your Eyes Only*
1961 *Thunderball*
1962 *The Spy Who Loved Me*
1963 *On Her Majesty's Secret Service*
1964 *You Only Live Twice*
1965 *The Man with the Golden Gun*
1966 *Octopussy*

The Short Stories:

1960 *For Your Eyes Only* "From a View to a Kill, Quantum of Solace, Risico, The Hildebrand Rarity"
1966 *Octopussy* "The Living Daylights, The Property of a Lady"

Fleming's Other Works:

1957 *The Diamond Smugglers* (nonfiction)
1963 *Thrilling Cities* (nonfiction)
1964 *Chitty Chitty Bang Bang*

His Words Were Their Bond: Broccoli & Saltzman

"What Ian Fleming wrote were paperbacks for all the little suburban people who spent every day travelling backwards and forwards to work on a train and needed something for a thrill," opined British filmmaker Peter Hunt, who, as one of the original architects of James Bond's cinematic foray, laid an indelible foundation upon which all subsequent Bonds would be built. "Fleming's books were written very much in that fast, paperback pulp style. So I remember I said to myself, 'Well, why can't we have *paperback films*?'"

As editor of the first five Bond films and director of the sixth, Peter Hunt was instrumental in crafting the visual style and brisk pace that immediately distinguished James Bond from other films. Along with Ken Adam's inspired production design, Terence Young's stylish direction, Maurice Binder's sensual title sequences, and John Barry's electric 007 scoring, a unique behind-the-scenes alchemy was achieved that would forever transform cinema. Of course, all the elements would never have fused so brilliantly were it not for two hungry and tenacious producers eager to jump-start their careers: Albert R. Broccoli and Harry Saltzman.

Spy vs. Spy: Ian Fleming's early apprehensions about Sean Connery playing his literary hero were long vanquished by the time of this conversation on the set of From Russia With Love in 1963

By 1961, Ian Fleming had grown weary of the many failed attempts to bring James Bond to the big screen. The British film industry had shown little interest in Bond during the '50s, preferring instead the grim social realism of kitchen sink dramas and World War II adventures. And across the pond, America's flirting with the idea had yielded disappointing results. The closest Fleming came to a major deal occurred when his trusted friend Ivar Bryce introduced him to Kevin McClory, an eccentric young Irish director who had just completed his first film — *The Boy and the Bridge.* Fleming was impressed by McClory's enthusiasm, and the three of them soon decided to put together their own Bond production: Fleming would pen the screenplay, Bryce would produce, and McClory would direct. The project would film in the Bahamas, where they would benefit from the Eady Subsidy Plan — a financial incentive for filmmakers shooting in Britain and the Commonwealth countries.

Instead of adapting one of Fleming's already existing novels, it was decided to create an entirely new adventure, one with a more exaggerated cinematic bent. Aided by screenwriter Jack Whittingham, Fleming and McClory fleshed out the tentatively titled *Latitude 78 West*, which involved the hijacking of atomic bombs from a jet aircraft.

But their collaboration collapsed when circumstances forced Bryce to withdraw as financier, and McClory couldn't persuade any U.S. studios to pick up the proposed $3 million project. It was a failed effort that would have enormous repercussions, haunting Fleming the rest of his life and proving a never-ending thorn in the side of future Bond producers for decades. With the *Latitude 78 West* project suddenly dead in the water, Fleming returned to Goldeneye in 1960. He began work on his eighth Bond novel and introduced the sinister crime organization known as SPECTRE — Special Executive for Counterintelligence, Terrorism, Revenge, and Extortion — run by Ernst Stavro Blofeld. But some elements of the *Latitude* treatment lingered in Fleming's mind, and he incorporated them into the book he entitled *Thunderball*.

When McClory read an advance copy of *Thunderball* in early 1961, he and Whittingham sued Fleming for infringing on their joint copyright. Since there had been no definitive agreement signed by the parties during their preproduction work on the project, publication of the novel proceeded. However, the judge in the case eventually awarded McClory and Whittingham screen rights to *Thunderball* as well as cocredit on all future editions of the novel. The bitter court battle — which would drag on for three years — took a severe toll on Fleming. He suffered his first heart attack on April 12, 1961, only days into the long-running ordeal.

Then in June 1961, as he lay recuperating at the London Clinic, Fleming finally received word that James Bond was indeed going to live twice. Canadian film producer Harry Saltzman sent Fleming a get-well greeting and a note, detailing plans for a James Bond deal at United Artists in the States. It was the best news Fleming had received in a long time.

Born in Saint John, New Brunswick, Saltzman spent his formative years in Sherbrooke, Quebec, and then New York City, where he developed a strong passion for vaudeville. At 15, Saltzman ran away from home and joined a traveling circus, where he was schooled in the art of flashy showmanship. It would be a skill put to good use when he began booking and promoting his own vaudeville acts up and down the East Coast. He eventually upped the ante by moving to Paris, where he continued his vaudeville endeavors in the French music halls. When World War II broke out, Saltzman joined the Royal Canadian Air Force and later the Office of Strategic Services (oss), reportedly serving as an Intelligence field officer in Europe.

After the war, Saltzman moved back to New York City and resumed booking entertainment acts, eventually segueing into the burgeoning world of television. By the mid-'50s, Saltzman had produced *Robert Montgomery Presents* and *Captain Gallant of the Foreign Legion* for American TV. But with his sights set on the film business, Saltzman figured he could make a bigger splash in a smaller pond by moving to England, where he soon formed an independent production company with director Tony Richardson and playwright John Osborne in 1956. Dubbed Woodfall Productions, their partnership was responsible for three of England's most critically acclaimed films of the era: the adaptation of Osborne's play *Look Back in Anger* (with Richard Burton), *The Entertainer* (with Laurence Olivier), and *Saturday Night and Sunday Morning*, which not only made a star of a young Albert Finney, but was also hailed as the finest of the kitchen-sink dramas dominating British cinema at the time.

Despite the success of his social realism films, Saltzman sensed that moviegoers would soon be looking towards more escapist fare, and he wanted to be at the forefront. His plans, however, conflicted with those of his partners', and Saltzman ended up resigning from Woodfall in late 1960. Seeing a potential bonanza in the James Bond novels, Saltzman arranged to meet with Ian Fleming through their mutual lawyer — Brian Lewis. At London's West End club Les Ambassadeurs, Saltzman sold Fleming on a deal of $50,000 for a six-month option on all the Bond novels (except for *Casino Royale*, which Fleming had already sold to Gregory Ratoff). Saltzman also pledged to pay Fleming an additional $100,000 per Bond film made, plus a percentage of the net profits (reportedly five percent).

But Saltzman's ambitious dreams for a big-screen Bond bonanza were quickly dashed in the wake of the apathetic response from financial backers. Bond was still considered an unproven commodity at that point, and, with significant capital invested, Saltzman was at wit's end as his six-month option was rapidly running out. With only weeks remaining on the deal, Saltzman received a pivotal telephone call. His friend, writer Wolf Mankowitz, told him that another producer — Albert R. Broccoli — was also a Bond enthusiast and eager to secure the rights. Broccoli — who, along with his producing partner Irving Allen, had produced such films as *The Cockleshell Heroes* and *The Trials of Oscar Wilde* — had coincidentally tried to purchase the Bond rights from Fleming two years earlier, but the venture had been quickly vetoed by Irving Allen, who didn't view Bond as a viable screen endeavor. Broccoli had severed their partnership shortly thereafter and decided to take a solo go at producing. When Mankowitz arranged a meeting between Broccoli and Saltzman in June 1961, Broccoli was determined to buy out Harry Saltzman's Bond option. But Saltzman had other ideas.

Born in Queens, New York, in 1909, Albert Romolo Broccoli became better known to his friends simply as "Cubby" — a nickname given to him as a youngster by a cousin. Cubby's father and uncle had emigrated from Calabria, Italy, at the turn of the century and began importing the vegetable that bore their name. Albert spent his childhood working in the family's garden, where he would help pick, wash, and pack the vegetables at their Astoria farm and then deliver them to the produce market in Harlem via horse-drawn cart.

But laboring as a broccoli farmer was a family tradition young Albert did not wish to continue. After his father, Giovanni, died, Albert began taking odd jobs in New York and eventually went to work selling coffins at his cousin's casket company, later becoming manager of the establishment. It was a comfortable living, but Broccoli had loftier dreams. At the invitation of his Los Angeles-based cousin Pat DeCicca (who was married to actress Thelma Todd), Broccoli moved to Hollywood in the mid-1930s, where he supported himself selling beauty supplies and Christmas trees. He would soon land a job in the mailroom at 20th Century Fox, and later a chance encounter with the legendary Howard Hughes would provide him with an entree into film production. Hughes was producing the 1941 film

A candid 1976 shot of Bond producer "Cubby" Broccoli on location in Egypt for The Spy Who Loved Me.

The Outlaw, starring his girlfriend, Jane Russell, and offered Broccoli a job as an assistant to the director, Howard Hawks. After that, Broccoli continued to work on various films before joining the war effort in 1942 by enlisting in the U.S. Navy, where he eventually earned his lieutenant's stripes.

Returning to Hollywood after VJ Day in September 1945, Broccoli joined Famous Artists, a thriving talent agency run by Charles K. Feldman. Always a quick study, Broccoli learned the business side of Hollywood and soon became a successful agent in his own right. Broccoli started making some real money and would often gamble it away in Las Vegas, accompanied sometimes by pal Howard Hughes. After years of brokering deals and contract negotiations, Broccoli was itching to tackle the more creative aspects of filmmaking — namely producing. But there was little room in Hollywood at the time for independent producers. Frustrated by the lack of opportunity, Broccoli teamed up with an old high school friend — Polish-born director Irving Allen — and the pair moved to London, where they established a company called Warwick Pictures (they took the name from the New York hotel they stayed at while formulating their game plan).

Armed with their considerable Hollywood contacts, the benefit of Britain's Eady Subsidy plan, and Howard Hughes agreeing to bankroll their first film, Broccoli and Allen signed Alan Ladd to a three-picture contract

(left to right) "Cubby" Broccoli, Roger Moore, and director John Glen relax in Greece on the set of 1981's For Your Eyes Only. (Photo courtesy of John Glen)

and secured Columbia Pictures as their principal distributor. Their first film was *The Red Beret* in 1953, which turned a tidy profit and gave them a foothold as producers. Incidentally, *The Red Beret* would prove significant in another respect: its crew included future James Bond director Terence Young, screenwriter Richard Maibaum, and cinematographer Ted Moore.

Over the next seven years, Warwick churned out 20 films, mostly slick adventure movies — among them were *Hell below Zero, No Time to Die, The Cockleshell Heroes, Interpol,* and *The Killers of Kilimanjaro* — and established expat Americans Broccoli and Allen as Britain's reigning independent producers. But the enormous commercial failure of 1960's *The Trials of Oscar Wilde* dealt a major financial blow to Warwick, further deteriorating the already strained relationship between the two men. Later that year, they agreed to dissolve their partnership and went their separate ways. Broccoli had never quite gotten over Allen's refusal to support him on the James Bond proposal in 1958 — something he was quite passionate about, so, when the opportunity arose again through Saltzman, Broccoli jumped at the chance to make his mark as a solo producer.

But Saltzman wasn't interested in selling Broccoli his screen option on James Bond. Despite his discouraging failure to secure a production deal, Saltzman was still anxious to produce a 007 series — so he suggested to Broccoli they go into business together. With only 28 days left on the option, Broccoli agreed to a 50-50 partnership split with Saltzman, and they formed Eon Productions (long believed to stand for "Everything or Nothing" — although that assumption has been challenged by Broccoli's stepson Michael Wilson).

Well acquainted with the studio hierarchy at Columbia Pictures, Broccoli approached them first. But Coumbia's studio heads, like their many predecessors, turned the Bond project down. With time quickly ticking away, Broccoli then hastily arranged a meeting with Arthur B. Krim, the president of United Artists. Broccoli and Saltzman, as well as their wives, Dana and Jacqueline, and Broccoli's 12-month-old daughter, Barbara, flew to New York on June 20, 1961. Walking into their meeting the following day, Broccoli and Saltzman were surprised to find 10 members of the UA board of directors waiting for them, including chairman Robert Benjamin. Fortunately, a young David Picker — who had just been promoted to head of production — was also in attendance. Picker was very familiar with Fleming's work and an admitted James Bond fan. Buoyed by Picker's enthusiasm, which was echoed by UA London chief Bud Orenstein, Krim hammered out a six-picture deal with Broccoli and Saltzman in less than an hour. Even more remarkably, it was all sealed by a handshake.

Now that they were officially in the Bond business, Broccoli and Saltzman's next step was to form Danjaq (an abbreviation of their wives' first names, Dana and Jaqui). Danjaq was a Swiss corporation that would hold the Bond film rights, while Eon Productions — a subsidiary of Danjaq — would actually produce the films. Broccoli and Saltzman proposed a budget of $1.1 million for the first Bond film, but United Artists trimmed it back to just under a million dollars. However, they were all in agreement that *Thunderball* should be the first 007 adventure to launch the series — it was the most recent of Fleming's novels, and the plot line, which involved the theft of atomic bombs from NATO, added a thrilling Cold War relevance. But the escalating McClory-Whittingham *Thunderball* litigation against Fleming presented too many legal entanglements, so they chose Fleming's 1958 novel, *Dr. No*, instead.

Screenwriter Richard Maibaum — who had already worked for Broccoli on a number of his Warwick adventure films — was signed on to adapt the novel alongside Wolf Mankowitz (who would later drop out of the project and request his name be removed from the credits). Meanwhile, the search for an appropriate British director with a strong visual style began in earnest. Original choice Guy Hamilton (who would later direct *Goldfinger*) was interested, but family concerns prevented him from a long absence on location in Jamaica. Directors like Ken Hughes, Guy Green, and Bryan Forbes were also offered the job, but all politely declined. Finally, Broccoli and Saltzman settled on Terence Young, who had helmed some of Broccoli's earlier films for Warwick. Little did they realize what a pivotal role Young would play in transforming Bond into a cinema icon.

With the main crew slowly assembling in the late summer of 1961, the only question remaining was who would play James Bond. Broccoli was adamant that he be an Englishman but one who was rugged and not afraid of fisticuffs in order to appeal to American audiences. Cary Grant expressed interest, as did James Mason, but both were reluctant to commit to a series of 007 films. Other names that surfaced as possibilities were Richard Burton, Peter Finch, Rex Harrison, Trevor Howard, and Fleming's personal choice: David Niven. Niven had been a friend of Fleming since World War II, when the actor also had served in the British Secret Services. But a limited budget, coupled with their desire for a long-term commitment, made it clear to Broccoli and Saltzman that they'd have to forgo a big star in favor of an unknown whom they could cultivate in the role. Up-and-coming actors like Patrick McGoohan and Richard Johnson were considered, as was a young Roger Moore, who also had Fleming's approval.

Meanwhile, speculation was growing in the British press as to who would land the coveted role. A poll in the *Daily Express* invited readers to vote on their favorite choices, and among the top contenders were Roger Moore — who by then was already signed to a TV contract and therefore no longer available — and a little-known Scottish actor named Sean Connery.

Connery had already been brought to the attention of Broccoli and Saltzman through editor Peter Hunt, who suggested the actor as a possibility in October 1961. "I had actually known Sean a long while because when we were making *The Admirable Crichton* [1957] Sean Connery and our star of the film, Diane Cilento, were having an affair," recalled Hunt. "They were practically living together, so I used to see him quite often. Flash ahead a few years, and one night a group of us were having dinner at the Polish Club in London, and Harry Saltzman started talking about this film he was going to make called *Dr. No* and that they were looking for an actor to play Bond. And at the time, I was doing a film with Sean called *On the Fiddle* for producer Ben Ficz. Alfie Lynch was the star of the film, and Sean was the second lead. So I offered to send Harry a reel of Sean's work and let them have a look at him. I was still in the midst of cutting the film at the time, so I just put some pieces together and sent it over to Harry and Cubby. And that's how it all started."

What prompted Hunt to suggest Connery for the role of Bond was that "he not only had extraordinary presence and was very handsome and masculine, but he always reminded me of a sort of young Clark Gable," explained Hunt. "And having already read several of the Bond books, I was pretty familiar with the material and felt Sean could do a really good job in the part."

Broccoli then also took a look at Connery's 1959 Disney film *Darby O'Gill and the Little People*, and both producers soon agreed that the 31-year-old Connery could be their man. The deciding vote ended up coming from Broccoli's wife, Dana, who deemed Connery "a very sexy guy." Broccoli and Saltzman quickly called in Connery for a series of interviews at their South Audley Street offices. They were immediately struck by his assertiveness and his bearing. They also liked the way he moved. After Connery left one of the early meetings, Broccoli and Saltzman went to the window and watched him cross the street. There was grace yet undeniable determination in his stride or, as Broccoli would later describe it, "a pantherlike prowl." It would be that walk across the street that sealed the deal for Connery. Though it took some convincing, Broccoli and Saltzman eventually sold United Artists on the unknown actor, and they signed Connery to a five-year contract, with one of his few provisions being that he be allowed to make other films in between Bonds. On November 3, 1961, it was announced to the world that Sean Connery *was* James Bond.

One of Broccoli and Saltzman's first steps was to polish the rugged Scotsman from Edinburgh's working class into the dashing yet debonaire Englishman of Fleming's novels. The task fell on the shoulders of director Terence Young, who himself possessed all the panache and savoir faire of Fleming's fictional hero. "Terence really was James Bond," chuckled Hunt, recalling the urbane Irish filmmaker, who was a contemporary of Ian Fleming. "In fact, I think he was more like James Bond than even James Bond!" Young immediately began grooming Connery in his own image, taking him to his personal tailor and boot maker. He escorted Connery to many fittings, from the Savile Row suits meticulously crafted by famed tailor Anthony Sinclair to the hand-woven shirts and neckties from Turnbull & Asser. Not only did Connery have to look the part, but Young insisted he also live the part. Young introduced Connery to the exclusive world of the St. James Club and took him to some of the most expensive restaurants in Mayfair, schooling him on everything from vintage wines to culinary delights. "Terence never really got the full credit, but he really did mold the screen version of James Bond," related director John Glen, who began his long-running association with the Bond films early in the series. "Terence was a real English gentleman, very well educated, and knew everything about the finer things in life. He was the perfect man to take Sean and knock him into shape."

Though filming was due to begin in Jamaica in January 1962, Broccoli and Saltzman still had to cast Bond's leading lady — the seductive seashell collector Honey Ryder, whom Bond first meets on the beach of Crab Key. But the search suddenly halted when a photograph of a stunning young Swiss beauty passed across Saltzman's desk. It was a shot of

A State of Andress: Sean Connery with Ursula in a 1962 publicity photo for Dr. No.

One of cinema's most indelible screen entrances: Ursula Andress emerging from the sea singing "Underneath The Mango Tree." In the book, Honey Ryder rises from the water wearing only a knife belt, but on screen, that was considered a Dr. No-no.

then-little-known actress Ursula Andress — dripping wet and clad in a soaked-to-the-skin white shirt — taken by her husband, actor John Derek. At first reluctant to take the role — Andress thought the script was silly — she was eventually persuaded by Derek. (Coincidentally, Derek's third wife — blonde bombshell Bo Derek — would be approached years later by Broccoli to appear in the 1981 Bond film *For Your Eyes Only*. Bo politely declined the offer.) The emergence of Ursula Andress from the Caribbean sea singing "*Underneath the Mango Trees*," wearing a white bikini and a hunting knife on her hip, became one of cinema's most breathtaking and memorable introductions. Sexy, scantily clad, and supremely resourceful, Andress's Honey Ryder set the standard for all Bond Girls to come. Next to the opening gun barrel sequence, Andress remains the most iconic image of the entire Bond series. Andress's only feature that didn't make it to screen, however, was her voice; her accent was deemed too pronounced, and Peter Hunt had to hire actress Monica Van der Zyl to redub her vocals in post-production (Van der Zyl would go on to loop a number of Bond actresses, including Claudine Auger in *Thunderball*).

Ursula Andress and Ian Fleming in conversation on the Jamaican beach set of Dr. No, nearby to Fleming's Goldeneye retreat.

Returning to Pinewood Studios in late February to begin interior shooting, two actors then joined the production in what would become key roles: British character actor Bernard Lee as Bond's no-nonsense superior "M" and Canadian-born actress Lois Maxwell as his superbly efficient, love-lorn secretary Miss Moneypenny. Lee (who passed away in 1981) would go on to portray M for the next 10 Bond films, while Maxwell would continue as Moneypenny for 13. Along with Desmond Llewelyn, who would be introduced as "Q" in the second Bond film, *From Russia with Love*, Lee and Maxwell became beloved, venerable fixtures in the cinematic world of 007. The role of Moneypenny came at a crucial juncture in Maxwell's life; her husband, Peter, had fallen ill, and she was in dire need of funds to help care for their two young children. "My husband had a heart attack and was quite sick for months," recalled Maxwell at her home outside London. "So I was forced to ring several directors and producers with whom I had already worked and ask them for a job. I told them how terribly ill Peter was, and with two little children I desperately needed the money. I said I would play anything. And Terence was the first one to respond."

After 58 days, *Dr. No* finally wrapped principal shooting on March 30, 1962. Despite a limited budget, the behind-the-scenes craftsman worked wonders. "I remember all of us who worked on the film went to a screening of the rough cut and thought it was marvelous," smiled Maxwell. "Instead of just being an ordinary spy film, there were all these amusing bits. There was a tongue-in-cheek sense of humor that took the mickey out of the spy genre. That was very much Terence, really."

UA wasn't as amused when it viewed the film. "United Artists didn't like it at all, quite frankly," recalled Hunt with a chuckle. "They thought it was a piece of rubbish!" As a result, United Artists decided to banish *Dr. No* to the drive-in circuit and second-run movie houses in America's Midwest. No Hollywood or New York premieres were planned. The lackluster studio reaction was not a sentiment shared by *Playboy* publisher Hugh Hefner — noted cinephile and one of Bond's first American champions — who secured an early print of *Dr. No* and gave it his stamp of approval. "We ran *Dr. No* at the Playboy Mansion in Chicago about four or five weeks before it actually opened in America," recalled Hefner. "And I was particularly impressed by the extent of the character, of the structure, and how they were able to get so many things right in that very first movie. It was all there." But the nominal American release troubled Broccoli and Saltzman tremendously. If Bond didn't catch on in the U.S., then their plans for a long-running franchise were doomed.

Nevertheless, the star-studded U.K. premiere went ahead as planned on October 6, 1962. The overwhelming response quickly put Broccoli and Saltzman's fears to rest. *Dr. No* was a box office success, becoming the second-highest-earning film in Britain in 1962. American audiences were equally enthusiastic, and with U.S. box office receipts piling up United Artists gave the go-ahead for a second Bond film. Bolstered by JFK's public endorsement of *From Russia with Love*, UA decided to adapt that novel for the next outing. *From Russia with Love* was given twice the budget of *Dr. No*, and filming began on April 1, 1963, with Terence Young once again at the helm. The demand for Bond was so great that the film held its world premiere only two months after filming wrapped, on October 10, 1963. It quickly became the highest-grossing film in British cinema history. "We were all working for the same ends in those days," reflected Peter Hunt. "Everybody contributed ideas, and we all built on each other. There weren't any egos involved — it was always about making the best possible film." On the other side of the Atlantic, *From Russia with Love* pulled in an astonishing $24 million — an enormous sum at the North American box office in 1963.

Reflecting on that surprising embrace of James Bond, Connery offered his theory: "I think it had a great deal to do with timing," he surmised. "For example, the reason the books became such a success in England initially was that they came along after the war, at a time when England had just finished rationing. And here was Fleming, writing about an eccentric character with a great finesse and taste in wine, women, and food, living extremely well. There was a great fantasy element, with all the sort of sexual fantasies of the healthiest, most virile bachelor. Then when the films came along, after many sociological dramas and kitchen-sink dramas dominating the screen, Bond was seen as pretty straightforward fun, with a very basic theme of good against evil. There was also a lot of sex, a lot of color, but all tastefully done . . . sort of sadism for the entire family."

United Artists no longer viewed Bond as a one-off adventure and soon shared Broccoli and Saltzman's vision of an extremely lucrative franchise. And while James Bond would form a permanent relationship with United Artists, the alliance between Broccoli and Saltzman proved less stable. Despite a strong mutual respect, they had very different personalities. Essentially, their only bond *was* Bond. "It was a very complex relationship between Cubby and Harry," explained Guy Hamilton, who was hired to direct the next Bond film, *Goldfinger*. "Cubby just wanted to concentrate solely on producing the Bond films. And Harry wanted to take over the world. He would say stuff like 'Metro is going for sale, why don't we buy that, Cubby?' That is how their split began to develop."

Bond screenwriter Tom Mankiewicz echoed Hamilton's thoughts. "For Cubby, Bond was his baby. He absolutely loved it, and that became his mission in life. He didn't want to own General Motors, he didn't want to have his own studio. He just wanted to do Bond movies. But for Harry, Bond was his grubstake to an empire. He was an empire builder and wanted to produce every film, control every studio, and run the businesses of the world."

Meanwhile, Sean Connery was beginning to feel left out of the enormous profits generated by Bondmania around the globe. "Sean had a problem on *Goldfinger*," related Guy Hamilton, "which was that *Dr. No* had been a success, *From Russia with Love* had been an even bigger success, and yet Sean was still under a five-year contract. He was very unhappy about the

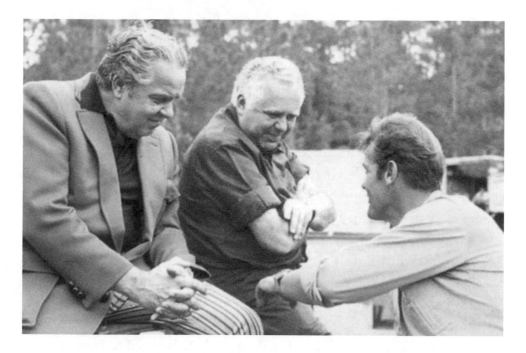

Gentlemen Prefer Bonds: (left to right) Cubby Broccoli, Harry Saltzman, and Roger Moore on location in the Louisiana Bayous for 1973's Live and Let Die.

amount of money he was receiving now that he was such a big attraction. And as I said to Sean, 'If I controlled the money, I would give it to you. But I'm not the paymaster. You've got an agent, you've got a business manager — they're the ones who have got to sort this out.' So there was quite a lot of 'sorting out' going on backstage, and the contract was later revised."

After *Goldfinger* broke all box office records in 1964 and firmly established 007 as a global phenomenon, Broccoli and Saltzman's next headache became Kevin McClory. The director started touting a rival Bond production based on his co-ownership of the *Thunderball* rights. Though Broccoli and Saltzman had commissioned Richard Maibaum to write a new treatment for *Thunderball*, they reluctantly gave McClory a producer credit and percentage of the profits on the 1965 film. It was a decision meant to forestall any possible legal action, but more importantly it was intended to protect their series from any outside competition.

As *Thunderball* took Bond to spectacular new heights, the clamor for anything 007 became relentless by the mid-1960s. Film and TV imitators began popping up regularly, like *The Man from* UNCLE, *I Spy,* and the Mel Brooks spoof *Get Smart* on television and *Our Man Flint* and the Matt Helm series on the big screen. From uncertain beginnings, the Bond films had exploded into the greatest box office force of the '60s. The impact of Bond on the cultural landscape cannot be overstated. It stretched far and wide, crossing language barriers and political boundaries and ideologies into the upper echelons of government. Even the real spy world began taking cues from Bond. Though not permitted to be publicly screened in the Soviet Union, the 007 films became compulsory viewing for all KGB agents. Bond's ingeniously lethal gadgets were being duplicated for use in the field, and his exploits were regarded as inspirational espionage techniques. Future 007 Roger Moore told me of one such confession from a high-ranking Intelligence official. "I was at lunch one day with the ex-head of French Intelligence, and he was telling me how he used to sneak out to see the Bond films," marveled Moore. "But he couldn't watch them in Paris; he had to fly to Geneva to see them because it wouldn't look good for the head of French Intelligence to be caught watching a bloody 007 movie!"

The Bond films had thoroughly captivated audiences through their exotic locales, fascinating characters, outrageous stunts, ingenious gadgets, thrilling action, and titillating sex scenes.

Less ecstatic with the 007 phenomenon, however, were film censors on both sides of the Atlantic. Their opposing mandates towards the rigorous violence and brazen sexual innuendoes forced them to work overtime in negotiating acceptable cuts with the filmmakers. In *Dr. No,* Bond's cold-blooded shooting of Professor Dent had to be trimmed from six shots to only two, while United States censors fought unsuccessfully to change Pussy Galore to "Kitty" Galore in *Goldfinger.* However, the name of Pussy Galore was eventually banned on *Goldfinger* publicity and promotion materials in America, which referred to her instead as simply "Miss Galore" or "Goldfinger's personal pilot." Censors were always on high alert trying to decipher subtle offenses slipped into the Bond films. Though an aggravating ordeal, the filmmakers soon took delight in their attempts to outwit censors.

Pussy in the Sky with Diamonds: Honor Blackman as Goldfinger's personal pilot, which caused problems galore with film censors in 1964.

"The British censors were only concerned about the violence, and they gave us a hard time on every film," related Guy Hamilton. "So we used to show them the film without the full dub or the sound effects. Without the full effect of bone-crunching and grunts and impacts, those fight scenes suddenly seemed rather innocuous. On the other hand, the American censors were only concerned with the sex — to the point of lunacy. If you look in one of the scenes, behind Bond a hundred yards away there are a couple of girls running past, and you can see a flash of a bare breast. But the censor spotted that immediately. So what I would do is put things in for him to cut out, and then I'd roll on the carpet saying 'But that ruins the whole scene!' By doing that, it would come down to 'Okay, you can get your two cuts' — which I didn't want anyway — 'if I can keep the other three which you're making such a fuss about.'"

Frequently more problematic, however, were Maurice Binder's electrifying and risqué title sequences. Binder's trademark of acrobatic nude female silhouettes flowing sensually amid stunning visual pyrotechnics continually pushed the boundaries. "The titles were actually the raciest things about the Bond films," chuckled Roger Moore. "Maurice was always getting into trouble for showing too much. I remember going down to watch him shoot one day, and there were all these wind machines and naked girls, and he'd be having to smear down their pubic hairs with Vaseline because they were blowing in the wind." Behind the scenes, Binder became equally famous for delivering those title sequences at the last minute. "We used to sometimes only get the titles just the night before the premiere of the film," grinned Peter Hunt. "He drove us mad." But Binder's logic seemed to be an attempt to prevent any possible censorship. It didn't always work. "In some countries, my film *On Her Majesty's Secret Service* wasn't directed by anybody," laughed Hunt, "because underneath my directing title Maurice put four beautiful nude girls that slid into the frame with their nipples pointing straight out. The censors quickly took the scissors to it. So the film ran without a director's credit in some places."

The greater dilemma that soon faced Broccoli and Saltzman was how to continually top themselves after cultivating such voracious appetites in moviegoers. Audiences had enormous expectations for each new Bond film, and the producers weren't about to disappoint them. Broccoli and Saltzman were always faithful to that old show business adage of giving audiences what they want. Huge budgets soon pushed the scope and scale of 007's adventures to outlandish proportions. Where James Bond had previously relied on his wits and cunning to outwit and outmaneuver opponents, he was becoming little more than the means to introduce eye-popping hardware and stunning visual effects. Connery was not happy. "I remember when I was asked to do *Goldfinger*, I started sensing a dangerous trend," explained Guy Hamilton, "in that Bond was becoming this Superman in a way. I was very concerned about that. Because there's no excitement if you know he's going to win every time. That was one of my prime concerns and is why I emphasized, for example, that there was no way Bond could physically beat Oddjob. Bond had to *outsmart* him."

By 1967's *You Only Live Twice*, Connery had had enough. Bond had overtaken his life, and he felt suffocated by his infamous alter ego. Connery was also frustrated that the lengthy shooting schedules weren't allowing him to do many film projects outside Bond. When he announced that he would not be returning for the next 007 film, *On Her Majesty's Secret Service*, Broccoli and Saltzman had to begin a search for a worthy replacement. Unfortunately, novice actor George Lazenby wasn't what the Bond audiences wanted in

1969. The film's disappointing box office only fueled Saltzman's increasing restlessness with the Bond films. Already distracted by other business ventures and side film projects, Saltzman decided that he and Broccoli would alternate producing chores on future Bond productions. "They started quarreling on my film and began not speaking to each other," recalled *On Her Majesty's Secret Service* director Peter Hunt.

Broccoli's success in securing Connery for one more turn as Bond in 1971's *Diamonds Are Forever* helped stabilize the series once again. Co-screenwriter Tom Mankiewicz related a tense moment early in production: "Sean, I think, had it in his contract that Harry was not allowed to be on the set if he was going to do the movie; he hated Harry. And because of that, Harry showed up in Las Vegas the first night of shooting, and everybody went '*Oh, boy* — that's all we need is Harry Saltzman! Now Sean is going to walk off the picture.' So here we all were, huddled in Sean's trailer as shooting was about to start, and suddenly Harry strode up and knocked on the door. Sean opened the door and said 'Harry!!' and gave him a big kiss on the forehead.'" Mankiewicz couldn't help but laugh at the memory. "Harry immediately turned bright red and flew back the next day."

Though Broccoli and Saltzman had their differences, they still made a formidable producing team. "Harry was absolutely full of ideas . . . some of them completely ridiculous," chuckled Peter Hunt. "You kind of had to hold him back. But he was a great raconteur and could laugh at himself. Cubby was the more relaxed of the two — rather kind-hearted, who could soothe anyone's hurt feelings." Essentially, they were a superb good cop–bad cop team, each savvy enough to reach his objectives through opposing means.

"Though Cubby had an avuncular appearance, Cubby was *nobody's fool*," related Roger Moore, who ushered in a new era of James Bond with 1973's *Live and Let Die.* "As a producer, Cubby was very caring, and everyone loved him. So much so that, if he said to the crew 'Jump over that cliff,' they would. He won their total respect. I remember oftentimes he would be out all night with us on location and would go into the kitchen and cook spaghetti for the entire crew.

"Frequently, when we were on location, we were near casinos," continued Moore. "Cubby loved to gamble, so we all would be there, and I

Spaghetti Western: Cubby "Mangia! Mangia!" Broccoli serves up his famous pasta dish to cast and crew on location in Cairo for The Spy Who Loved Me. Meanwhile, Roger Moore tries his best to stir, not shake, the Bolognese sauce.

remember one time he started noticing the crew were losing all their money in the casino. So he had the accountant only let them have 50% of their salary, so that when they got home they would get the rest and wouldn't be broke. And oftentimes I'd see him go from table to table where the boys were playing roulette or black-jack, and he'd hand them all a pile of chips. Cubby was a very generous man."

"Cubby wanted everyone to enjoy in his success," added Mankiewicz. "I remember he would always give a great tip wherever he went. I once said to him, 'Wow, that's an out-rageous tip,' and he said, 'Remember this: for every dollar you give away, you'll get a hundred back. And for every buck you steal, you'll lose a thousand.' I never forgot that."

Saltzman, meanwhile, wasn't being as wise. Bored with his Bond duties, he was focusing most of his energies on outside ventures, including the purchase of Technicolor — an idea that didn't interest Broccoli but that Saltzman went ahead with anyway. It soon became his undoing. "Harry was a very bright man, but he started making one bad investment after another," explained Mankiewicz. "And part of the bylaws of their company Danjaq was that you couldn't put up stock in Danjaq as collateral for loans without telling the partner. You couldn't do it, but somehow Harry did. Harry was convinced that, when his train came in and he made a huge fortune, it would all be just fine.

"Then one day, the United Bank of Switzerland called him and wanted their money," continued Mankiewicz. "He didn't have it, so they said, 'Then we have to take your stock in Danjaq.' When Cubby found out, he said, 'Wait a minute — you can't take his stock in Danjaq because he had no right to put it up!' Harry was now bankrupt, and the only way he could get out of bankruptcy was to sell his half of Danjaq."

In 1975, just 15 years after first optioning Ian Fleming's novels, Saltzman sold his stake in the Bond partnership to United Artists, leaving Broccoli as the sole producer. Saltzman's last film would be 1974's *The Man with the Golden Gun*. Litigation entanglements delayed the next Bond film until 1977, but *The Spy Who Loved Me* and then 1979's *Moonraker* became the biggest Bonds of the entire series. At the 1982 Oscars, Broccoli was awarded the prestigious Irving J. Thalberg Award in recognition of his legendary producing career. Nearly five years later, Broccoli would receive the Order of the British Empire for his outstanding contributions to the British film industry, as well as the French Commandeur des Arts et des Lettres.

Broccoli continued to pilot the films with unwavering enthusiasm and dedication throughout the '80s, even as Fleming titles began to run out, even though Kevin McClory released rival Bond film *Never Say Never Again* with Sean Connery, and despite the fact Roger Moore was replaced by new 007 Timothy Dalton. All the while, Broccoli had been keeping Bond in the family by mentoring stepson Michael Wilson in the business of Bond since the mid-'70s. Along with his half-sister Barbara Broccoli, Wilson assumed the producing reins just as 007 number five Pierce Brosnan helped propel the franchise to its biggest box office returns ever.

Cubby Broccoli poses in front of the under-construction 007 Soundstage at Pinewood Studios in 1976.

Saltzman and Broccoli eventually reconciled in the 1980s. In 1994, Saltzman died of a heart attack at the age of 78. Broccoli was in failing health himself at the time but was anxious to see footage of the still-in-production *Goldeneye* before he passed away in June 1995 at the age of 87. Broccoli had always insisted that Ian Fleming's name would be honored in the credits of every Bond film. The Broccoli family has continued that tradition and added another one — every Bond film will also bear the title "Albert R. Broccoli's Eon Productions presents."

Shortly before he died, Cubby was still concerned about his beloved Bond franchise. He cautioned Barbara and Michael, *"Don't let 'em screw it up."* As James Bond's film father, Cubby was most fearful of disappointing his audience. He fought to maintain enormously high standards and never once forgot his responsibility to always entertain. His legacy is secure as James Bond continues to do just that into the 21st century.

Bond . . . Sir James Bond: Sean Connery

There is good news and bad news concerning Sean Connery's much-anticipated return to the James Bond films. The good news is Connery may be interested. The bad news is reportedly no one has made him an offer.

Ever since Pierce Brosnan resuscitated the Bond series, rumors have been flying that Connery will make a return to the series. Not as 007, however, but as James Bond's *father*. Or perhaps even a villain. The Bond camp has slyly alluded to it, Brosnan told me he was hopeful, and fans rejoiced at the news of the unique casting twist. I have interviewed Connery a number of times since 1983, and the subject of Bond frequently and inevitably arose. My most recent visit with Connery in his hometown of Edinburgh found the Oscar winner contemplating — and not necessarily discounting — a James Bond reunion.

"I keep hearing about my supposed return every year now," confessed Connery, relaxing on the top floor of the stately Caledonian Hotel, which sits in the shadow of Edinburgh Castle — the dark and brooding essence of Scotland's martial past — looming dramatically above the city. Dressed neatly in a black golf shirt and black pants, the silver-haired, 70-year-old

Sean Connery strikes a Bondian pose for an early publicity shot.

Scot still cuts an imposing figure. No matter how large the room, Connery seems to fill it. It's a physical authority, due in part to his lean six-foot-two frame, but mostly a giant persona from four decades in the elite of worldwide superstardom. When Connery sits down to talk, he immediately clears the table of obstacles — glassware, a floral arrangement — to give himself an unobstructed channel of communication. Hunched over, with elbows on the table and fingers clasped, Connery means business, whether talking movies or politics.

"There have been no official overtures made to me [regarding Bond], so I don't know," shrugged Connery. "Nobody has called. They haven't offered me anything yet. I would certainly consider it, look at it . . . I don't know if I could avoid it, really.

"But quite frankly," he added with his characteristic wry grin and arched eyebrow, "I don't think they could afford me."

The fact that Connery would even consider an offer is a feat in itself. While he certainly defined the role, his ability to transcend it took a lot longer than he'd expected. As a result, Connery has always had a love/hate relationship with his famous alter ego. It did make him a global sensation and was certainly the biggest break of his career. But when Bondmania swept the planet in the mid-'60s, Connery was trapped in the center of a storm that had taken on Beatlesque proportions. In fact, James Bond and the Beatles were the two biggest pop culture icons to emerge during that decade. "And there were four of them to kick it around," he said, admitting it took years for him to recover.

Born to humble beginnings, Thomas Sean Connery grew up in a poor and rugged part of Edinburgh, near a rubber mill and a brewery. "The place smelled of rubber and hops," remembered Connery. His father worked at the mill 12 hours a day, and his work ethic rubbed off on his son. "It's blind allegiance, in a way. Therefore, I couldn't wait to go to work."

Shortly after his brother Neil was born, nine-year-old Sean began rising at 6 a.m. to deliver milk before going to school. It was war time, and, while his father worked in a munitions factory in Glasgow, Sean was doing his part to keep the family afloat. "I never thought of myself as underprivileged," he said, "because, really, I had nothing to compare my situation with."

Connery said he recalls life being "disruptive" growing up. Still, he managed to see a few movies on Saturdays, trading jam jars and beer bottles, he says, for tokens to the local movie house. He says he loved Flash Gordon, the Three Stooges, and American cowboy flicks. He dropped out of school at age 13 and joined the navy at 16. Stomach ulcers — which he blames on his inability to deal with discipline — got him discharged at 19. After attending a British Legion training school, he became a furniture polisher, which led to a job polishing coffins.

In 1955, while working in a London newspaper printing plant, he joined a body building club. His height and rugged good looks soon earned him jobs as a swimsuit model. When he entered the Mr. Universe competition the same year, he was invited to audition for the touring company of *South Pacific*. Connery wound up in the male chorus, going from town to town singing "There Is Nothing like a Dame," he recalled. He graduated to a small speaking part and, on the road, made up for lost school time. Every day for a year, in almost every town, Connery hit the local library, reading voraciously. He also worked on his diction by reading into a tape recorder. Back

Connery's acting headshot from the 1950s.

in London, he immersed himself in theater by studying at the Old Vic.

He applied himself to repertory theater and television work, making a mark for himself in a BBC presentation of *Requiem for a Heavyweight*, playing the battered protagonist. Then came a role opposite Claire Bloom in *Anna Karenina*. Signed to 20th Century Fox, Connery appeared with Lana Turner and Barry Sullivan in *Another Time, Another Place*. He had just played a vicious killer in *Tarzan's Greatest Adventure* and had crooned in Walt Disney's Irish fantasy *Darby O'Gill and the Little People* when he got a call from two American producers — Albert Broccoli and Harry Saltzman — that would change his life forever. They had acquired the rights to several of Ian Fleming's popular James Bond novels, and they were interested in seeing the young Scotsman.

For the role of Bond, the producers had been considering more polished contenders, but in came Connery with that walk of his, a kind of fluid swagger that Broccoli later described as "the threatening grace of a panther on the prowl." Poorly dressed and with his thick Scottish brogue, Connery delivered his theory of Bond, pounded the desk to make his points, then sauntered out, leaving the two men dumbfounded.

"I used strong and commanding movements," explained Connery of that fateful day. "Not with weight, but to show how Bond is always in control of a scene."

It worked. As did his fee of only $16,500, compared to those of the bigger names, who were just too pricey for the million-dollar budget of *Dr. No*.

Connery ran with the part, adding a blue-collar arrogance to the character written by Fleming as a superbly efficient and self-assured upper-class Brit. Fleming, however, wasn't too happy with the casting decision. "You have to remember, the ideal Bond for Fleming would have been a young David Niven," explained three-time Bond screen-writer Tom Mankiewicz, whose father was famed Academy Award-winning director and screenwriter Joseph L. Mankiewicz. "Fleming was obsessed with the fact, at least in the books, that Bond was

"To try and erase the image of Bond is next to impossible," admitted Connery about his iconic alter ego.

English. And when Sean Connery was first cast, with his thick Scottish accent, Fleming was appalled. It was the purist in him. And I think he referred to Sean as that 'great snorting lorry driver.' But by *Goldfinger* time, Fleming was so impressed with Sean, and so fell in love with him as Bond, that in his last book, *The Man with the Golden Gun* — in which Bond retires at the end — he gave Bond Scottish ancestry. That was Fleming giving com-plete kudos to Sean Connery." Connery also injected another ingredient largely alien in Fleming's Bond: humor. It came in the form of teases — Miss Moneypenny, the secretary of Bond's boss, became the most frequent target — and racy double entendres. In bed with yet another knockout dame — golden girl Shirley Eaton — in *Goldfinger*, Bond answers the phone and declines a dinner invitation with "something big's come up." Connery's Bond combined levity with casual brutality and was light-footed enough to dodge the campy punches — not to mention dagger-tipped kicks and razor-edged bowler hats.

"I look for humor in whatever I'm doing," mused Connery, "as long as the humor fits the character and the story." His early role models were Spencer Tracy, Cary Grant ("probably the most underrated actor to appear on screen"), Marlon Brando ("the most watchable of American actors"), and Sir Ralph Richardson. "I adored his acting," he said. "He always found something quite humorous in his way of doing things."

Students of pop culture attribute the 007 phenomenon to America's need for a suave hero after the assassination of President John F. Kennedy. On the threshold of the sexual revolution in the '60s, the Beatles were taking care of the girls, but all women wanted Bond, and all men wanted to be Bond. The sole exception was Connery himself. As Bondmania became an international phenomenon, Connery grew concerned the character was smothering his acting career. No matter how good he was at essaying the role, he grew increasingly worried that he would be stamped as 007 forever, and he was never comfortable with the frenzied adulation and attention. The press followed his every move, and any semblance of a private life was nonexistent. On one occasion — while on location in Tokyo shooting *You Only Live Twice* — Connery was at dinner, and after retreating to the men's room he looked up from the urinal to find a photographer snapping photos of him relieving himself. For Connery, that was the last straw. The privacy invasion had become intolerable.

"The problem was that Bond was just so damn popular, the public only wanted to see me doing that," Connery explained. "All I can do now is what's interesting and rewarding for me. To try to erase the image of Bond is next to impossible."

Connery admits the series became a straitjacket for him. The films often did not start shooting on schedule, and it was impossible to get a completion date, so Connery never knew when he might be free to make a non-Bond movie. And he desperately wanted to.

"For me, what became wrong with the Bond films was that they just got further and further into the technological and science fiction stuff, which was not very interesting for me," admitted Connery. "It was always important for me to use the humanity of the character as a base because however original the gadgets were, James Bond still had to figure his way out. It's the human being, with all his human instincts, who must overcome the obstacles. But they kind of lost that in the plots, in terms of having some sort of story."

So after shooting completed on *You Only Live Twice* in 1967, Connery said never again and announced his departure. But after George Lazenby's less-than-successful outing as 007 in 1969's *On Her Majesty's Secret Service*, Connery was lured back for 1971's *Diamonds Are Forever* with an offer he couldn't refuse. United Artists film executive David Picker committed to back two of Connery's personal film projects as well as pay the actor a much-deserved sum of $1.4 million, plus a percentage. "It was an unprecedented deal in those days," stated *Diamonds* co-screenwriter Tom Mankiewicz. Connery made it known that he was donating his entire salary to charity — the Scottish International Educational Trust — which not only served to create awareness for the organization, but also substantially aided its efforts in helping underprivileged Scottish children (to this day, Connery has continued to donate a yearly sum to the charity).

But after *Diamonds Are Forever*, Connery again said never again and ripped up his license to kill. But as production for *Live and Let Die* geared up, Broccoli was still hoping to entice Connery back for yet another outing, just as he had with *Diamonds Are Forever*. Tom Mankiewicz was charged with the task of trying to persuade Connery over lunch one day at the White Elephant. "I was pretty young at the time — only like 28 or 29 years old — but Sean and I had developed a nice relationship on *Diamonds*, and he took to calling me 'boyo,'" smiled Mankiewicz. "So I remember at the end of our lunch, I worked up the courage and said, 'You know, Sean, this next Bond film is going to be so much fun — there's crocodiles, and wild boat chases, and. . . .' And he said to me, '. . . *and I have an obligation to my public to play James Bond?*' And I sort of gulped and said, '*Well. . . .*' And he then said to me, 'Well, when does that obligation stop? Seven films? Ten films? Twenty films? I've been playing this part for a decade or more — when do I no longer have an obligation to the public to play James Bond?' Then he took a pause and said to me, 'Let me tell you something, boyo —

"There was a certain amount of curiosity about the role, having been so long away from it," said Connery about his return to Bond at age 53.

Bonds Have More Fun: Sean Connery enjoys his leading ladies Barbara Carrera (left) and Kim Basinger (right) from 1983's Never Say Never Again.

there's only two things in the world I've ever wanted to own and now have them both: a golf course and a bank.' So I had to agree with him. When does that obligation stop? We really couldn't expect him to keep playing Bond for the rest of his life."

With Roger Moore asserting himself successfully in his debut as Bond in 1973's *Live and Let Die*, Connery finally felt he was one step closer to shaking his past and wandered his way through the decade, turning in terrific performances in diverse films like *The Great Train Robbery, The Offence, Robin and Marian, The Man Who Would Be King*, and *Outland*. Then in 1983, Connery made *Never Say Never Again*, which marked his return to the role he had seemingly turned his back on forever. Produced by Irish movie entrepreneur Kevin McClory — who had the rights to remake *Thunderball* because of his onetime collaboration with Ian Fleming on the story back in 1959 — *Never Say Never Again* was positioned as an antidote to Moore's more lighthearted take on the Bond character. The project had come together after years of untangling the rights by Jack Schwartzman, an American film producer with a background in entertainment law. Connery said it was actually his wife, Micheline, who finally persuaded him to revisit Bond after so many years — she had even coined the film's title as an ironically sly jab at Connery's past declarations.

"When Jack Schwartzman came to me to ask me to do *Never Say Never Again*, Micheline encouraged me to think about it carefully," explained Connery. "'Why not play the role? What do you risk? After all these years, it might be interesting.' The more I thought about it, the more I thought she was right. There was also a certain amount of curiosity in me about the role, having been so long away from it."

Although audience enthusiasm was high, the rival Bond production failed to match the mighty box office of *Octopussy*, Eon Production's official Bond installment of that year. Behind-the-scenes production turmoil on *Never Say Never Again* and clashes with director Irvin Kershner left Connery disheartened by the whole experience, and he ended up staying away from films until the mid-'80s. He then reemerged in top form with some impressive work in *The Name of the Rose, The Hunt for Red October, Indiana Jones and the Last Crusade*, and *The Untouchables*. Eager to work

(left) Sean Connery backstage at the 1988 Academy Awards with his Best Supporting Actor Oscar for The Untouchables. "His code of ethics is quite strong and I really respected that in him," said Kevin Costner of working with Connery in The Untouchables (right).

with director Brian De Palma and playwright David Mamet, who supplied the screenplay, Connery jumped at the chance to join the cast of the stylish crime drama, where he shared the screen with Kevin Costner and Robert De Niro. Connery stole the film with his brilliant characterization of Jimmy Malone, the veteran and gruff Irish beat cop who teaches the naive Elliot Ness how to fight organized crime "the Chicago way" during the brutal reign of Al Capone in the Roaring Twenties.

The things he appreciated about the character of Jimmy Malone were its paradoxes. "I like contrast in my roles," explained Connery. "I like it when an actor looks one thing and conveys something else, perhaps something diametrically opposite. With Malone, I tried to show at the beginning he could be a real pain in the ass, so that you wouldn't think he would be concerned with such things as Ness's feelings or Ness's family, and then show he was someone else underneath, capable of real relationships." Working with the venerable screen icon on 1987's *The Untouchables* left a lasting impact on the young Kevin Costner. "One never knows what to expect, but for me Sean really matched up with every expectation you'd want," explained Costner, who ended up forging an off-screen friendship with Connery as well. The two reunited again on Costner's 1991 hit *Robin Hood: Prince of Thieves*, where Connery made a surprise cameo as King Arthur.

"I have to say, however, that it's outside the lines of acting where you come to really respect Sean," continued Costner. "His desire to be fair is really important to him. And when he's unhappy about something, rather than lash out, he makes a list to make sure he's thinking correctly — sort of a checks and balances list. 'Cause I remember on *The Untouchables*, when at one point he was unhappy about a situation, he ran this list by me in his desire to be fair. His code of ethics is quite strong, and I really respected that in him." Connery's charismatic performance wound up earning him an Academy Award for Best Supporting Actor and once again shifted his career into high gear. Hollywood had realized that Connery was one of the very few older actors whom young moviegoers still found exciting and relevant and, more importantly, whom they respected.

Yet, young filmmakers today still can't resist trying to re-create some of that old Bond magic, trying to cast Connery — much to his chagrin — as the action hero, even though he's now past 70. Such was the dilemma Connery encountered with his 1999 art heist movie *Entrapment*, which the director tried filling with extensive helicopter chases and lots of gunplay. It became too reminiscent of Bond, and Connery was forced to fire the original director during production and bring in John Amiel to helm a revamped, more character-driven story.

In the film, Connery plays an aging and elusive art thief who teams up with an undercover insurance investigator (played by Welsh beauty Catherine Zeta-Jones), who's posing as a fellow burglar. As they plan the heist of the century, the two engage in a romantic dance that defies the generation gap. "We had the opportunity to make a movie that was much more about romance than about sex," explained Amiel. "It was an intense love story that didn't need to be physicalized and didn't need to be the 'lets-all-pretend-that-he's-not-in-his-late-60s-but-just-a-prematurely-old-looking-35-year-old.' It was not a last-ditch attempt to re-create James

(left to right) Sean Connery, Catherine Zeta-Jones, and director John Amiel on the set of 1999's heist-thriller Entrapment.

Bond. It was more about what would happen to a James Bond-type character if he really was in his 60s and how he could still do what he does with dignity and intelligence, without pretending he's something he's not."

Playing the romantic leading man with a woman half his age didn't faze Connery. "If I had any reservations about the part, I would've said, 'Well, I'll just produce the film and get someone else to play the part,'" Connery confessed. "But I didn't. I most certainly will know when it's time for me to say 'Ahhh, not for me anymore.' But we dealt with the age difference immediately in the script. So the audience knew the rules and conditions from the beginning, but in spite of them a different relationship develops. She's a modern woman who was most certainly a match for him."

Of course, that's not to say Connery has a problem still playing the action hero, but only when he feels the need arises, as evidenced in the past few years by *The Rock*, *The Avengers*, and, to a lesser degree, *Entrapment*.

"Today's action scenes are much more scientific now, especially the stunts," said Connery, reflecting on his years of action work and the numerous on-set injuries he's suffered as a result. "The stunts have just gotten so much more unusual and spectacular, and the audience obviously adores it, so you have to have a few in the movie, and each one must be better than the last. But they are certainly much more carefully prepared now and cost a lot more money. Much more than in the '60s with the Bond films. . . .

"But I'm still game, and still try to do as much as physically possible without breaking my neck," he added with a laugh.

Connery says he's constantly offered action scripts, "where it's all action, action, action, right to the end. But my personal choice is for something much more than just that. Not that I'm convinced audiences are fed up with action movies, because you can never tell what they're going to go for."

He relates an incident during the filming of *Goldfinger* that illus-

"He's a complex guy," Harrison Ford told author David Giammarco about working with Sean Connery on 1989's Indiana Jones and The Last Crusade. "He brings intelligence and emotion and also unique craftskills at expressing ideas. He's an interesting guy and, consequently, that's why I think he's such an interesting actor. I had a great time working with him . . . I mean, he's Sean Connery – you can't get any better than that. I'm looking forward to working with him again on the next Indiana Jones."

trates how people can react in radically different ways to the same movie. "They were shooting in a junkyard, and they took this beautiful new car, and they smashed it into the size of a box," recalled Connery. "The guy who was working the crane on the last shot nearly fell out of the box with laughter. Meanwhile, the manager who was running the place, all he could think was 'Jesus, *destroying* a car like that?' It was two distinctly diverse reactions. . . .

"So I could never tell you what makes an audience like what they like," he added with a shrug. "I've just always tried to use my own compass, or barometer, in a sense."

Connery admitted he hadn't really seen the new Bond films with Pierce Brosnan. "I've seen only bits and pieces of them on airplanes, and that's certainly not a fair way to judge them," he confessed. But he's quick to add that, "even for my own Bonds, though, I think I only saw two or three of the ones I did in the cinema."

But from what he has seen, Connery gives top marks to Brosnan's portrayal. "I know Pierce well, and actually just saw him at Pinewood last week," smiled Connery. "And as I said, like back in the mid-'80s, when Pierce was doing *Remington Steele* and they were talking about him for the role of Bond, that he was indeed a very good choice. I'm not surprised at all with how well he's done.

"But it was really much more in the hands of the combination of him and who was going to direct it, I always felt. And who, if not either of these two, was going to supply a good script," offered Connery on what he felt was needed to resuscitate the Bond films. "The Bond films certainly needed a complete rethinking. I suggested they should get someone like [Quentin] Tarantino and make a real departure. But then again, look at what a big success the last few have been. . . ."

And what would be his own favorite Bond film?

"I guess I'd have to say *From Russia with Love* — heavy on intrigue and light on technology," said Connery without hesitation.

At his age, Connery could certainly be resting on his stature and success, passing the time by just soaking up rays at his beachfront home or working on his golf game. But he continues to act because, as he related simply, it makes him happy. "It gives me the opportunity to be somebody better and more interesting than I am," he smiled. "I guess I've never really had a problem with lack of appetite or desire to work. I've sometimes taken three years off at a time, but retiring just doesn't work for me.

"But I've always felt that, if it all went wrong or wasn't working anymore," he continued, "I would just walk away, I suppose."

One thing Scotland's most famous son insists he would never walk away from is his support of the Scottish National Party (SNP) and the fight for an independent Scotland. Connery was front and center in a campaign to help push the SNP to victory in the country's fiercely contested 1999 elections. Though the SNP lost, Connery continues to urge Scots to make decisions for themselves — not in a Labour Parliament controlled by London. "I've supported the SNP for over 30 years," explained Connery, "and I've seen Scotland change for the better in that time. Now I and many millions of

Scots want to see Scotland's Parliament working for Scotland's future."

Connery elaborated, saying the Labour Party had destroyed the spirit and enthusiasm that had surrounded the decision to create Scotland's first Parliament in 300 years. He said he detected a real change in the political atmosphere since he last campaigned in the devolution referendum. "When I campaigned with Labour, the snp, and the Liberal Democrats — there were no Tories, of course — for the referendum vote, there was a spirit and a positive enthusiasm," explained Connery. "Well, the control freaks have blown it away. They have replaced it with fear and intimidation, the very same way that others have before them."

Just before the election, Connery gave a rousing speech to over 300 snp members and supporters in Edinburgh, delivering an impassioned yet dignified morale booster that saw the actor occasionally overcome with emotion. He stated that anything he has ever done for Scotland was for "her" sake and not for his own. "And I defy anyone to prove otherwise." All he ever wanted, he said, was for Scotland to be nothing less than an equal of all the other nations in the world. "My position on Scotland has never changed in 30-odd years. And snp's plans for our future are made in Scotland by Scotland for Scotland. New Labour is controlled by Tony Blair. And in our Parliament, with New Labour in charge, all the decisions are still made in London.

"I mean, we've waited nearly 300 years," added Connery, who had "Scotland Forever" tattooed on his right arm as a teenager. "My hope is that it will evolve with dignity and integrity and [that] it will truly reflect the new voice of Scotland."

In a bid to encourage tourism in Scotland, Connery insisted that parts of his film *Entrapment* be shot in the picturesque west coast Isle of Mull. The actor, who was refused a knighthood in 1997 because of his determination to see Scotland march alone to full independence, contributes generously — and without fanfare — to his country, from the Scottish International Education Trust to a reported half a million dollars in snp donations. And to boost Scotland's economy and fledgling film industry, Connery is trying to establish the first Hollywood-style film studio in Scotland, to be built 10 minutes outside Edinburgh and housing half a dozen sound stages. "Right now, it is in the hands of the government because certain conditions have to be abided by," he explained. "There are a lot of restrictions. But we're about two-thirds of the way done with that. It would be part of a triangle with Pinewood and Shepperton studios in London and ours here in Edinburgh."

And in a reversal of the original knighthood snub, Connery was finally bestowed the honor in July of 2000 by Queen Elizabeth II. Considering his longtime support of the film industry and the immeasurable PR he gave Her Majesty's Secret Service over the years, it was an act of appreciation long overdue. The formal ceremony was conducted at the Palace of Holyrood House on Connery's home turf of Edinburgh, and Connery wore a kilt, bearing the MacLean tartan of his mother's clan. "It was very moving," said Connery of his knighting. "It is a great honor for me and for Scotland as well."

Is it conceivable that *Sir* Sean Connery could better effect change for Scotland by simply running for political office himself? "No, no, no," he insisted, shaking his head. "I am not a politician, and I have no intention of being one." But as Connery has learned before, you should never say never.

DR. NO *(1962)*

It remains one of cinema's most famous introductions:
A sultry brunette is losing her edge at a high-stakes game of chemin de fer at the Le Cercle casino. As she anxiously seeks additional coverage for her bets, she locks eyes with the dark, tuxedo-clad figure across the table repeatedly drawing better cards from the shoe. He reaches for his silver cigarette case.

"I admire your courage, Miss. . . ."

"Trench," she replies rather tersely. "Sylvia Trench." Her curiosity piqued by this mysterious rival, she volleys back. "I admire your luck, Mr. . . ."

"Bond." The lighter snaps shut as the now-lit cigarette hangs casually between his lips. "James Bond."

And with those immortal words the most successful film series of all time was launched.

Directed By: Terence Young

The Mission: On behalf of international criminal organization SPECTRE, twisted scientist Dr. Julius No constructs an elaborate nuclear base off the coast of Jamaica with the aim of destroying the burgeoning U.S. space program.

Locales: Jamaica, Crab Key, London

The Villain and Accomplices: Dr. No (Joseph Wiseman), Professor Dent (Anthony Dawson), Miss Taro (Zena Marshall)

The Bond Girls: Honey Ryder (Ursula Andress), Sylvia Trench (Eunice Gayson)

Theme Song: "The James Bond Theme" by Monty Norman and orchestrated by John Barry

A View To Kill: The first glimpse of Sean Connery as James Bond in 1962's Dr. No.

Score: John Barry

Memorable Lines:

Honey Ryder: "Are you looking for shells?"
Bond: "No, I'm just looking."

Dr. No, as Bond attempts to use a bottle as a weapon: "That's a Dom Perignon '55. It would be a pity to break it."
Replies Bond: "I prefer the '53 myself."

Dr. No, dismissing Bond: "Unfortunately, I misjudged you. You are just a stupid policeman — whose luck has run out."

Peter Hunt (Editor): "It was a cheap film to make — well under a million dollars. We ended up going over budget a little bit because we had terrible weather in Jamaica. Absolutely dreadful. The location shooting ended up being more extensive than it should have been. We had a lot of problems in production. But when you haven't got very much money and you're making a film without any big stars — you're just making a little British film — those things matter very much. We eventually pulled it off with a great deal of ingenuity and a great deal of encouragement on Terence Young's part. But we certainly didn't think this was going to be a series — we thought it was just a onetime thriller."

Monty Norman (Composer): "Cubby Broccoli had been one of the main financial backers of a stage musical I'd done in London, and so a few months later he called me in to meet with Harry Saltzman and discuss doing the score for a project they were planning. At the time, I knew a little about James Bond but not that much. So I'm sitting there with Cubby and Harry, and they say, 'We've just acquired the rights from Ian Fleming for most of his books, and we're hopefully going to turn them into a series of movies. The first one is going to be *Dr. No* — would you like to score?' Now I wasn't immediately saying yes because I was in the middle of doing two stage musicals at the time. So just as I was about to say 'Well, let me think about it,' Harry said, 'Look, we're doing our locations in Jamaica, why don't you come out and absorb the atmosphere and maybe write some of the Caribbean stuff there. Bring your wife too, all expenses paid.' And that was the clincher. I thought, 'Well, I'll have some money in the bank, and, if this film is a flop, at least we'll have had some sun, sea, and sand.' On such small things destiny turns."

Lois Maxwell (Miss Moneypenny): "Terence Young originally offered me the choice of two roles: the glamor girl Sylvia Trench or Miss Moneypenny. When I read the *Dr. No* script, Bond arrives back to his flat, and he hears a noise in the corridor, and he sort of creeps along the wall, pulls out his gun, flings open the door, and there is Sylvia Trench in his pajama top putting a golf ball down the corridor. Well, I didn't fancy myself just wearing a pajama top on screen, and what's more I'm ambidextrous, so it would almost have been impossible for me to putt a ball down the corridor. So I said, 'I'd prefer to play Miss Moneypenny.'

A Penny For Your Thoughts: Lois Maxwell shares a tender moment with Sean Connery on the set of Dr. No.

And Terence Young later said to me, 'You know, you've made the right decision, because if this takes off it's going to be a series of Bond films.'"

Monty Norman: "The first scene shot in Jamaica was the three so-called Blind Beggars walking towards the house, which became the first assassination in a James Bond film. And I was watching it and thought, 'Why not do a calypso "Three Blind Mice"?' Then I wrote 'Jump Up' for the big dance sequence, which later went on to become quite a hit in Jamaica. And, of course, 'Underneath the Mango Tree' I wrote out there as well, and having Ursula Andress singing it as she comes out of the water and Sean on the shore singing it back to her is now such a classic moment. That was such a magical day when they shot that sequence. It really was amazing. When Sean sang back to Ursula, I remember thinking what a nice singing voice he had and wondered to myself if I could get him to do one of my musicals. But I think he moved too fast for that. And I still remember the name of that beach we shot on: it was called 'Laughing Waters,' and it was actually located not too far away from Ian Fleming's house."

Peter Hunt, on the now iconic gun barrel opening trademark:
"Maurice Binder was a tremendously imaginative and inventive guy. He designed the gun barrel shot after seeing the film, and it was the very last thing shot. Because we had already finished filming at that point, Sean wasn't available to do the gun barrel walk, so we used Sean's stunt double, Bob Simmons. We actually didn't shoot Sean doing the gun barrel walk until we switched to CinemaScope for *Thunderball*. But Maurice always

regretted not copyright-
ing the gun barrel
design, because it is used
over and over and over
again. He would always
say to me, 'Dammit, why
didn't I copyright it!' In
Dr. No, the titles used all
those dots, which we
then had to cut and sync
up to the music. And
then we got John Barry,
who did such marvelous
work on the James Bond
theme, which I then
shoved all over the film.
But I remember Maurice
Binder was always work-
ing right up until the very
last minute on the open-
ing titles for all the films.
But he really did put
quite a stamp of his own
on the Bond films. I've always been a big fan of his work."

No Can Do: Dr. No (Joseph Wiseman) refuses to let Bond and Honey Ryder leave his fortress alive.

Monty Norman, on his inspiration for writing the James Bond theme: "I was back in England at that point, and I was playing around with ideas when Harry suggested the possibility of putting 'Underneath the Mango Tree' at the top of the film because it seemed so magical. But Cubby and I thought that wasn't a good idea because it had nothing to do with James Bond himself. And, of course, it was set in the Caribbean, and, if Bond was going to go on for other films, there was no way that would make sense. But around that time, I suddenly remembered a piece of music that I'd written for my musical follow-up to *Irma La Douce*, which I had tucked away in my bottom drawer. I dug it up, and it was called 'Bad Sign/ Good Sign.' I then realized that, if I split the notes in the piece of music, it would have the exact feeling of the character and the ambience of James Bond. And that's where it began. I split the notes, and it suddenly became '*Dun da da da dun, dun dun dun dun da da da dun.*' So from that, the rest of the piece just flowed very organically. With that sort of number, if you can get the first two bars and it really hits, then the rest is relatively easy."

Dream Theme: A recent photo of Monty Norman, composer of what is arguably one of the most famous pieces of music in the world: The James Bond Theme.

Ken Adam (Production Designer):

"The last two days of shooting, somebody came up and said, 'We've still got to shoot that scene in Dr. No's complex where he's interviewing Professor Dent.' It was an afterthought, because it was never in the original script. But by that point, we had run out of money. So I had to design and build that set very quickly and very cheaply. I think the whole thing only cost something like £450. I came up with this stylized concept of just a bare room with this circular grilled opening in the ceiling, a chair, and a table with the tarantula's cage, and you just hear the disembodied voice of Dr. No. No one told me what the picture was going to look like, and, because I was left very much alone while they were all on location, I decided to try something new, to use new materials and be slightly tongue-in-cheek. I was fed up with always using the same set construction techniques and the same materials. And it was very stimulating to be surrounded by the construction team at Pinewood, who said, 'Anything you design, Ken, we will build it.' So by the time everyone came back from shooting in Jamaica, I had three or four stages full of sets ready to go. If they hadn't liked them, I would have been in serious trouble! But Terence Young was very enthusiastic. Since then, at exhibitions I've had and in articles, people always talk about that set from *Dr. No*. It was a simple set but a very effective and dramatic one. I didn't realize it at the time — but now I do — that it really set a style for the rest of the Bond pictures."

Monty Norman, on working with Cubby Broccoli and Harry Saltzman: "They were very good, but they were chalk and cheese. You had this wonderful Italian-American and Jewish-Canadian combination. Harry was quite spiky and could be very difficult. But Cubby was always a gentleman in every sense of the word. I mean, he could be a tough businessman, but he was truly a lovely man, no question. He really did engender a family atmosphere on set. I even remember Barbara, who probably wasn't any more than two or three years old, being with him on set the entire time we were in Jamaica."

Hawaii Five 0-07: Jack Lord would be the first of many actors to portray Bond's CIA contact Felix Leiter, a character Fleming based on his Washington-based friend John Leiter. Incidently, Leiter's wife Marion was the one who first introduced Fleming to JFK in 1960.

Peter Hunt: "If you analyze *Dr. No*, there were many sequences that we didn't shoot, which we should have shot on location. And we had to make them work with inserts and lots of bits and pieces of shots back at Pinewood Studios. If you look at the film today, you'll see how the editing of it gave it its briskness and style. Also, remember all those people sitting around in the club in the beginning, talking about *Strangeways* and the plot of the film? They were all amateurs Terence had picked out in Jamaica just to fill in the parts. I had to revoice all of their roles by real actors once we got back to England. We had to do all sorts of things like that to try to make the film work. And in the end, it did work. But it was a lot of hard work. *Dr. No* certainly was the most difficult Bond film to edit."

North American Gross: $16.1 million

Overseas: $43.5 million

An assassin is put through his paces in the guise of James Bond for a SPECTRE Island training exercise in the opening of From Russia With Love.

FROM RUSSIA WITH LOVE (1963)

Directed By: Terence Young

The Mission: Only months after the Cuban Missile Crisis, SPECTRE is intent on avenging the murder of Dr. No and creating another Cold War crisis by the theft of the prized Soviet Lektor decoding machine.

Locales: London, Venice, Istanbul

The Villain and Accomplices: Ernst Stavro Blofeld "SPECTRE NO. 1," Rosa Klebb (Lotte Lenya), Donald "Red" Grant (Robert Shaw)

The Bond Girls: Tatiana Romanova (Daniela Bianchi), Sylvia Trench (Eunice Gayson)

Theme Song: Matt Munro

Score: John Barry

Memorable Lines:

"Well, I've just been reviewing an old case." — *Bond to Moneypenny, when her phone call interrupts his tryst with Sylvia Trench.*

"Red wine with fish. That should have told me something." — *Bond, held at gunpoint by Red Grant aboard the Orient Express.*

"You may know the right wines, but you're the one on your knees." — *Red Grant to Bond.*

Peter Hunt (Editor): "Terence Young was very nervous. Doing the second one was not easy. After you've had a success with the first one, you go into the second one and just hope to God it's going to be all right. But as it happened, it wasn't just all right, it got better. Everything in it was better. After that, everyone was much more confident. Attitudes were better, and people were looking forward to the challenge. Budgets were suddenly bigger, and one was able to try more adventurous stuff. And it also allowed us to take a little bit more time, perhaps, and a bit more money was allowed for us to indulge and experiment."

Lois Maxwell (Miss Moneypenny), on meeting Ian Fleming: "My husband, Peter, was in the Indian Army and had commanded the viceroy's bodyguard in New Delhi. So Peter had known Ian during the war. But I had never met Ian before. So when he met me for the first time, he came up and said, 'Oh, Lois, when I first wrote Miss Moneypenny, I visualized a tall, elegant woman, and you, my dear, are exactly that! And once more, you have the most kissable lips in the world!' And he was leaning forward to kiss me — or at least I assumed he was going to kiss me — when his wife, Anne, suddenly walked up and said, 'IAN!!' So I never got that kiss."

Peter Hunt, on staging the bone-crunching brawl between Bond and assassin Red Grant aboard the Orient Express: "It took some real sleight of hand. We were fortunate in having a set of the train at Pinewood, with double compartments and the back projection through the windows. Terence used three cameras; I had a handheld camera on one side and Terence was on the other side with the steady cameras. We shot it for two days, and then I went in the cutting room and put it together. We looked at it and realized we needed some more material, so we did another shot here and another shot there. A week later, we shot some more, and in all it took about three weeks. We put it together piece-

Jaws-breaker: SPECTRE *assassin Red Grant (Robert Shaw) is about to have his strength put to the test by Rosa Klebb (Lotte Lenya).*

meal, very methodically, knowing exactly what we wanted each time. But you have to really fight with a film to make it work. That's what I've always loved, I remember sometimes I'd wake up at four in the morning and suddenly have a brilliant idea about how the fight scene should work, and I'd put on my clothes and go down to the studio and try it. We were also able to build up this wonderful tension in the scene with that briefcase. The scene just grew and grew and ended up work- ing tremendously well. So

Sean Connery and Italian actress Daniela Bianchi in a candid moment on the 1963 Istanbul set of From Russia With Love.

much so, that people thought the fight scene was too brutal and too realistic for audiences to stomach. But it was all done for real with Sean and Robert Shaw; there was only one little shot we did with stuntmen. It turned out to be one of the most memorable fight scenes in cinema."

Sean Connery: "The stamp Terence Young put on the film was immeasurable. I don't think anyone else got closer. It's always been my favorite Bond film."

North American Gross: $24.8 million

Overseas: $54.1 million

Laser Scream: Bond is seconds away from castration by the man with the Midas touch — Auric Goldfinger.

GOLDFINGER *(1964)*

Directed By: Guy Hamilton

The Mission: "Operation Grand Slam" is billionaire industrialist Auric Goldfinger's plot to increase the worth of his vast gold holdings by detonating an atomic bomb inside Fort Knox, thereby contaminating the entire gold supply of the United States.

Locales: Miami, London, Switzerland, Washington, Kentucky

The Villain and Accomplices: Auric Goldfinger (Gert Fröbe), Oddjob (Harold Sakata), Mr. Solo (Martin Benson), Pussy Galore (Honor Blackman)

The Bond Girls: Pussy Galore (Honor Blackman), Jill Masterson (Shirley Eaton), Tilly Masterson (Tania Mallet), Dink (Margaret Nolan)

Theme Song: Shirley Bassey

Score: John Barry

Memorable Lines:

"Shocking. Positively shocking." — *Bond after electrocuting an assassin by tossing him, then a heating lamp, into a bath.*

"Sorry, I can't. Er, something big's come up." — *Bond, declining a dinner invitation over the phone while in bed with Jill Masterson.*

Bond, facing castration by laser: "Do you expect me to talk?"
Goldfinger: "No, Mister Bond. I expect you to die."

"My name is Pussy Galore."
Bond, regaining consciousness after being tranquilized: "I must be dreaming."

Honor Blackman (Pussy Galore): "At that point, I was very hot after doing two solid years on *The Avengers*. I was also the first woman to be doing judo, so I think that's why I was cast as Pussy. When I had to do that piece of judo with Sean in *Goldfinger*, it was a piece of cake. They were piling up the hay and mats all over to make sure I wouldn't get hurt. I thought, 'This is wonderful,' because I was so used to doing judo on the cement floor of the studio for *The Avengers*. This was a real luxury."

(left) Miami's Fontainebleau Hotel as it looks today. "I might've known M wouldn't book me into the best hotel in Miami Beach out of pure gratitude," laments Bond after mission instructions interrupt his poolside tryst with Dink (Margaret Nolan).

Guy Hamilton (Director): "I remember whilst we were shooting second unit — just Ken Adam, the cameraman, and myself — in Miami at the Fontainebleau Hotel we decided we would go to Fort Knox on the way back to have a look around. Well, that turned out to be a joke, because even the president of the United States is not allowed in Fort Knox. I still laugh remembering this, 'cause we got within about 50 yards, clicking away with cameras, and they rushed up to stop us and said, 'You mustn't take pictures!' And so I moved forward and said, 'Oh, why not?' and as I did Ken continued to quickly snap off more pictures. But we ended up reckoning that it was pretty dull inside. However, the great trick was, since no one has ever seen the inside of Fort Knox, we could go bananas with the set, which Ken did brilliantly."

Ken Adam (Production Designer): "I got a call from Stanley Kubrick, who was very impressed by the look of *Dr. No.* Kubrick was so fascinated by the big Bond movies — he was like a child when it came to Bond. But he was about to do *Dr. Strangelove* and thought I was the right man for that picture. So I didn't do *From Russia with Love.* But I came back on *Goldfinger* and really went to town. What was an interesting challenge was Fort Knox, because we could copy exactly the exterior of Fort Knox — which we built on the backlot of Pinewood Studios — but nobody is

A Lesson In Hard Knox: Goldfinger (Gert Fröbe) and Oddjob (Harold Sakata) prepare to handcuff Bond to the activated atomic bomb.

allowed inside the place. So I visited the vaults at the Bank of England and decided to make the interior of Fort Knox very theatrical — a complete stylization. I felt here is the biggest gold depository in the world, the audience wants to see gold. That is what Fort Knox should look like. But over the years, I found that the difficult thing was not in building or designing a set, it was convincing a director or producer of your concept. And particularly on *Goldfinger* it was difficult because Harry [Saltzman] and Cubby [Broccoli] said to me, 'Come on, Ken, it looks like a fuckin' prison!' And I said, 'But that's exactly what I want to do! I want it to rise up 40 or 50 feet behind giant bars.' And it was Guy Hamilton who said, 'I think Ken has a point.' After that, the rest was smooth sailing more or less. The audience completely accepted it. And I remember United Artists got so many letters after *Goldfinger* came out, asking how we were allowed to film inside Fort Knox when even the president of the United States was not allowed inside. It's funny, I even got a letter from the director of Fort Knox, who said he admired my imagination, and he hated to disappoint me, but Fort Knox looked nothing like that inside!"

Peter Lamont (Draftsman): "*Goldfinger* was my first introduction to Ken Adam, who became my mentor. He didn't know me, but he knew my reputation. So I remember one day he came over and handed me this package of photos of the exterior of Fort Knox and said, 'Draw this up!' It was a baptism by fire for me. For the next month, I drew all the details, and when I finished it was figured it was going to cost just under £60,000 to build it. Well, the most expensive set up until then in England had been about £30,000, so I thought for sure I was going to get fired! But then Guy said, 'Well, if we take out this little bit and that little bit, we could take it down to £45,000.' At that point, Cubby simply said, 'Build it!'

Guy Hamilton: "We realized we had to shoot more footage of the Pussy Galore's Flying Circus air raid over Fort Knox. It was now July, and the picture was opening in September — there was an absolute rush on because the schedule was so hurried. So Cubby, [cinematographer] Ted Moore, and I flew to Kentucky and stayed at a motel outside of Louisville. We got in a helicopter the next morning and flew over the nearby army barracks and filmed the troops on the ground. Well, when we landed, there were screams and yells, and Cubby said to me, 'You can only go up once more to film, so do it quickly because the general is sending the police because we didn't have the permission to fly over the joint.' So we did that, and then in the afternoon we bribed a sergeant in the platoon to let us shoot them all in exchange for something like 10 bucks and a beer each. They agreed, but we only had an hour window to shoot. So I said, 'Okay, this is it, fellas — you march along, and when I blow my whistle you all look up, and when I blow my whistle the second time you all fall down dead.' Well, they all thought it was hilariously funny. They had no idea what it was all about. But for 10 bucks and a beer, they did it. So we rushed around all over the place shooting this platoon, and then we got the hell out of there."

Guy Hamilton: "The joke about Pussy Galore's Flying Circus was they were all crop duster pilots smoking these enormous cigars. So we made them all wear these wigs we bought from Woolworth's, and when they flew within camera range we instructed them, 'Take off your Stetsons, put your wigs on, and for God's sake take those cigars out of your mouths!' But when we looked at the footage later, there were a lot of shots we couldn't use because, as the planes came into view, you could plainly see these guys

One of the sexiest "Bond Girls" ever: Honor Blackman in an early '60s publicity photo, and (right) together with author David Giammarco in London (2002).

still chomping on those cigars. That was Pussy Galore's Flying Circus!"

Honor Blackman: "I had read Ian Fleming's book beforehand, and I was just sorry that they didn't put in the fact that Pussy Galore was a lesbian to begin with, because we could have had some real fun with my flying team! But I always hated being referred to as a 'Bond Girl,' because a 'Bond Girl' implies that she was a bimbo. And Pussy was by no means a bimbo. But it's funny, I remember there were quite a few interviewers in America who wouldn't even say the name 'Pussy Galore.' They were so puritanical. So when they would just say 'your character,' I would always pipe up, 'Oh, you mean *Pussy Galore*?' It was fun to get a rise out of them."

Guy Hamilton, on casting Gert Fröbe as Goldfinger: "Cubby asked me to come and see a German film that Gert Fröbe was in where he played a pedophile. He was deliciously evil and wicked. Gert was a

James Bond and his Slazenger gets into the swing of things with Goldfinger on the links at Stoke Poges.

wonderfully accomplished actor, so I said to Cubby, 'Yeah, I think he's tremendously good. But what's his English like?' And Cubby said, 'Oh, his agent said he speaks perfect English.' So after Gert was cast, I met him, and he said, 'How do you do, Mr. Hamilton? It is a great pleasure to meet you, and I look forward to our film.' And then I said, 'What hotel are you staying at?' And he said again, 'How do you do, Mr. Hamilton? It is a great pleasure to meet you.' He didn't understand a word I said — he only knew that one phrase! Well, that became quite a problem, as you can imagine. But he had a dialogue coach, and he studied his scenes very hard. I made a point of not making them too long and had lots of cuts in them. He learned his dialogue phonetically, and the only thing I had to do was getting him to speed up because he was enunciating everything very slowly. If I hadn't sped him up, you could have gone and gotten popcorn and come back, and he still would have been on the first sentence. So he started rattling off this dialogue very quickly, and when Cubby and Harry saw the rushes they went bananas. They said, 'We can't understand one word he's saying!' And I said, 'Don't worry — we will revoice him in postproduction. The main thing is the mouth is moving at the right tempo.' And we did dub him, and the actor [Michael Collins] did a tremendous job of imitating Gert. But there actually are some bits of Gert's real voice in the film, because by the end of the shoot he was speaking much better."

Sean Connery poses with the Aston Martin DBV. Ken Adam, Guy Hamilton, and screenwriter Richard Maibaum dreamed up ideas for the car's gadgets, which were all fully functional except for the tire scythes — an optical effect added in later. The total cost was £15,000 and the extras added 300lbs additional weight to the vehicle.

Honor Blackman: "The funniest thing about *Goldfinger* was when I first met Gert Fröbe. He said 'How do you do?' and then we sat down to rehearse our first scene. He said his first line, and I couldn't understand one word! I panicked a bit, but I waited until his mouth stopped moving and then I said my line. Then he started saying his next line, and I thought, 'My God, what is this?' So when we finished rehearsing, I said to Guy, 'What is going on? No one is going to understand a word he's saying.' And Guy said, 'Oh, don't worry, he's going to be dubbed.' And what Gert was trying to say was 'Operation Grand Slam will make you a very rich woman, Miss Galore.' But I can't tell you what that line came out sounding like!"

Guy Hamilton, on the gadget-loaded Aston Martin DB-V: "Ken Adam thought the whole idea was very silly, and we had to convince him otherwise. And it was [special effects supervisor] Johnny Stears who had the job of constructing it. But the revolving number plates were my idea, because I was getting a lot of parking tickets at the time, and I had rather fancied the idea of just driving away. There were a lot of bits and pieces that went into brainstorming that weren't in the script. I remember the original script had Q saying, 'Now you see that little red button there? Whatever you do, don't touch it!' And you faded out on that. We shot it on a Friday afternoon, and Cubby was sitting on the set, and he said, 'No, no, no — you've got to tell the audience what the red button does.' And I said, 'Cubby, if you do that, then you're going to spoil all the fun because then they'll know what's going to happen.' So we went on about it for a while, and I thought, 'Well, we can always cut it out.' So I sat down and wrote the lines very quickly about the ejector seat and how it worked — with Sean finally saying 'Ejector seat? You're joking!'— and handed it to Desmond [Llewelyn] and said, 'Right, we're going to shoot this in a couple minutes.' Poor old Desmond was terribly flustered having to learn it all so quickly. He usually needed a lot of time to learn his lines. So he went off in a corner, memorized it, and it was our last shot of the day. Now, I have to say that Cubby was 100% right. You tell 'em what you're going to do, and then you do it. That's one of the occasions where I have to give Cubby full marks. My instincts were wrong on that one."

Honor Blackman: "Sean Connery was very professional, very twinkly. He has to be, without doubt, the sexiest man I've ever met. A lot of natural authority and charisma. We certainly had a lot of fun in the hay, because we had to lie about for such a long time. But there was no starry-star with Sean. He didn't behave like a starry-star, and he wasn't treated like one. I mean, there's always pressure on a movie, but on a Bond movie even more so because there's a lot of money being spent. And in those days, they were the films that spent the most money of any movie made in Britain."

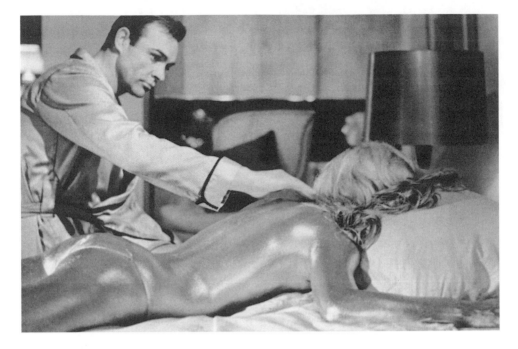

On Golden Blonde: Bond discovers Goldfinger's lethal brush strokes on Jill Masterson (Shirley Eaton).

North American Gross: $51.1 million

Overseas: $73.8 million

THUNDERBALL (1965)

Directed By: Terence Young

The Mission: "SPECTRE NO. 2" Emilio Largo captures two atomic bombs by hijacking a British Vulcan aircraft during a NATO training mission off the coast of the Bahamas. Unless SPECTRE's demands for £100 million ransom are met, a major British or American city will be destroyed.

Locales: France, London, Bahamas

The Villain and Accomplices: Ernst Stavro Blofeld, Emilio Largo (Adolfo Celi), Vargas (Philip Locke), Fiona Volpe (Luciana Paluzzi), Count Lippe (Guy Doleman)

The Bond Girls: Domino (Claudine Auger), Patricia Fearing (Molly Peters), Paula Caplan (Martine Beswick)

A Looming SPECTRE: Emilio Largo (Adolfo Celi) keeps an eye on Bond and Domino (Claudine Auger) in the Bahamas.

Theme Song: Tom Jones

Score: John Barry

Memorable Lines:

"I think he got the point." — *Bond, after harpooning henchman Vargas to a tree.*

"It's your SPECTRE against mine." — *Bond quips to Largo at the baccarat table.*

Domino: "What sharp little eyes you've got."
Bond: "Wait till you get to my teeth."

"Mind if my friend sits this one out? She's just dead." — *Bond, depositing Fiona Volpe at a table after she takes a bullet on the dance floor.*

Ground Control To Major Bond: 007 gets propelled out of a sticky situation at Jacques Boitier's French chateau thanks to a Bell jet pack in Thunderball's opening teaser.

Peter Hunt (Editor): "After *Goldfinger*, we realized how formidable the task was in topping ourselves. By the mid-'60s, everyone around the world was anxiously awaiting each new Bond film — it was always the talk of the town. But we had such a great group of minds working on the Bonds. The producers were very open to suggestions. We would have conferences and throw out ideas and discuss them. And fortunately for *Thunderball*, we had a pretty good book as source material. But *Thunderball* took the longest to shoot because of all the underwater scenes. It was also our biggest budget yet — $11 million."

Ken Adam (Production Designer): "On *Thunderball*, I'll always remember the swimming pool with the sharks. I couldn't get enough Plexiglas in the Bahamas; all they had were four-by-eight sheets in Nassau. So we ended up with this four-foot gap. We were working with Ivan Tors — the underwater expert who was doing the *Flipper* television series — and I had one of his guys stationed in the pool, and of course I didn't tell Sean there was a gap. We used enormous sharks, but they were pretty tired because they'd already been in the pool for some time. And I knew it was going to happen: this shark took one look at the gap and went right for it. I don't know where the underwater guard was. We saw all this from the top, but Sean didn't realize what had happened, so we started screaming at him to get out of the water. You've never seen someone get out of a pool so quickly. He literally walked on water!"

Thunderball's final underwater battle took six days and 60 divers to shoot in the waters off Nassau.

Peter Hunt, on the elaborate underwater fight sequences:
"Underwater scenes are a very tricky thing to do. They can really slow down the pace of a movie. We had to speed up all those scenes. We did a lot of tests as to what speeds we could reach without it looking ridiculous. That was the secret of the film, and we had to be very clever about it. Not every shot was speeded up, but most were in order to make it all work. And also don't underestimate the enormous advantage of having John Barry's score. John's music contributed a great deal to those scenes, as it did in all the Bond films he worked on."

Peter Lamont: "I was promoted to chief draftsman on *Thunderball*, and one morning Ken Adam came into the art department and said, 'We're going to the Bahamas, so you better learn to swim underwater.' So I had

The Domino Theory: Raquel Welch was originally signed by Cubby Broccoli for the role of Domino, but she was tied up filming Fantastic Voyage. Former Miss France Claudine Auger would fill out the part quite nicely.

to learn to scuba dive, because I was in charge of dressing all the underwater sets and the Vulcan bomber. I even ended up having to double Sean for one shot where he retrieves Domino's brother's dog tags from the submerged Vulcan. They needed that shot, but it was Sean's last day, so they said to me, 'You know what to do, Peter, you do it.' It's a brief shot at the end of the sequence, but that's me in the cockpit."

Ken Adam: "On *Thunderball*, the challenge wasn't so much the sets but building that Vulcan bomber full size down in the Bahamas. For Largo's superfast yacht the *Disco Volante*, I found a hydrofoil down in Puerto Rico and bought it for $10,000. We took it back to Miami, and I redesigned it and doubled its length by building the 50-foot catamaran that cocooned around it. All the naval experts were worried and didn't think it could work. But I used two one-inch slip bolts on either side that held the cocoon to the hydrofoil so they could move independently. And once they separated and the hydrofoil was revealed, the cocoon became a floating arsenal with the type of armament you found on a destroyer ship, like the antiaircraft cannon, machine guns, and armor plating. Everyone said we were going to have a disaster, but it worked beautifully."

North American Gross: $63.6 million

Overseas: $77.6 million

YOU ONLY LIVE TWICE *(1967)*

Directed By: Lewis Gilbert

The Mission: Ernst Stavro Blofeld is revealed as the mastermind behind an elaborate bid for world domination by simultaneously sabotaging U.S.- and Soviet-manned spacecrafts, causing the two superpowers to blame one another and triggering World War III.

Locales: Hong Kong, Japan, outer space

The Villain and Accomplices: Ernst Stavro Blofeld (Donald Pleasence), Mr. Osato (Teru Shimada), Helga Brandt (Karin Dor), Hans (Ronald Rich)

Rocket Man: Blofeld (Donald Pleasence) shows off his wares inside the volcano lair, as audiences saw Blofeld for the first time.

The Bond Girls: Aki (Akiko Wakabayashi), Kissy Suzuki (Mie Harma), Ling (Tsai Chin)

Theme Song: Nancy Sinatra

Score: John Barry

Memorable Lines:

Bond: "May I smoke?"
Blofeld: ". . . it won't be the nicotine that kills you, Mister Bond."

Blofeld: "They told me you were assassinated in Hong Kong."
Bond: "Yes, this is my second life."
Blofeld: "You only live twice, Mister Bond."

"You're late as usual — even from your own funeral." — *Moneypenny to Bond, after he surfaces from his fake burial at sea.*

"Bon appétit!" — *Bond, after flipping Hans into Blofeld's piranha-infested pool.*

Ken Adam (Production Designer): "I always liked big challenges, and *You Only Live Twice* was certainly that. By this point, I was really very confident, maybe over-confident, that anything I could draw somebody could build. So when we were flying all over Japan looking for locations, we flew over this volcano area, and everyone got very excited, saying wouldn't it be fun if Blofeld was headquartered in this extinct volcano. I thought it would be great fun to design, and I did a quick scribble. When I start designing something and I know I'm on to something really good, it's almost like having an orgasm. The volcano set was like that for me. But you have to remember the pressure we were all under, because we had no script. The writer had been fired, and then they brought in Roald Dahl to write the new screenplay. In those days, the studio had very firm release dates, and our release date was only five months away, and we had nothing. So when I showed Cubby my scribble of the volcano set, he said, 'It looks interesting,' and then said, 'How much is it going to cost?' I said, 'I have no idea.' So he said, 'If I give you a million dollars, can you do it?' I said, 'Of course.' Because in 1966, a million

Author David Giammarco with Oscar-winning Production Designer Ken Adam at Adam's home in London.

dollars was quite a lot. So he said, 'Well, you've got it.' Well, that's when my worries really started. How am I going to do this? Am I crazy to try something so gigantic? And even though I covered myself by calling in experts and structural engineers, they were just as much in awe of a sliding crater lake 120 feet up with a 60-foot diameter made of fiberglass and 700 tons of structural steel and a full-size helicopter flying through there. It took real courage. But I had a great team of people, who by now had worked with me on several Bonds, and that was very encouraging. Early on, we were considering doing the volcano set as a model, but we all realized that would be cheating the audience. And Cubby never wanted to cheat the audience; he wanted to give them as much reality as we could, and we always kept to that. However, I do remember a doctor ended up having to put me on Valium while I was building that set. Looking back now, I think I was slightly mad."

Peter Hunt (Second Unit Director and Supervising Editor): "The script for *You Only Live Twice* had four different car chases in it. [Director] Lewis Gilbert just threw all the car chases at me and said, 'You can do those as second unit.' And I said, 'Oh, God, how can you be clever over *four* car chases?' I was very upset because I didn't know what to do to make these car chases different and interesting. I was hoping something would come up or something would happen. So we were in Japan location scouting, where every day we went out in a helicopter looking for a castle on the island — which is how Fleming's book ends — but there was no such thing in Japan. But one day when we were flying over this area that was full of something like 21 defunct volcanoes, I suddenly said, 'Why don't we use these?' They just looked so spectacular from the air. Out of those conversations came 'Why can't Blofeld be headquartered underneath a volcano?' And it was then that I got the idea of how to get rid of one of the car chases: we could have a *helicopter* chase instead. Harry [Saltzman] said, 'Great! Bond can be chased by five helicopters!' And I said, 'Whoa, wait a minute! *Five* helicopters?' But that was typical of how Harry was. No idea was too fantastic. He said, 'If he's Bond, he's got to be chased by more than just one helicopter!' I realized what a big job that was going to be. So we started to write it, and when Harry went back to London he picked up an *Aero* magazine and saw that gyro-copter. He picked up the telephone and said, 'I want this gyro-copter. Get it down to Pinewood, I want to look at it.' And so when we got back from location weeks later, Harry had the gyro already and was as excited as a little child with his new toy. He kept saying to everyone, 'Look what we've got!' And that's how the Little Nellie gyro-copter scene came about."

Keeping it on the QT: Desmond Llewelyn and Sean Connery in rehearsals for the Little Nellie gyro-copter scene in Japan.

Ken Adam: "I remember listening to the BBC one morning while I was shaving, and I heard Wing Commander Kenneth Wallis giving an interview about this gyro-copter he had invented. So I rang up the BBC and asked to get in touch with Wallis. I was delighted when I saw the gyro-copter at Pinewood and thought, 'I'm going to make a war machine out of this.' I don't know why, but I always had a knack for designing things like planes, cars, boats, and underwater craft. And at the time, my wife was designing handbags in Italy and exporting them, and she said, 'Wouldn't it be funny if you did the gyro-copter like a do-it-yourself kit, all in very chic crocodile luggage with velour inside.' Everyone was getting into the spirit of things."

Vic Armstrong (Stuntman), on his first Bond assignment, doubling as a Ninja warrior rappeling into the volcano:

Kung-Fu Fighting: During martial arts training, Bond comes to blows with a Ninja infiltrator.

"If you watch the film, I was the first guy to hit the ground off the ropes. The Japanese didn't want to do it; they were fighters, not really stuntmen as such. They were more karate guys and not too crazy about the height of the jump. So we had to do it. It was a funny feeling, because you're 125 feet up in the air, and you had to crawl between the roof and the girder, which was a gap of only about three feet. So imagine your toes are on something three feet below your head, and you're hanging on with your hands and your ass sticking out and having to shuffle sideways along an I-beam onto your rope, and then you've got to very quickly slide down that rope. My God, you could never do that nowadays with Health and Safety! But *You Only Live Twice* was a very special moment for me as a kid new to the business. I remember I earned 90 quid, and I bought my first car with the money. And now all these years later, I'm spending 20 or 25 million of their money on the film."

North American Gross: $43.1 million

Overseas: $68.5 million

A Winning Hand: Sean Connery and Lana Wood show plenty for the camera in Las Vegas.

DIAMONDS ARE FOREVER (1971)

Directed By: Guy Hamilton

The Mission: Ernst Stavro Blofeld has kidnapped reclusive billionaire Willard Whyte and uses his empire to secretly amass vast quantities of diamonds in the construction of a laser satellite for destroying major cities.

Locales: London, Las Vegas, Japan, Egypt, Amsterdam, South America, South Africa, Los Angeles

The Villain and Accomplices: Ernst Stavro Blofeld (Charles Gray), Mr. Wint (Bruce Glover) and Mr. Kidd (Putter Smith), Peter Franks (Joe Robinson), Bambi (Donna Garratt), and Thumper (Trina Parks)

The Bond Girls: Tiffany Case (Jill St. John), Plenty O'Toole (Lana Wood)

Theme Song: Shirley Bassey

Score: John Barry

Memorable Lines:

"Hi, I'm Plenty."
Bond: "But of course you are."
Plenty: ". . . Plenty O'Toole."
Bond: "Named after your father, perhaps."

"I'm afraid you've caught me with more than my hands up." — *Bond, alongside Plenty O'Toole, surprised by gangsters in his hotel suite.*

"Refreshing to hear there's one subject you're not an expert on." — *M, after Bond admits to limited knowledge about diamonds.*

"Klaus Hergersheimer — G section." — *Bond's alias when caught in a top-secret military laboratory.*

Faced with twin Blofelds, Bond determines the real Blofeld by kicking the white Persian cat to its rightful owner. "Right idea, Mister Bond," *Blofeld gloats after 007 mistakenly shoots his double.*
"But wrong pussy," *concedes Bond.*

Blofeld to Bond: "Surely you haven't come to negotiate, Mister Bond? Your pitiful little island hasn't even been threatened."

"My God, you've just killed *James Bond*," *says a shocked Tiffany Case to Bond, who bumps off diamond smuggler Peter Franks and then switches identities with him.*
Bond: "Is that who it was? Well, it just proves no one's indestructible."

Guy Hamilton (Director): "*Diamonds Are Forever* was a big responsibility because Lazenby's film hadn't worked so well, and the goose that laid the golden egg was wobbling a bit. I was aware of what they wanted: they wanted Sean back, and they wanted me. I was asked to do *Thunderball*, and I said 'No' because I had run out of ideas. I think you've got to approach the Bond films very fresh. And by *Diamonds*, I then had some ideas because I had put enough distance between *Goldfinger* by then."

Guy Hamilton, on Sean Connery's return as Bond: "It turned out he liked the script very much, and once he agreed to the deal the only thing that concerned him was whether it was going to overrun, because he wanted a very firm stop date. But that was not a particular worry to me, because I was always careful about keeping to the schedule. And we finished exactly at four o'clock on the last day of his contract. The production had advanced very smoothly indeed. I think the only stipulation was that in the contract it was more or less stated that Sean got time off to play golf once a week."

Viva Bond Vegas: Sean Connery strikes a pose on location along the Vegas Strip for Diamonds Are Forever.

Tom Mankiewicz (Co-Screenwriter): "I met Sean for the first time in Las Vegas two weeks before we started filming. We had a script reading together, just Sean, Guy, and myself, and Sean had like 30 or 40 notes over the 130 pages. Some were very little notes, like about a certain line, or 'Bond wouldn't use this word.' But what I was so impressed by was that more than half the notes were for the other characters; they weren't about him. He would say, 'Are you sure Blofeld would say this?' or 'Wouldn't it be more fun if Tiffany Case did this?' I was shocked. It was the least self-centered script meeting I'd ever had with an actor, much less a star of his magnitude."

Guy Hamilton: "Tom Mankiewicz and I had many conversations about how we were running out of Fleming books. Things like villains on a train, chases in helicopters, these were very exciting, modern things when Fleming first wrote them. But 15 years later, every TV show had helicopters buzzing about. These are no longer climaxes for a Bond movie. When you come to film the book years later, all those elements are passé in spades. So that was always one of our main considerations. Also, where do you take Bond? He had been all over the world. The book takes place mostly at Saratoga Racetrack, but there's nothing happening there anymore. But I had been to Las Vegas a lot after *Goldfinger* and liked the place very much, so that became an obvious choice. I remember I even had an idea for a chase sequence in Disneyland, where all the villains are in costume. We approached the Disney organization about that, and, well, you can imagine what their reaction was."

Tom Mankiewicz: "James Bond is this wonderful character, but the problem the films were going through was that Bond had started out as just this side of a paid assassin in *Dr. No* and *From Russia with Love*. A really tough guy. You know, 'That's a Smith & Wesson, and you've had your six . . . boom, boom, boom, boom.' By the time *Diamonds Are Forever* came along, I couldn't have written a scene like that. In other words, Bond couldn't have killed a guy in cold blood. My theory has always been that, the minute that Aston Martin came on screen in *Goldfinger*, movies changed forever. The minute the audience roared with laughter at the ejection seat, the machine guns, the oil squirting, Bond suddenly became 'Can you top this?' The audience now wanted to see new and bigger gadgets. But the Fleming books, while fun to read, are really much closer to *Dr. No*. There was no way you could make Ian Fleming's *Diamonds Are Forever* anymore given the audience expectations of what Bond should be."

Tom Mankiewicz on censorship: "The Bond films were PG movies, but PG was much stricter in those days. You couldn't say 'fuck' in a PG movie or show any nudity whatsoever. And, of course, Americans are only concerned about the sex, and the British are only concerned about the

Breakfast With Tiffany: Sean Connery and Jill St. John (Tiffany Case) kill time Vegas-style between camera set-ups in the Ken Adam-designed bridal suite.

violence. So in *Diamonds Are Forever*, we were threatened with losing our rating because in one scene Mr. Wint dropped a live scorpion down the dentist's throat. That was fine with the Americans, who don't care about violence, but not with the Brits. On the other hand, a one-half-second glimpse of Lana Wood's breasts, which was fine in England, we had to cut out."

Guy Hamilton, on Howard Hughes's involvement: "We were *persona* very much *grata* in Las Vegas, because it takes special permission to shoot a film there, especially inside the casinos. Let's just say Cubby had very good connections that went all the way to the top. Howard Hughes was a very great friend of Cubby's — they went back a long, long time. That's what helped us get into Vegas so smoothly. But I always thought it so sad that Hughes had become such a recluse. Cubby said he would just get messages from Howard, saying that he wanted to see his Bond films. Cubby said he knew he would always run them, so I said to Cubby, 'Well, that's it — send him the new one, and then halfway through the reel put in an insert shot that says, "Howard Hughes, you prick! Why don't you call me? Love, Cubby" and maybe wake him up. And Cubby said, 'No, you don't know Howard.' So we never did get to meet him."

Ken Adam (Production Designer): "I was intrigued because the Willard Whyte character was loosely based on Cubby's friend Howard Hughes. It gave me a very enjoyable opportunity to imagine and design what his penthouse would possibly look like. It was a very interesting set, but I was disappointed that it was hardly used in the film. It was quite beautiful. I mixed antique with very modern furniture, and it seemed to work. I don't mind if a set is well shot and then it's struck. But if it's not well shot, or you don't see enough of it in the film, then I find that upsetting. And then there was Bond's bridal suite, which I wanted to make very kitschy because Las Vegas is vulgar. The big waterbed became the central part of the suite, and I thought it would be fun to fill it with tropical fish and having the fish all swimming around the waterbed in Plexiglas aquariums. It ended up easier said than done. But I had fun doing that."

Tom Mankiewicz: "It's no secret that Cubby loved to gamble. *Diamonds Are Forever* was the worst location for him, because we were in Las Vegas for months. And I used to sit next to him at the baccarat table, and I would think that on an average evening Cubby never won or lost less than $50,000. And I remember we were in one of the last mob-owned casinos, the Riviera, when one night Cubby said he wasn't going to gamble anymore — just keno cards from now on. And then he would proceed to buy 10,000 keno cards! It's like the guy who says, 'I'm not drinking hard booze anymore,' and then you watch him down 25 beers in a row. So I said, 'Cubby, why don't you just go back to the baccarat table?'"

Tom Mankiewicz, on the fake moon landing staged on a secret Nevada military installation: "At the time, the rumors had just started circulating that we hadn't really landed on the moon. So we were just trying to do a kind of wry nod to that without hitting it too hard. We thought it would be funny if Bond came crashing through there. It was the first time I started getting mail from audiences. But I got really angry mail because of the line near the end of the film, when Blofeld is about to shoot the laser and asks, 'Where is the laser now?' and they say, 'Over Kansas,' and he says, 'Well, if we destroy Kansas, the world might not hear about it for years!' I can't tell you how many letters I got from people in Kansas saying, 'You son of a bitch . . . we're never going to see another Bond movie again!' In those days, *everybody* went to see the Bond movies, and they all had opinions they would write to us about."

North American Gross: $43.8 million

Overseas: $72.2 million

For One Bond Only: George Lazenby

His Bond only lived once. But in the more than three decades since his sole outing as James Bond in 1969's *On Her Majesty's Secret Service*, George Lazenby knows that the mark of 007 never dies.

"I didn't want to do another Bond film because I didn't want to be known as James Bond for the rest of my life," explained Lazenby with a wry grin, "which, as it happens, I have been anyway. . . ."

The story of how the 29-year-old George Lazenby — born and raised in rural Goulburn, Australia — won one of the most coveted roles in motion picture history and then summarily tossed it away is a scenario as intriguing as it is unimaginable.

It was 1967, and the times they were a changin'. Haight-Ashbury. Carnaby Street. The Summer of Love. The Peace Movement. The escalating war in Vietnam. . . . And Sean Connery throwing in the towel on one of the '60s most potent pop culture phenomena. After *You Only Live Twice*, Cubby Broccoli and Harry Saltzman were faced with the stark reality that Sean Connery was sticking to his guns, and nothing they did could persuade him to stay. So the hunt was on for a new James Bond. Could the franchise still survive? Would the public accept a different 007? Broccoli and Saltzman were cautiously optimistic. High on their wish list to take Connery's place were Roger Moore (who had been one of the original choices for the role and had subsequently become a household name through his '60s TV series *The Saint*) and a young Timothy Dalton, fresh from an impressive performance as Philip II of Spain in *The Lion in Winter*. But Moore was still in a television contract, and Dalton considered himself much too young to play Bond. Hundreds of other actors were being screen-tested for the coveted role throughout late 1967 and early 1968.

Meanwhile, a world away, George Lazenby was a tall and rugged Aussie outdoorsman who had done a stint in the army and then moved to London in 1964. Acting had never crossed his mind. He was working as a car salesman when one of the customers — photographer Chard Jenkins — persuaded Lazenby to try his hand at modeling. Lazenby ended up being quite successful, appearing as the Marlboro Man and in numerous other print ads, as well as gaining some notoriety on TV for his Big Fry Chocolates commercials. Lazenby was happy with the money he was making and had no ambition for an acting career. At least not yet.

But a good pal of Lazenby's, who happened to be an aspiring actor, was caught in a double-booked dating bind one night and asked for Lazenby's help. "He said, 'There's an agent that I was going to go out for dinner with tonight, but now my girlfriend has come back into town — can you take her out?' So I said, 'Sure.' We went out, and she was so impressed by me and kept saying she thought I would make a good James Bond."

The agent turned out to be Maggie Abbott from the ICM talent agency and, unbeknownst to Lazenby, was quietly championing him for the Bond role. She later telephoned Lazenby in Paris and asked him to return to London to screen-test for a film. But she couldn't divulge the nature of the project. Recalled Lazenby: "So I more or less told her, 'Look, if you can't tell me the name of the movie, I'm not coming over.' And she said, 'Well, I can't tell you on the phone.' And so I said, 'Well, I'm not coming over then,' and I hung up.

"Then when I got back to London a few weeks later, my friend said Maggie had been searching everywhere for me, and had I spoken with her?

By George: Australian model George Lazenby had the formidable task of stepping into the shoes vacated by Sean Connery for 1969's On Her Majesty's Secret Service.

And I said, 'Yeah, she was talking about a film, but she wouldn't tell me the name of it, so I hung up on her.' And he said, 'Well, let's go see her,' and I said, 'No, fuck her.' So we went out for a walk, and he ended up purposely guiding me by her office and said, 'Go on! Go in and see her.' So I went in, and that's when she finally told me about the James Bond thing and thought I had a really good shot at it. Apparently, they had been looking for a guy for a year or more and had done 300 different screen tests and were not satisfied with what they'd seen.''

So Lazenby went to the casting office but was turned away because he didn't have an appointment. Lazenby tried again later and this time happened to catch the eye of the film's casting director, who just happened to be on the phone with Harry Saltzman at the time. 'He said to Harry, 'I think I've got someone here who looks interesting.' So he hung up and asked me some questions, and I told him my life story — which was all bullshit.''

Lazenby's bluff included conning the casting director into believing he was a karate expert, a race car driver, a ski instructor, and "an actor who'd done movies in Russia and Germany and God knows what other places that they couldn't check on," remembered Lazenby with a chuckle. Lazenby was promptly whisked over to Saltzman's office, "and when I got there Harry said, 'Tell me your life story,' and I said, 'I've already told this guy — let him tell you.' So he proceeded to tell Harry the story just as if it were for real." Lazenby admits that halfway through the meeting his nerves started getting the best of him, and he feared the ruse was about to be exposed. "I just wanted to get the hell out of Harry's office. I thought to myself, 'The bullshit has gone too far — I can't handle it anymore.' I didn't want to go through with it."

But Saltzman was intrigued. Lazenby's fear had come off as arrogance, and Saltzman asked Lazenby to return the next day and meet Peter Hunt, the director of *On Her Majesty's Secret Service*. Lazenby panicked and refused the offer. Figuring he would assuredly be busted by the director, Lazenby lied and said that he had to return to Paris the next day for a job. Saltzman pressed him further, saying, "'How much is it going to cost to keep you here?' And I told them, and they said, 'We'll give you a check — *now* will you stay here?' And I said, 'Yeah, okay.' Next thing I know I've got a check for $500 — which was a lot of money in those days — to come back the next day and test!

"So I called up Maggie and said, 'They've given me a check to test.' And she said, '*What?!*' And I said, 'Yeah, they've given $500 to come back to test tomorrow and meet the director.' And she said, 'Jesus, they've never given anybody anything! Do it!' And I said, 'I was actually going to give the check back to them — they're going to find out I'm a phony because I've never acted before and never spoken in front of a camera. I've lied to them.'"

Eventually, Lazenby decided he would go to the meeting and confess his sins. "I told Peter Hunt the truth. I said, 'Peter, I've never acted before. I just told them a whole lot of bullshit, and when you test me you're going to find that out.' And Peter's response to me was '*You've fooled the two most ruthless guys I've ever known — you've got to be an actor!* Just stick with your story, and I'll make you the next James Bond.'

"And I never understood at the time why he did it, but Peter's thing was that, if he used a nonactor, he would get all the credit. That was explained to me years later — I had no idea what he was up to," shrugged Lazenby.

He indeed tested, and Hunt then sent Lazenby to a vocal coach to help extinguish his Australian accent. Lazenby was asked to stay in London for a retainer of £150 a week and was put through a battery of on-screen tests with various other actors. The testing process lasted four months. "It gave me a lot of experience, because at the end of the four months I didn't feel uncomfortable in front of the camera anymore," said Lazenby.

By late spring 1968, Broccoli and Saltzman had narrowed their choices down to five actors: John Richardson (who had starred opposite Raquel Welch in *One Million Years B.C.*), Anthony Rogers, Robert Campbell, Hans de Vries, and Lazenby. They, along with many young actresses, were all being tested at Pinewood Studios. In the end, it was Lazenby's physicality and skill with hand-to-hand combat that won him the role. Lazenby's test-fight footage had duly impressed both Saltzman and Broccoli, as well as United Artists. They finally announced they had found their new James Bond. The 29-year-old Lazenby would be the youngest actor to ever play Bond.

But the seeming ease with which Lazenby landed the role of a lifetime was far from effortless. "I concentrated really hard on what I was doing to

A recent shot of George Lazenby at his home in Los Angeles.

get that part," he insisted. "I didn't do anything else but focus on getting that role. I put all my energy into it, because I felt it was important for me. It's not at all like it was easy or I got it slipped to me on the side. I had no distractions at the time. I didn't go out anywhere through it all. I just concentrated on getting that part, otherwise I wouldn't have had a shot. I mean, the other guys probably lived their normal life and were distracted and fragmented, but I was totally centered on getting that part. And that's why I eventually got it, I think."

In hindsight, Lazenby admits now that he was driven for probably all the wrong reasons. "I think it was more that I just wanted to be important . . . more important than I was," he said with quiet reflection. "That really appealed to me, because I remember being at a hotel in St. Tropez and not being able to get a room as a male model. Guys were walking past me who were doctors and dentists and whatever and getting rooms. And I thought, 'There's a game here that I can't play.' Because I haven't got any initials after my name, I'm not anybody. And I thought [Bond] would establish me on this planet as *somebody*. It was a practical thing more than an ego thing, you know what I mean? It was almost like, 'Hey, this could make me be *someone*' . . . I was always a very practical person."

But once *On Her Majesty's Secret Service* filming commenced, there was little bonding for the new 007. During the first week of shooting, a major rift reportedly developed between Lazenby and director Peter Hunt that remained unresolved during the entire nine-month shoot. According to Lazenby, it happened when he was asked by the crew to kick some of Hunt's friends off the set who were getting in the way. "It was upsetting the crew, so they said to me, 'All these guys are running around here, and we can't say, 'Anyone who's not needed on the set, please leave. But *you*, being the star, *could*.' So I stood up and said, 'Anyone not needed on the set, please leave!' And so these three guys left, and they told Peter that I said that. Now I had no idea what was going on. I just thought I was doing the crew a favor. . . . I had no idea I was shooing off some of Peter's friends.

"Next thing I know," continued Lazenby, "Peter is pissed with me, thinking I knew what I was doing. So then he didn't show up for dinner that night at a party we were having, and from then on he wouldn't speak to me. Every time I tried to talk to him, he just looked at me as if I knew what I was doing, and I shouldn't have done it. It was as simple as that. He took it as I was taking aim at him, and I wasn't. And that's how the whole thing started."

In fact, Lazenby said that while filming there was no communication at

"I didn't do anything else but focus on getting that role," says Lazenby.

all between him and Hunt — any direction was conveyed via the assistant director. "The AD would come over and say, 'Peter would like to do that take again,' and that's how we did it." And Lazenby just figured all directors worked that way. "I didn't know any different," he said. "I didn't know whether the director was supposed to talk to the actors or the assistant director was — I had no clue. I'd never been on a film set before."

Peter Hunt's recollections differ. "Oh, that's just silly," he laughed incredulously. "How on Earth can you make a film without speaking to your lead actor? It's absolute *nonsense*. We spoke all the time. I think what George got upset about was I wouldn't take his side on anything.

He was making demands on the producers. He wasn't getting his own way, and suddenly he said he didn't want to do the film anymore. In fact, it was only about four weeks into the film when he came to me and said, 'I'm not coming in tomorrow — I'm not going to shoot anymore.'

"And I kept telling him," continued Hunt, "'You've got to make this film, because it's to your advantage. We make it well, and then you've got something. You don't make it, and you haven't got anything. After the film, *then* you can fight with them.'"

However, Hunt did keep a distance from Lazenby as a technique to provoke a performance from the novice actor. Hunt said he wanted Lazenby to feel the isolation and loneliness inherent to the character of Bond. And the only way he figured he could generate some depth and emotion from Lazenby was to shake him up somewhat. But Lazenby insists that, even after filming wrapped, Hunt's silence continued. "In fact, I remember one day I saw Peter walking past my house in Eton Square, and I said, 'Hi, Peter! How are you?' and he kept walking. So I said, 'Peter, it's *me* !' And he said, 'I *know*' and just kept walking."

A strained relationship also developed between Lazenby and his costar Diana Rigg, who played Tracy de Vicenzo. Lazenby insisted the British tabloids made a mountain out of a molehill when they reported that Rigg purposely ate garlic before their first love scene to annoy Lazenby. "'The Garlic Incident', as it became known, was just a hoot," laughed Lazenby. "I mean she was in the commissary at Pinewood Studios, and when Diana ordered something with garlic in it she said to me, 'I'm eating garlic, so I hope you are too.' Well, the press got a hold of it and blew it all out of proportion and said, 'DIANA RIGG EATS GARLIC BEFORE LOVE SCENE WITH BOND!' It was ridiculous. Contrary to the press reports, Diana and I did not hate each other. But she was an accomplished actress, and I was not an actor. And there I was, sowing my oats all over the film set. And she got pissed off at me, you know, screwing everything that moved. But I never had a problem with her. Ever."

Five-time 007 director John Glen, who kicked off his Bond association as editor and second-unit director on *On Her Majesty's Secret Service*, recalled shooting stunt sequences with Lazenby as a hassle-free experience.

"He was fine with me," said Glen, "I never had a problem with him. He was always very cooperative. But we were doing stunt work, which was easy for him. On the main unit, he was required to act, and he wasn't a trained actor by any means. And he was working alongside a fantastic actress in Diana Rigg. . . .

"He freely admits now that he was a bit stupid. He was behaving like a spoiled boy who had lots of money and was famous as a male model. He had girls flocking after him all the time, and I think he took this kind of baggage along with him onto the movie. I think he would've done a lot better to have been a bit more humble, in some respects, in his relationships on set."

Despite the on-set tensions, Lazenby said he came away from the shoot with some enjoyable memories — albeit mostly *off* set, he was quick to point out. "Every night I would enjoy myself," he grinned. "But during the day, there was always something going on that was someone else's problem. I never had a problem, really. Everything for me was on the up and up. I mean, how can I go from being just a guy off the street from Australia — just this little country boy Australian male model — to James Bond and have a *down*? Every night, somebody was doing something that was fun for me. I had a good time."

Lazenby soaked up the perks of his new celebrity with reckless abandon. "I certainly didn't know how to handle the fame very well," he admitted. "I mean, there was no one to compare me with. No one had stood in something that was so developed and so famous. You were considered like one of the Beatles being James Bond. Suddenly, you go from nothing, as far as fame is concerned, to VERY FAMOUS. You're all of a sudden invited to places that you would never get into. Suddenly, David Niven is on one side and Princess Grace is on the other, and you're having dinner together. And then you've got Sammy Davis Jr. wanting to invite you to dinner, and you've never met him, but he knows who you are. It was very strange. People like Frank Sinatra, Jill St. John — wherever you go, you're with the A-group while under contract for that two-year period. Your agent tells people that the new James Bond is in town, and tickets for everything were suddenly available; limos were at your disposal; party invites every night."

Why, then, would Lazenby walk away from the role? Granted, stepping into the well-worn shoes of Sean Connery wasn't an easy task for anyone, but Broccoli and Saltzman were committed to their new star. They had even offered Lazenby a lucrative seven-year, seven-picture contract. "But I wouldn't sign it," confessed Lazenby. "I got some bad advice from a guy named Roan O'Reilly, who was my adviser then. He was the guy who ran the pirate radio station 'Radio Caroline,' which was pretty much responsible for all those English pop groups — the Rolling Stones, the Who, the Beatles — getting off the ground. They got their airplay on 'Radio Caroline,' which got their records sold in England. They couldn't get airplay before that. So I thought he was a smart guy, and I trusted him. And he convinced me that the Bond films were not my gig; it was Sean Connery's gig. That they weren't going anywhere and that I was going to be a big movie star all on my own, so why get mixed up with those guys?"

Lazenby paused and recalled the pivotal decision. "I remember very clearly him saying to me, 'There's a *new era* coming. Look at all the hippies. They're not interested in conservative people like James Bond. They're more into *Easy Rider*. Bond isn't the image young kids are into. Being a government agent who drinks martinis wasn't exactly *peace and love*, you know? People are all about nonviolence.'

"So I pulled out of the deal," stated Lazenby. "I was convinced that now that I was famous I was better off on my own anyway." Lazenby said Harry Saltzman tried to convince him to stay on. "He offered me money under the table, and United Artists offered me any movie I wanted to do in between Bond films that they owned. But this guy O'Reilly — who was supposed to be my mentor and manager — kept turning it all down. He kept shooting me dialogue that those guys are going to control me and get me into a big house with big payments and a Hollywood actress for a wife, and you'll need a lot of money to live that way. He gave me the whole spiel. And it was, at that time with the hippie movement and everything, not very appealing. It wasn't *cool* to have money back then. . . .

"Today, it would be," he added with a laugh.

When did Lazenby realize he had made a big mistake? "Oh, I pretty much realized it when I was doing it. But I just didn't have my heart and soul in one spot. If someone gave me lines like that today, I would just laugh at them! But I was a kid from the bush in Australia who hit it big and was learning as I went. I thought this guy was on my side. But what I didn't realize was he wanted me to be in *his* pocket rather than United Artists."

"Unfortunately," sighed Hunt, "George could've gone on to a huge career. Considering he had never acted before, I think he did a wonderful job. But he got some bad advice, and he behaved very badly. He was the wrong personality for this great opportunity given to him. He didn't know how to handle it."

Though Broccoli and Saltzman never doubted they could continue the Bond franchise without him, the bitter feelings still continued, according to Lazenby. "I bit the hand that fed me," he acknowledged. "I don't think they wanted that experience to happen ever again. They spent millions on me, publicizing me as James Bond and all the rest of it, and then I just said, 'I'm not doing it anymore.' It was all my own fault, and I blame myself."

As a result, the media tore Lazenby apart, labeling him difficult and unmanageable. And he soon found producers pulling out of film deals as the bad press started swirling around him. "I certainly didn't deserve the blacklisting I got," he emphasized.

To clear his head and escape the white-hot media spotlight, Lazenby disappeared on a 15-month sailing expedition in the Mediterranean. But he revealed an incident that occurred in 1971 in Malbere, Spain, finally humbled him. "My feet had been off the ground for those years, but then a very strange thing happened. One night I drank a little too much vodka and experienced death. I stopped breathing. Went through a tunnel and saw this bright light, the whole bit. I mean, I was a vegetarian at the time and wasn't eating properly, and I was drinking all this vodka, and the lights finally went out on me. A few people who were in the house, as well as my ex-wife — who was my girlfriend at the time — heard me fall in the bathroom and found me lying on the floor. They lifted me up, and eventually I started breathing again. Suddenly, the lights came back on, and I was out of this tunnel. And for two years after that, I was really, really weak. I couldn't walk a hundred yards without having to take a rest. . . .

"But from that day on," continued Lazenby, "I became a much wiser man. I started feeling really good about myself and about the world. I got a brand-new sense of life."

Unfortunately, Lazenby's new lease on life didn't include a continuation of his fame and fortune. Lazenby had returned to find himself virtually unemployable because of all the negative press he had received during his absence. So Lazenby accepted an offer from Bruce Lee and moved to Hong Kong to work on low-budget kung fu films like *A Man Called Stoner* and *The Man from Hong Kong*. Over the years, Lazenby made guest shots on various shows like *Hawaii Five-O, Hotel, Kung Fu: The Legend Continues*, and *VIP*, and he played a pivotal role in Peter Bogdanovich's *Saint Jack*, all the while pursuing alternative ventures in real estate.

While always living in the shadow of Bond, Lazenby's most heroic role would end up occurring off-screen, as his priorities suddenly shifted to that of his dying son, who in 1984 was diagnosed with brain cancer. Lazenby spent the next nine years caring for Zack, who finally succumbed to the disease in 1994 at age 19. That same year, Lazenby's 24-year marriage dissolved, and Lazenby began immersing himself full time in activities like motorcycle racing, mountain biking, golfing, and tending to his 600-acre ranch in the California desert. Lazenby also maintains a residence in Brentwood and continues to keep his foot in the acting door. "I've been available all this time, but I don't want to scratch the dirt to get a job," he admitted. "I've got enough to take care of myself because I'm not a big spender. And I enjoy life. I live moment to moment. Because you know, at the end of the day — meaning in 100 or 200 years — who gives a shit?"

On June 12, 2002, Lazenby married tennis pro Pam Shriver, whom he met in 2000 at Wimbledon. He still enjoys globe-trotting adventures ("Oh, I get around," he chuckled) and in fact had just returned from an invitational tournament at Stoke Poges before one of our conversations. Stoke Poges is, of course, the prestigious golf course outside London where *Goldfinger* filmed. "I'll probably run into Sean [Connery] one of these days," he laughed. "I keep hearing that we've been playing on the same links."

As for another go-round at a Bond film, Lazenby says he's game. "I offered to play a villain in one of the new ones," he said, "but I imagine they're still pretty sore at me."

Bond, But Not Forgotten: George Lazenby in now happier times.

Nonetheless, Lazenby remains ambivalent about making any kind of splashy Hollywood comeback. "After my death experience, I didn't really give a damn anymore about fame," he shrugged. "When you realize how important *breathing* is, fame doesn't come very high on the totem pole anymore. I'm not one of these guys who needs to go out and be number one. A lot of these actors have *got* to be number one, no matter what. Well, I lost that drive a long time ago. Been there, done that. My drive is happiness — pure and simple."

How does Lazenby feel about *On Her Majesty's Secret Service* all these years later? He revealed that he only watched the film recently, having not seen it since its 1969 premiere. "I had a great laugh," he admitted. "I mean, I couldn't even *recognize* myself, I looked so damn young."

The Lazenby Bond

1969

James Bond (George Lazenby) – in disguise as Sir Hilary Bray – investigates Piz Gloria's main assets.

ON HER MAJESTY'S SECRET SERVICE
(1969)

Directed By: Peter Hunt

The Mission: From his mountain-top headquarters at Piz Gloria in the Swiss Alps, Ernst Stavro Blofeld plots to unleash biological warfare on an unsuspecting world.

Locales: The Italian Riviera, London, the South of France, Geneva, the Swiss Alps

The Villain and Accomplices: Ernst Stavro Blofeld (Telly Savalas), Irma Bunt (Ilse Steppat), Grunther (Yuri Borienko)

The Bond Girls: Contessa Teresa di Vicenzo "Tracy," later Mrs. James Bond (Diana Rigg), Ruby Bartlett (Angela Scoular), Nancy (Catherine Von Schell)

Theme Song: Louis Armstrong

Score: John Barry

Memorable Lines:

"This never happened to the other fella." — *new Bond George Lazenby after winning a fight but losing the girl.*

After Ruby quietly uses her lipstick to write her room number on Bond's thigh during dinner, Irma Bunt asks if anything is wrong. Replies Bond: "Just a slight stiffness coming on."

"We have all the time in the world." — *a distraught Bond as he cradles his mortally wounded bride, Tracy.*

Peter Hunt (Director): "A great deal of discussion went into how to address the issue of a new James Bond. Everyone had different ideas about how to handle Sean's exit from the role. There were all sorts of lines and scenes being discussed when finally [screenwriter] Dick Maibaum said, 'Why are we playing around with this? Why don't we just take it as a matter of course?' We were all scratching our heads about how to start it, and I believe it was Dick who came up with the line 'This never happened to the other fella!' We all agreed that we should just get on with it right away, because no matter what you do you come back to the same thing — you're changing the actor, not the character. We weren't changing the style of film nor the stories. So we figured the more quickly we got it out of the way the better."

Peter Hunt, on casting the leads: "Diana Rigg was absolutely marvelous. I very carefully arranged that she should meet George Lazenby way before we signed him. So I took them out to dinner, and beforehand I said to Diana, 'Talk to George this evening, but if you don't like this boy, then we won't go with him, and we'll make some other arrangements. It's important you should like him and should get on with him, because I'll

Diana's Rigors: Diana Rigg as Tracy di Vicenzo became the one and only wife to James Bond . . . with unfortunate results.

need a lot of your help.' So after dinner, they came back to my house in London, and we all had drinks and got to know one another. The next morning, she rang me and said, 'Thanks for dinner — it was lovely.' And I said, 'Okay, tell me the truth — what do you think?' And she said, 'Oh, I like him. I think he could do it very well. I'll give you all the help you need.' I said, 'Are you sure?' and she said, 'Absolutely.' And she did. She was so professional and helpful. Without Diana, it wouldn't have been the same at all."

George Lazenby: "There are times in the movie where I felt I was very shallow in my thought patterns as an actor. I think I look a bit dumb at times. It's because I just didn't have the sophistication or experience of the trials and tribulations of life. I didn't have the life experience, plain and simple. I think if I played the role today it would be completely different. If you're not honest and straight up with yourself, you don't know who you really are. The only way of telling who you are is by being who you are at all times. And I didn't realize that when I was playing James Bond. Now I do."

Sean Connery, on his replacement: "My feeling about the Lazenby picture was that, if he had kept his mouth shut, he might have come out a lot better. I thought for somebody who had no previous acting experience he did quite a good job."

The opening teaser of On Her Majesty's Secret Service: Bond tries to save Tracy on the beaches of Portugal.

George Lazenby: "For me, the most difficult scenes were the fight sequences because they never did just one or two takes. It was always something like 12 takes, and sometimes I'd be badly injured and just had to keep going. I heard later that Connery and Moore never did their fight scenes, but I did all mine. No one stood in for me. The only thing I wasn't allowed to do was the skiing because it was written into the contract that the lead actor doesn't do his ski scenes. But that was really me hanging off those cables for the cable car scene. I ended up dislocating my shoulder and had ultrasounds done and treatment trying to get back into shape. I jumped 20 feet out of a helicopter for one scene and ended up breaking my ankles. But I didn't know that you didn't do your own stunts. That's how naive I was."

John Glen (Second Unit Director/Editor): "George was always very cooperative. I think he enjoyed hanging out with us because we were an

Who Doesn't Love Ya', Baby: Telly Savalas as Blofeld disovers Bond's true identity.

action crew. He was very keen to do all the stunts. In fact, he was an embarrassment for them because he wanted to do all the ski scenes too and kept insisting he wanted to put on the skis. I said to him, 'If you do that, George, I'm going to get the sack because, if you break a leg, I'll be the one held responsible.' And he would just laugh. Fortunately, he never did ski. But I was a very worried man, I'll tell you."

Lois Maxwell (Miss Moneypenny): "Poor Peter Hunt, who was our editor — our *super* editor — on all the early Bonds. He was finally made director for *On Her Majesty's Secret Service* and then had to work with this difficult actor who thought he was the cat's meow and was throwing his weight around. In the end, it was remarkable the performance he got out of George Lazenby. I thought he was very good, and I think *On Her Majesty's Secret Service* is one of the best Bond films that's been made."

John Glen: "Peter Hunt's editing flair had created a new type of editing in motion pictures. It didn't rely on continuity so much as moving the story along at breakneck speed. If something was boring, he cut it out. So in all the early Bonds, if Sean just looked towards the door, the next moment he was in the corridor. Every film uses those kinds of techniques today, but in those days it was unheard of."

Peter Hunt: "Editing is all a question of timing. And music is a great education, because from music you learn timing. I studied music at the London College of Music and came from a very musical family, so that was very instrumental in teaching me how to pace the drama and the action. Today in movies, they employ teams of editors to work on films. But you can't have seven or eight different people editing a film — you get a mess because there are so many different styles. One man alone has to sit at that machine and edit. Otherwise, you don't get the personality in the film. It would take six months to edit the Bond films, to change performances and make it all work. If we had a performance that didn't work, we *made* it work. It takes time to shape a film to its absolute best. But today, the moment they finish shooting a film, the next week they want it in the cinemas."

John Glen: "Peter and I talked the same language because we were both editors. One morning at Pinewood, he asked me to direct the bobsleigh-run sequence for *On Her Majesty's Secret Service*, and five days later I was on a plane for Switzerland. It was extremely exciting shooting the bobsleigh scenes. Every time we had a spill, an accident of some sort, I filmed it and would then rewrite the script around it, and Peter really encouraged me to do it. Willy Bogner, the brilliant German skier and cameraman, came up with the astonishing idea of actually skiing inside the track behind the bobs, filming the action with a handheld camera. Then he said, 'I'll get right in the bob run and stand on the inside of the curve — it'll be a fabulous camera position.' And I said, 'You can't do that, it's too dangerous.' And he said, 'Not at all — it's the safest place to be because the centrifugal force will take the bob to the outside wall.' Willy got some unbelievable shots of the action that way. You couldn't plan for some of the things we got. And when there were some mishaps, your heart would jump a beat, but when you looked at the material later you would think, 'Well, if I do this and do this and do this, I can work it into the movie.'"

North American Gross: $22.8 million

Overseas: $41.8 million

5

Moore the Merrier: Roger Moore

"If you're fortunate enough to be born looking like a hero, you remember most of your lines, and you don't bump into the furniture, you can get away with *anything*," joked Roger Moore about his record-breaking 12-year reign as James Bond from 1973 to 1985.

Grossing over $1 billion at the worldwide box office, Moore's seven 007 escapades propelled the series to some all-time highs (and lamentable lows according to some Bond purists). With tongue planted firmly in cheek, Moore injected even larger doses of humor into the role while imbuing it with the more suave and sophisticated polish of Fleming's Eton-educated literary creation. However, Moore never took the role too seriously and didn't expect audiences to either.

"To me, the character is not real. . . . Bond has nothing to do with the real spying world," chuckled Moore, after spending the morning skiing the slopes near his home in the picturesque resort town of Crans Montana, Switzerland. "This man is supposed to be a spy, and yet *everybody* knows he's a spy! Any bar he walks into, the bartender immediately says, 'Ahhh, Mr. Bond — *a martini, shaken not stirred*?' Spies are supposed to be faceless

*Have Gun Will Travel: Roger Moore took James Bond to all-new box office heights during his
12-year rein as 007 from 1973 to 1985.*

people or at least have an excellent cover as something else — hardly
unlikely it would be as a poncing actor!"

It was Moore's comedic bent that so endeared him to moviegoers —
"although certainly not to the critics," he dutifully pointed out — and won
the 007 series millions more new fans. The '60s had been a tumultuous
decade driven by political and social upheaval — the Kennedy and King
assassinations, civil rights unrest, and growing opposition to the escalating
war in Southeast Asia — and then came Watergate and the Vietnam deba-
cle. All this meant audiences of the '70s were starved for some escapism and
fantasy. They enthusiastically embraced Moore's lighthearted and jocular
take on what had been the brutal business of Connery's day. And the sober-
ing congressional and Senate investigations into the murky world of the CIA
and other Intelligence agencies didn't exactly inspire the romantic notions

of Bondian espionage. Instead, shock and outrage were felt as the dirty laundry of the spy world unfolded daily in newspapers and on the evening news throughout the '70s. Nefarious plots and schemes — some successful, some not, some heinous, some unintentionally comical — were exposed and served to further tarnish the ideal of a noble gentleman spy like James Bond.

Moore's flair for self-mockery was in tune with the times. The increasingly fantastical plots of the Bond films, which by 1979's *Moonraker* had approached outright parody, dovetailed nicely with the increasingly big-budget, special-effects extravaganzas of the era. Audiences ate it up, and *Moonraker* quickly became the biggest moneymaker in the series, even though its flippancy infuriated some Bond aficionados, who felt the films had been reduced to the big-screen equivalent of a Wile E. Coyote/Road Runner cartoon.

"To me, the Bond situations were so outrageous that I had to treat the humor outrageously as well," explained Moore. "The audience all knows James Bond is going to win. *I* know I'm going to win. So it became rather a wink at the audience, saying, 'Hey, look at this! How are we — not how am I — how are *we* going to get out of this now?'"

As the Moore merriment continued, so did the frustration of critics at the perceived diluting of Fleming's creation, although no one denies Roger Moore revitalized the series after the departure of Sean Connery. No easy task for any actor, but Moore breathed new life into the long-running institution. "I think Roger was largely responsible for keeping the films going," surmised Maud Adams, who starred with Moore in both *The Man with the Golden Gun* in 1974 and 1983's *Octopussy*. "One of the reasons Roger's Bonds were so popular was because of his humor. In the past, Sean had been pretty straightforward, and it was more of a dangerous take on the role, whereas Roger had more fun with it. And by doing so, he took it to a new level. Because by then, the Bond films had started having so much competition from other action adventures with also a tremendous amount of stunts. So I think the humor is what really carried the Bond films through."

These days, Moore is taking his new mission in life with deadly seriousness. Now in his 70s, the still dapper and witty Moore continues to spend

Roger That: A recent shot of Roger Moore (Photo courtesy of Jerry Pam)

his time globetrotting to exotic locales but for far different reasons. Since 1991, Moore has dedicated himself almost exclusively to his role as UNICEF goodwill ambassador, following in the tradition of such luminaries as Audrey Hepburn, Sir Peter Ustinov, and Danny Kaye. In his nonpaying role, Moore travels extensively to the far ends of the world, raising funds for UNICEF and at the same time promoting the plight of underprivileged children. From Costa Rica, El Salvador, Honduras, and Guatemala to the Philippines, Mexico, Slovenia, and Ghana, Moore can usually be found in the world's impoverished regions visiting local UNICEF projects to rally the troops, witnessing official commitments to protect the rights of children, and creating media awareness of the dire circumstances. "Unless it's the headline — the front-page news — people forget about what is happening to the children," explained Moore, who skillfully uses his worldwide notoriety for a much greater good. "I'm very grateful for James Bond, because it gave me the fame or celebrity to be of some use in the work I do today. It's very helpful in getting the press to listen to you when you talk about children's issues."

The permeation of James Bond into virtually every culture around the world also serves Moore well when it comes to gaining an audience with leaders of many foreign countries, where the former 007 actor is regarded as visiting royalty. Moore is aware the Bond mystique opens doors that otherwise would remain closed to pleas for policy change. Once inside, Moore relies on his wits and some good old-fashioned Bond savvy to accomplish his goals. "Usually, you get in to see them because a lot of times they're curious to see what a stupid, friggin' actor is doing running around the world as a goodwill ambassador," smiled the typically self-deprecating Moore. "They're very curious when I show up. But it doesn't take them very many seconds to find out that I've come to discuss some very grave issues."

Moore also actively campaigns for the Kiwanis on behalf of another charity. He's honorary chairman of the campaign to eliminate iodine deficiency disorder (IDD), which causes conditions such as goiter, cretinism, dwarfism, and low IQ. "It's something that affects one-fifth of the world's population," explained Moore, "but it's so easy to cure — just one teaspoon of iodine is needed throughout our lifetime. The easiest way is using iodized salt, which in most of the developed countries is automatic. But in a lot of countries, where they say the salt is iodized, it's actually not. It's madness that so many lives are ruined by something so simple."

Moore recounted a visit with the president of Indonesia about the IDD issue that found him in the midst of some political treachery. "Here I am, sort of chatting away with him, and he kept intimating — in these rather hushed tones — that he wouldn't be president much longer because they were trying to get rid of him," revealed Moore, who then employed some quiet diplomacy to ensure the IDD situation remained a priority with the new regime. "We then went to see the vice president, knowing that she would be president, and then to the leader of the house, just in case he became president too! Indonesia is a country that has a big problem, and I had to make sure the issue was recognized and reinforced on all levels."

Moore dismissed any fears for his own safety while visiting some of these war-torn and politically volatile countries. "Nahhh . . . I *was* James Bond after all," he smirked. But he did admit remorse for not taking action sooner. "You know, I used to go to these countries for the Bond films, and I look back on it and feel a terrible guilt that I wasn't more concerned about the things that were going on around me," confessed Moore. "When you're shooting a film, you don't have time to really think of anything else. You're aware of the poverty around you, but you're too worried about your own agenda. Now I see things through much different eyes with UNICEF."

"So The Bartender Says . . .": Roger Moore brings some laughs to underprivileged children as part of his wide-ranging duties as UNICEF Goodwill Ambassador. (Photo courtesy of Roger Moore)

In recognition of his humanitarian services, Moore was presented by Queen Elizabeth II with the Commander of the Order of the British Empire (CBE) Award in January 1999. And what 'oo' agent couldn't use assistance from another 'oo' agent in the field? In December 2001, new Bond Pierce Brosnan was appointed as a special patron of UNICEF Ireland. "It's something I have wanted to do for a long time, to give something back," said Brosnan on following in Moore's footsteps. "I am especially interested in highlighting the tragic impact of war on children, who are always the innocent casualties of conflicts around the world."

The son of a London policeman, Roger Moore was born in Stockwell, south of the Thames, in October of 1927. He was signed up for one school, but World War II was breaking out, so instead he was evacuated to Worthing Sussex, and later to Chester, in the north of England, with his mother. Hitler's "phony war" lulled everybody into a false sense of security, and, as nothing happened and no bombs dropped on the city, the evacuees began to drift back, including Roger and his mother, only to beat a hasty retreat to Amersham in Buckinghamshire a few months later when the war began in earnest. At Amersham, Moore attended Dr. Challoner's Grammar School and watched the distant fires burning at night in London, where his father, George, still worked at Bow Street Police Station.

"My father was one of the most multitalented people I knew," recalled Moore. "He was very clever with his hands. He was a wonderful sleight of hand magician; he built model railway trains, could play every musical instrument — string, woodwind, and piano — and was a wonderful athlete. Basically, he could do most things that I couldn't."

Art and drawing were Roger's best subjects in school, and when he left early to find a job he was given an introduction to Publicity Picture Productions — an animated cartoon studio — on D'Arblay Street in London's West End. For three and a half pounds a week, Moore worked as a tracer and filler-in, made tea, and ran errands. But he quite often made cold tea and worst of all made a costly mistake one day on some celluloid. He was fired as a cartoonist. "Being fired was the luckiest break, but it didn't feel like that at the time," recalled Moore.

A friend suggested the now unemployed Moore could make money as an extra on a film being made at Denham Studios — *Caesar and Cleopatra* (1946). "Anything remotely connected with acting had not occurred to me, but I went along to an office on Wardour Street in Soho, offered myself as an extra, collected a piece of paper, and made a long journey on a bus out to the studio," he remembered. "I did this highly pleasurable job for a few days, and on the third day as I walked through the gates a car stopped alongside me." Brian Desmond Hurst, the film's codirector, stuck his head out of the car window and asked Moore if he had ever considered becoming an actor. "It hadn't occurred to me not to be interested in acting, so from that moment on I was interested," remarked Moore.

Hurst offered to pay Moore's fees to the Royal Academy of Dramatic Art if the young man's family agreed to support him during his studies there. "Like a film script, isn't it? But that's the way it happened." Moore fondly recalled his days at RADA as among the happiest of his life. "There were four boys in each class of 16 girls," he smiled. "It was like going to heaven without dying." To conceal his lack of confidence on stage, the novice actor often used humor. It would eventually become a hallmark of Moore's persona — both on screen and off.

After three terms at RADA, Moore decided to leave and get some practical experience, joining the Cambridge Arts Theatre for a season of George Bernard Shaw plays. But 18-year-old Moore was soon called into service in the British Army and served in the rank of second lieutenant in occupied Germany at the end of World War II. Later he joined the Combined Services Entertainment Unit in Hamburg and found himself back among many of his fellow classmates from RADA. "As part of Rhine Army responsibilities, we had to travel around and supply entertainment to Italy and Austria as well," remembered Moore. "As an officer, I was frequently in charge of the traveling shows."

After his release from military service around 1948, Moore sought work in repertory, radio, and television but was often forced to support himself with an array of nonacting jobs, including modeling and sales. He eventually did get 30 days of work in a film called *Trottie True*, where he shared a dressing room with another unknown actor — Christopher Lee (who would eventually costar with Moore on screen as villain Francisco Scaramanga in 1974's *The Man with the Golden Gun*).

Moore's first big stage break came when he understudied David Tomlinson in *The Little Hut* in London. Bit parts in various plays followed, including the London stage run of *Mister Roberts* with Tyrone Power. Moore would make his American television debut soon after, portraying a French diplomat in a play with Diana Lynn and Phyllis Kirk. His television work continued until the major studios began calling. His American motion picture debut came in MGM's *The Last Time I Saw Paris* with Van Johnson and Elizabeth Taylor in 1954. Moore related his nerve-wracking first day on set: "It was April Fool's Day, and the joke was on MGM, I thought," he laughed. "It was rather intimidating having to work with Elizabeth Taylor and Van Johnson. And it was even worse because I had to punch Van Johnson in the mouth on the first day of work!" *Interrupted Melody* (with Eleanor Parker and Glenn Ford) and *The King's Thief* (with

Ann Blyth, George Sanders, and David Niven) came next, and then Moore starred opposite Lana Turner in *Diane* (1956), where he got his name above the title for the first time, playing King Henri II of France.

Soon a long-term contract was offered by Warner Brothers, who wanted to cash in on Moore's leading man good looks and affable British charm. He was cast in the 1957 syndicated TV series *Ivanhoe*, crusading as "a boy scout in shining armor," and then ventured into the savage American frontier of gold rush days as the con man in *The Alaskans*, before finally landing in the wild, wacky west as Beau Maverick — British cousin to James Garner's popular Bret Maverick character in the eponymous ABC television series. When Garner left in a 1960 contract dispute with Warner Brothers, Moore was asked to take over *Maverick* as the show's new lead. Moore explained, "I really didn't want to take over *Maverick*, but I was under contract, and so I had to do it. I had just finished doing *The Alaskans*, and I had not really signed with Warner Brothers to just go from television series to television series. I rather thought they were exploiting me in a one-dimensional way — the sort of Englishman as fish-out-of-water.

"They were tired scripts and blurred in my mind while I was doing them," he continued. "I was suspended by Warners because I refused to do them. Jack Warner called me in for a meeting, but I sent word back that I was sick and in Las Vegas doing therapy for my fingers at the crap tables.

"Eventually, I went in to talk. I told them I didn't think the scripts were any good. So they promised that they would tailor them the way I felt they should be. They didn't, so I left. I'd had enough of bucking broncos and a home on the range."

After making guest appearances in 1961 on *77 Sunset Strip* and *The Roaring 20s*, Moore decided to pack it in and return to Europe. "There was a sort of stigma attached to actors who did television series at the time — they could never go back to motion pictures," said Moore. "So I thought, 'I must look around and find something that is right for me, something that I can do and that will be profitable in television.'" Moore had expressed interest in bringing *The Saint* to television ("I figured that I might not ever work again, and I better find something of my own to do — *The Saint* seemed ideal for television, and I felt the part was made for me," he said),

Saint Misbehavin': Roger Moore as Simon Templar in the classic '60s television series The Saint.
(Photo courtesy ITC)

but author Leslie Charteris wasn't interested in selling the rights to TV. So Moore went to Italy, where he chose to make two potboilers, including *The Rape of the Sabines*. His costar was Luisa Mattoli, an Italian actress whom Moore later married (they split up in 1994 after 33 years together and have three children: Deborah, Geoffrey, and Christian). The couple were living in Venice in 1961 when Moore received a phone call that shot him to superstardom. Moore's London agent informed him that producer Lew Grade had succeeded in buying the rights to *The Saint* and wanted Roger to star as the dashing and debonair adventurer Simon Templar. It was a role tailor-made for Moore.

For the next seven years, *The Saint* completely dominated Moore's life. Charteris's best-selling novels about the gentleman rogue Templar and his acts of heroism had already acquired a huge following for almost 40 years, having also served as the basis for several films and a popular radio series. That built-in audience helped propel *The Saint* to become one of the most successful and widely viewed British series ever produced. And by the time filming ended in 1968, after 114 one-hour and two feature-length shows, *The Saint* had been syndicated to over 80 countries around the world. Assuming the slightly lopsided halo and angelic stance of Simon Templar provided a heavenly career for Moore. "But at the time, it seemed the equivalent of a nine-to-five job, really," reflected Moore, who became a wealthy partner in Bamore, Ltd., which then owned the series. "I lived close to the studio, had two young babies, and growing up with the series gave me my own production company. And I also directed a number of episodes too, so it was a time full of enthusiasm for me.

"But there were times at the end of the day when I would say, 'Oh, God, blimey, what have I been doing all this time?'" he added about the rigors of doing a weekly series. "Still, a great deal of satisfaction came out of it. And *The Saint* gave me an enormous worldwide television audience. . . . Even though I've done Bond, there are some people who still only think of me as Simon Templar. . . .

"And still more people don't think of me at all," he quipped.

After *The Saint* ended its successful run, it seemed a logical progression for Moore to step into the shoes of that *other* world-renowned British hero. After all, Ian Fleming himself had recommended Moore for the role of James Bond back in 1961. "I also heard that David Niven and Cary Grant were suggested as well," said Moore, "so I guess it's not bad company to be in." However, Moore had already committed to *The Saint* at that point, so the casting search continued, and Sean Connery was later signed. "But Cubby [Broccoli] and Harry [Saltzman] became good friends of mine," explained Moore. "Because while they were making all of those with Sean, we would sort of meet up once or twice a week at the gaming tables — back in the bad old days when I gambled — and we became pals, and they told me that I had been in line for the [Bond] role.

"But I certainly don't think I was ready for it then," added Moore with a chuckle. "Even though I'm older than Sean, I looked much younger — probably because I had a cleaner youth — and I still had this sort of baby face . . . but it was much better I did it at the time I did."

Moore's next opportunity to take over Bond in 1968 came to an even more abrupt end. After Connery announced his departure from the series after 1967's *You Only Live Twice*, Moore was lined up, and plans got under way to shoot a version of *The Man with the Golden Gun* as Moore's 007 debut. "It wasn't going to be *On Her Majesty's Secret Service* at that point — it was *Golden Gun* that was planned, and it was going to be shot in Cambodia," revealed Moore. "But then, when all hell broke out in Cambodia, that script just went into the ground." By the time Broccoli and Saltzman were finally ready to begin production on a new script — *On Her Majesty's Secret Service* — Moore had been contracted to other projects, and the producers were forced to hunt for a replacement. While George Lazenby temporarily filled the role for OHMSS in 1969, and Connery made a surprise save in 1971's *Diamonds Are Forever*, Moore was busy shooting the syndicated TV series *The Persuaders* as notorious playboy Lord Brett Sinclair alongside Tony Curtis. The action adventure — also produced by Sir Lew Grade — ended its run in 1971, and Moore was finally available to Broccoli and Saltzman. The producers hoped to put an end to the Bond musical chairs once and for all and signed Moore to a three-picture deal.

In October 1972, as Moore celebrated his 45th birthday, shooting began

on *Live and Let Die* in New Orleans under the direction of Guy Hamilton. From the out-set, it was clear this was going to be a much different Bond from Connery's. "All the things that Sean does very well Roger can't do, and there's lots of things that Roger can do rather well that Sean can't do," recounted Hamilton, who had previously helmed *Goldfinger* and *Diamonds Are Forever*. "With Roger, we knew we couldn't imitate Sean, so we just let him play himself."

Everyone was confident that Bond was in good hands with Moore. "In fact, the only

Roger Moore in an early publicity photo as the new James Bond.

direction I ever got from Cubby and Harry was to lose weight and cut my hair," recalled Moore with a smirk. "And Guy Hamilton just sort of avoided me saying anything that was completely Sean, like 'shaken, not stirred', which I never said in any of the films. . . ."

The only real Bondism that worried Moore, however, was his requisite — *required* — introduction in the film. "I guess the slight apprehension I had was saying the line 'My name is Bond, James Bond.' I was frightened it would come out [Moore imitates Connery's Scottish burr] '*My name ishhh Bond, Jhameshhh Bond!*'" Moore lets out a laugh. "Thankfully, that didn't happen."

Moore knew comparisons to Connery were inevitable, and he tried not to take any criticism personally, especially difficult considering "that when you picked up the paper every day you read that you couldn't possibly be as good as Sean," he admitted with a good-natured laugh. "I mean, I was getting bad reviews just for being *alive!*"

Connery's cold and calculated brutality was slowly giving way to the more cool cunning of Moore. The new Bond relied on his wits — rather than his fists — to disarm his opponents. Instead of throwing a punch, Moore was more likely to throw a punchline. Same intentions and objectives, just different tactics. Moore admitted he lacked Connery's killer instinct as he related an incident during the shooting of his next Bond film, *The Man with the Golden Gun.* "Guy Hamilton made me twist Maud Adams's arm in one scene, and she screams, 'You're hurting my arm!' and I said, 'I'll *break it* unless you tell me what I want to know!' Well, that's really not me. I don't think anybody believes me when I say it," he said. "And I think that's the difference between Sean and me: you *believe* Sean when he says he'll put a bloody bullet through your head. Whereas with me, you say, 'Bloody pussycat — he wouldn't do *that!*'"

Guy Hamilton chuckled as he recalled Moore's aversion to firearms as well. "As you know, Roger is a very relaxed human being," said Hamilton, "so don't put a gun in his hand. That's death, because he cannot fire it without turning away and blinking his eyes. It's not very Bondian at all. Roger absolutely abhors guns and explosions. It got to the point where you had to put matchsticks in his eyes in order to keep them open when the gun went off!

(left) James Bond takes aim in The Man With The Golden Gun and (right) together with former RADA classmate Lois Maxwell as Miss Moneypenny in Brazil for 1979's Moonraker.

"But he was so delightful, he never made a fuss about it," added Hamilton. "I knew he hated loud bangs, so one had to find a way around those problems. But Roger is one of the most fun persons to work with."

For actress Lois Maxwell — who played the lovelorn Miss Moneypenny for the first 14 James Bond films — *Live and Let Die* presented a welcome reunion with Roger Moore. The two had been classmates back at RADA, and Maxwell had also guested on a number of *Saint* episodes in the '60s. So how had Moore changed since they first met at 17?

"Not at all," she replied with a laugh. "I mean, he had lost the puppy fat he had when he was younger, but other than that Roger still had the exact same cheeky humor and twinkle in his eye. Nothing had changed about him. He was still the most charming man around. He's an absolute hoot to work with. He just makes everything so much fun."

Maud Adams echoed those sentiments. "Roger is an absolute doll," she smiled. "He's truly a Renaissance man. He's very intelligent. He reads voraciously. And he's a very self-deprecating kind of man who isn't one to give much credit to what he does. But I think, in a lot of ways, people knew it wasn't really true. I certainly knew it, and everybody around him knew it."

Yet Moore's penchant for self-deprecation seems terminal. "Yeah, I'm always being told off, 'You mustn't put yourself down!'" he agreed. "I mean, I tried saying I was great, but I wasn't very good at it . . . so anybody who

(left) Roger Moore in a shot from the 1976 film Shout at the Devil, directed by longtime Bond filmmaker Peter Hunt. (right) Moore with two-time Bond Girl Maud Adams in 1983's Octopussy.

wants to criticize, they can. Because I've already said it!"

Regrettably, Moore never really got to show more of his dramatic chops in the Bond films. Occasional scenes, however, did showcase his wider range as an actor. One such memorable display was in *The Spy Who Loved Me* between Bond and Russian agent Anya Amasova (Barbara Bach) after she discovers Bond was responsible for killing her lover. It remains one of Moore's most powerful, emotionally charged scenes in all his Bond films. One wishes we could've witnessed further glimpses of Moore's serious side, but, as he points out, "there wasn't really room for that sort of thing in Bond, it's more like a comic strip."

Other films, like *For Your Eyes Only* and *Octopussy*, would offer flourishes of Moore's greater depth, but for the most part the focus remained on action and laughs. "After he quit Bond, Roger did a couple serious movies which I thought he was quite good in," said Maud Adams, "but unfortunately the productions never quite lived up to his talent. He was never really given the opportunity to show his more dramatic skills. . . .

"I guess it always happens to you if you're beautiful," Adams added with a laugh. "It's not just women that suffer that fate. Certainly, when Roger was younger, he was absolutely gorgeous — probably the most beautiful man on screen ever!"

Yet as effortless as Moore's portrayal seemed (he once joked to me years ago that the only difference between him and Bond was "I don't wear a dinner jacket to breakfast"), it's no secret that James Bond is indeed one of the trickiest roles for any actor to pull off successfully. Moore made it all look so easy, and that is perhaps one of his greatest strengths on screen. But Moore did admit it took him three tries before he truly felt he had hit his stride. "I think after *The Man with the Golden Gun* we started letting a little more of my humor creep in," he said. "The first two Bonds I did were a little experimental, but with *The Spy Who Loved Me* it became a slightly different kind of Bond. I think we found the right ingredients, the right level of humor, the right locales, the right approach. Everything came together. Also, [director] Lewis Gilbert and I shared the same sense of humor, so we just had a ball."

The clowning around reached its pinnacle with 1979's *Moonraker*. Sending Bond into outer space stretched the boundaries to their breaking point, and it was decided to bring 007 back to Earth for 1981's *For Your Eyes Only*. The task of returning Bond to solid ground and restoring credibility fell on the shoulders of John Glen. "They realized they had strayed, and they wanted to get back to the harder-edge Fleming style," noted Glen. "That was my briefing."

It took some real persuasion for Moore to accept that darker side of Bond's personality. The cruelty and violence being reinjected into the films didn't sit well with Moore, especially after having made his Bond more saint than sinner. "Roger was very conscious of his audience, the younger kids and the families who went to see his Bond films," explained Glen, who made his 007 directing debut on *For Your Eyes Only* after serving as editor and second-unit director on a number of earlier Bond films. "On a couple of occasions, I had to have some big discussions with him to convince him that I was right to try and get this back to a more hard-edged Bond.

"And I think up until my pictures he hadn't had that hard edge that one associated with Connery and to some respect also Dalton," continued Glen. "A lot of people felt he was a fantastic Bond, and his humor was great, but you couldn't really imagine him killing someone, really. Whereas you could imagine Connery killing someone, couldn't you?"

(left) Roger Moore at a Friar's Club Roast with wife Luisa, Frank Sinatra, Dean Martin, and Cary Grant (Photo courtesy of Jerry Pam). (right) Hot Wheels: "Thank God it's a rental."

Moore and Glen proved a formidable team, collaborating again on the next two Bond films. Both *Octopussy* (1983) and *A View to a Kill* (1985) broke Bond box office records, yet Moore decided that *A View to a Kill* would be his swan song. Officially retiring from Her Majesty's Secret Service at age 58, Moore said he had no regrets about bidding Bond farewell. "No, I'd done seven — I had my whack," he said simply. "I mean, quite frankly, I think they were running out of girls who looked old enough to be playing opposite me, without it being sort of *Love in the Afternoon*. . . ."

Moore laughed and then added, "I also think they were running out of villains who looked feeble enough to be knocked down by me!

"I'm a realist," he continued. "I know that you can only do things for so long. And if you've got a short leading lady, and you have three chins when you look down at her, it's not very good. It's not the way people want to see Bond."

While his charity work for UNICEF remains his ongoing priority, Moore does still find time for the occasional acting role. In 2001, he shot the comedy *Boat Trip* alongside Cuba Gooding Jr., and in early 2002 he made a guest appearance on the ABC spy drama *Alias* as a shady SD-9 director.

Shortly thereafter, the former 007 jetted to Copenhagen, where, on March 9, 74-year-old Moore tied the knot in a quiet ceremony with his longtime love, 60-year-old Swedish beauty Kristina Tholstrup. Moore even admitted that, much like his fellow Bond actors, he would get a real kick out of returning to the Bond series as a villain. "They are the best roles to play," he offered. "I think I have such a Goody-Goody Two-shoes image around the world that it's about time I did something outrageous!"

Though Moore gives high marks to Pierce Brosnan, he admitted he hasn't kept up to speed on the current Bond films. "I've only ever seen two reels of *Goldeneye*," he remarked. "I knew people would ask me questions about them, and just suppose I didn't like them? Then people would say, 'Oh, it's sour grapes!'

"Because I always tell the truth," he quipped with a wink, "except when I'm *lying*."

The Moore Bonds

1973–85

Mirror Image: Roger Moore kicks off 12 years of good luck with his first shot at James Bond in Live and Let Die.

LIVE AND LET DIE
(1973)

Directed By: Guy Hamilton

The Mission: The execution of three MI6 agents is traced back to San Monique's de facto dictator Dr. Kananga (Yaphet Kotto), who leads a double life as drug baron Mr. Big. Aided by his band of voodoo cultists and tarot-card-reading clairvoyant Solitaire, Kananga plots to corner the world's heroin market with his island's massive poppy fields.

Locales: New York, New Orleans, London, San Monique (Jamaica)

The Villain and Accomplices: Dr. Kananga/Mr. Big (Yaphet Kotto), Baron Samedi (Geoffrey Holder), Tee Hee (Julius W. Harris), Whisper (Earl Jolly Brown), Rosie Carver (Gloria Hendry)

The Bond Girls: Solitaire (Jane Seymour), Miss Caruso (Madeline Smith), Rosie Carver (Gloria Hendry)

Theme Song: Paul McCartney and Wings

Score: George Martin

Memorable Lines:

M's surprise appearance at Bond's door in the middle of the night.
Bond: "Insomnia, sir?"
M, tersely: "Instructions."

Rosie: "I'm going to be completely useless to you."
Bond: "Oh, I'm sure we'll be able to lick you into shape."

Bond, hearing the transmission of CIA *agent Felix Leiter through a radio receiver disguised as a dashboard cigarette lighter:* "A genuine Felix Lighter — illuminating."

Solitaire asks Bond for another round after their first bedroom encounter.
Bond: "Absolutely. There's no sense in going off half-cocked."

A furious Sheriff J.W. Pepper, finally confronting Bond after he demolishes all his police vehicles in the Louisiana bayou boat chase: "What are you — some kind of doomsday machine, boy?" *After being informed Bond is a secret agent on a mission, Pepper screams:* "Secret Agent? On *whose* side?!"

Guy Hamilton (Director): "When they were hunting for a new Bond, I was very keen on Burt Reynolds. I insisted that Cubby meet him. I thought Burt had a lot of the qualities of Bond. He was a super stuntman, had a twinkle in his eye, but I remember Cubby and Harry said, 'We think he's a stuntman, and it's ridiculous . . . plus, he's an *American*! Bond must be

Bond screenwriter Tom Mankiewicz in 1973 during location scouting for The Man With The Golden Gun in Iran. (Photo courtesy of Tom Mankiewicz)

British.' I said, 'Yes, but in nine-tenths of the world Bond speaks Japanese, French, German, Italian. . . .' It was a crazy idea, but I am delighted that Burt became a very big star thereafter because I thought he had a lot going for him."

Tom Mankiewicz (Screenwriter): "Roger Moore was Cubby's choice to play Bond in *On Her Majesty's Secret Service*, but because he was doing *The Persuaders* they couldn't get him. So Cubby was quite determined to get him for *Live and Let Die*. With Roger, I was able to rely much more heavily on dialogue. Sean — in the best sense of the word — looked like a real bastard when he walked into a room. You just knew violence would erupt. There was always a mean twinkle in his eye. It's actually kind of interesting, but if you watch Sean closely when he's fighting on screen he always seems to have a smile on his face. It's like he really loves it. I always used to say that Sean could sit across a table from a woman and either kiss her or stick a knife in her under the table and then say, 'Waiter, excuse me — I have nothing to cut my meat with.' And you could love him for either one. Whereas Roger could kiss the girl, but he couldn't stick the knife in her because he would look nasty. However, one of Roger's greatest strengths was that he played the throw-away lines wonderfully. Sean played them wonderfully in his own way, which was he just threw them away. Sean played the part in Bond of a real prick, but Roger cannot play a prick; he looks like too nice a guy."

Roger Moore: "I read a number of Fleming's books, and I remember that one of them said that Bond had returned from a mission somewhere and had killed, but he didn't like killing. So that's the way I played Bond — as someone who really didn't like killing."

Jane Seymour (Solitaire): "I remember I was called into Harry Saltzman's office, and I was wearing a fur hat and a coat with a fur collar. Harry said, 'Take off your coat,' and I did. Then he said, 'Take off your hat,' and I pulled it off, and my hair came tumbling down. That was when Harry said, 'I want you to play Solitaire.' There was no audition. I got it on the spot. Then he said, 'I want to take you to see my partner, Cubby.' So we went across the street to Cubby's office, and the two of them then had this huge argument right in front of me about who had spotted me first. I had just been on a TV show at the time called *The Onedin Line*, so I put up my hand — as if I was at school — and said, 'Umm, excuse me — didn't you both see me at the same time? I was on TV at the same time in everyone's house.' And they were like, 'yeah, yeah, yeah.' Then one of the secretaries pulled me out of there and said, 'I think you better come wait out here.' So I sat there, and the next thing I knew they'd sorted it out amongst themselves. I was brought back in, and they said, 'Well, we definitely want you, and we'll call your agent.' There were politics involved, as I later found out, and since this was a 'Harry film' I only ever saw Cubby again once, which was when he invited me to his house and gave me my

Black Magic Woman: Roger Moore with Jane Seymour between takes at Pinewood for Live and Let Die.

first champagne and my first taste of caviar. I've never forgotten, because that was a big thing for me. I suddenly felt like, 'Gosh, I'm a *star!*'"

Tom Mankiewicz: "When I was writing the script, Solitaire was black in my original version. I was writing it for Diana Ross, and Cubby was very hot on the idea. Roger had been signed at that point. But halfway through I had a meeting with David Picker, who was head of United Artists by that time and, I must say, a really wonderful guy. But David said, 'We cannot have a black heroine.' And I went crazy. I was pretty left wing when I was younger — very much anti-Vietnam, very much into civil rights, the Black Panthers, and radical stuff like that. Jane Fonda was my neighbor at the beach, and we were all into that kind of stuff back then. So I said to David, 'Look, this film is all black villains — you've got to take the edge off it with Bond having an affair with a black woman.' And he said, 'First of all, this is none of your particular business, but there are about six countries in the world we won't be able to play the film in, including South Africa, which is a huge market. Also, 20 miles outside of any big city in the United States, it will really work against us.' The country wasn't quite up to speed yet on things like that. David said, 'You know, if Sean were still playing Bond, I'd take the chance, because it would be daring. But since this is a new Bond, I don't want to add anything more to the film.' He also said that because it's Diana Ross — who was one of the biggest stars in the world at that time — that it would be Diana Ross in bed with Bond, rather than Bond in bed with a girl. David Picker wasn't being insensitive; they were valid reasons at the time. He always felt that Bond was a port in this storm, a port where people could go to escape and be entertained. He didn't want to contribute to everything that was going on politically and socially at the time."

Tom Mankiewicz, on the casting of Yaphet Kotto: "Because it was at the height of the Black Panthers, Yaphet was very concerned about playing a black villain who gets inflated at the end and bursts like a giant balloon. At the time, Yaphet had been a star in films like *Across 110th Street*, and there were all those *Superfly* kind of movies being made then.

He said, 'God, my people are going to kill me!' And I remember saying to him, 'Yaphet, this is kind of a really specious argument. . . . Goldfinger was obviously Jewish, but nobody thought it was an anti-Semitic film. So nobody's going to think ill of this either; it's a James Bond film, for crying out loud.' But what I did was create multiple parts for him, where he was the heroin dealer in New York but also the head of the Caribbean country. So he loved that. And I must say the black actors had a ball on that picture. I remember Geoffrey Holder, who played Baron Samedi, was just wonderful. He took me to a voodoo ceremony up in the hills of Jamaica, where I drank something that I will never know what it was! I really started seeing people coming out of graves that night!"

Jane Seymour: "I was absolutely terrified when Geoffrey Holder took me to a voodoo ceremony one night in Jamaica. I've never felt so out of place in my life — certainly, there was no other white person even close to where we were. It was pretty scary. But Geoffrey was from Trinidad, and they respected him, so the fact that I was with him, I was very safe. But all the people were definitely in trances, and I witnessed the sacrificing of chickens and blood flying around. The women were all in white dresses, just completely out there. With the wild music and the pounding drums and

Roger Moore is flanked by Jane Seymour, Yaphet Kotto, and Julius W. Harris.

being in the middle of the jungle, it was all very intoxicating. I certainly got the idea of what we were trying to do in the film, so you could say I definitely did my research!"

Guy Hamilton: "I remember day one for Roger was at the airport in New Orleans, where he has to run outside the airplane hangars. Before we started shooting, Roger took me aside and said, 'I think there's something you should know about me.' And I said, 'What's that, Roger?' And he said, 'I can't run.' So I said, 'Don't worry — it's just one foot in front of the other.' I yell 'Action,' and he runs, and it's an extraordinary sight to behold. Suddenly, the crew all look at me, and I say, 'Cut.' Roger comes back and says, 'I told you!' So we had to film the scene with something in front of him every two yards so you would only occasionally glimpse him running."

Tom Mankiewicz: "Yeah, Roger has these very long legs, and when he runs he does kind of bound. I think Roger said he felt he looked like a giant deer when he ran. So I remember Guy Hamilton saying to Roger, 'Right, then. When I yell action, why don't you just *walk quickly*?'"

Voodoo Doll: The enchanting Jane Seymour as Bond Girl Solitaire. (Photo courtesy of Jane Seymour)

Jane Seymour: "When I first arrived in New Orleans, I went walking down Bourbon Street at four in the afternoon, just sort of window shopping, and just as I was about to cross the street somebody tried to steal my handbag. It was the first time I'd ever been mugged. As they were attacking me, I smashed them in the face with my handbag and ran. Which is, of course, exactly what I do in the Bond film! But it hadn't occurred to me that's why I did it. I realized I must have gotten the idea from Solitaire."

Guy Hamilton, on the double-decker bus chase: "I once saw a London bus driver doing a 360° skid, and I thought, 'That's an idea for a Bond film.' Bond is always hopping into Aston Martins, but suppose he stole something as ordinary as a bus to make a getaway? But I realized it needed a payoff. Then I thought, 'Ahhh, a low-bridge, and it shears the top off!' So we bought a secondhand London bus for about £500 and took it to Pinewood Studios. I measured the bridge in Jamaica very carefully, and on the lot at Pinewood we put up a steel bar at the same height. Then Johnny Stears and company went to work and took the top of the bus off. They installed two sliders with ball bearings on the top and soft metal at the front. We performed the stunt at Pinewood to solve any problems before we shot it in Jamaica. Like how many miles an hour are required to make the top fly enough feet so it lands like a tea cozy on the police car following the bus. All these things were worked out in advance so when we got to Jamaica we wouldn't waste endless time with a whole crew on location waiting for something to work. We ended up filming that stunt in only one take."

Jane Seymour: "I learned a big lesson on that stunt. Just before I got on the bus, I asked the stunt people, 'Have you done this before?' And they said, 'No, only with models.' And I said, 'You mean you don't know if this is going to work?' And they said, 'No.' Then I looked outside, and there were hundreds of press there, all on the side of the road with cameras pointing, ready to photograph this major stunt. I was too chicken to go out there and refuse to be in the stunt, so I did it, and all I remember as we were racing towards the bridge was 'I'm going to die!' I was completely terrified. Afterwards, I was very excited 'cause I was like, 'Yeah! I did a stunt!' But looking back now, I realize how foolish it was. When you're the size of a postage stamp on the big screen, there's really no reason for you

(left to right) Roger Moore, producer Harry Saltzman, and screenwriter Tom Mankiewicz watch the bayou motorboat jump on location in Louisiana. (Photo courtesy of Tom Mankiewicz)

to do it. That's why I've tried not to do any stunts since."

Guy Hamilton: "Oh, Baby Bernhardt [Seymour] loves to be dramatic! She was perfectly safe during that stunt."

Desmond Llewelyn, on Q's conspicuous absence from *Live and Let Die*: "I was supposed to be in it, but then I think Harry Saltzman thought there were too many gadgets or something. I'm not quite sure what happened, but I believe Harry felt he needed to change the formula slightly now that there was a new Bond."

Tom Mankiewicz, on the crocodile jump: "Guy and I were doing location scouting in Jamaica when we suddenly came across this huge sign in the jungle that said 'Trespassers Will Be Eaten.' It was a crocodile farm owned by someone named Ross Kananga, who was this weird guy with scars all over his chest, living with something like 1,500 crocodiles and alligators. I said, 'Did a crocodile do that to your chest?' He said, 'No, I used to have two lions to protect the crocodiles from poachers, but then the lions went after me one day.' Kananga was a white guy, but I used his name for Yaphet Kotto's character as president of San Monique. I immediately started writing a scene where Bond jumps over the backs of crocodiles to get off that little island. We wanted to use real crocodiles, so we tied their little legs down underwater so they couldn't move and then lined them all up. The stuntman who was doubling Roger — wearing his pants and alligator shoes — jumped, and he slipped on the first crocodile and fell into the water. One of the crocs whacked him with his tail and almost got him. Then Kananga tried it next, and he slipped too. We tried it again, and not only did Kananga slip again, but one of the crocs got hold of his foot. The stuntmen all said, 'We're not going to do this anymore — you'll have to think of something else. The crocodiles are just too slippery.' So we sat there in the middle of the jungle in Jamaica, and Harry says, 'Goddamn it — think of something!' Then suddenly one of the crew members said, 'I have a suggestion: if you went into Montego Bay and bought some shoes with cleats on them, I betcha' you wouldn't slip.' And Kananga said, 'Yeah, I'll do that.' So they got him these shoes with cleats, and he did it in the first take. But the reason that take looked so good was because we had already been stepping over their backs for three or four takes, so by the fifth attempt the crocodiles knew what was coming next, and they all opened their jaws and snapped their heads towards him. They were like, 'Here comes that guy again — let's get him this time!"

Guy Hamilton, on Paul McCartney's theme song: "We were shooting in New Orleans when Harry came up to me one morning and said, 'At 5:20, we've got to go to a recording studio. I've got a song from Paul McCartney and Wings.' So we're listening to it, and suddenly that crescendo of the music comes flying through the speakers, and Harry says, 'Well, it's not my type of music,' and I said, 'It's not mine either.' But Harry said,

Careful, It's Loaded: Tee Hee (Julius W. Harris) disposes of Bond's Walther PPK after his unwelcome visit to Harlem.

'Paul McCartney has recorded this at his own expense. George Martin has done the arrangement, and Paul is launching his new group called Wings. If we use the song for the film, I think it would be good for him, and it would be good for us.' Harry and I weren't about to argue with success, so that's how it happened. It may have been shortened by just a few seconds, but what you hear in the film is the identical song that we heard that day in New Orleans."

Jane Seymour: "I think Roger was a little nervous about taking over the role. I was certainly nervous too. But Roger, and his then wife Luisa, could not have been nicer to me. They really went out of their way to make sure I was all right, especially when Harry would sometimes be a little difficult with me. Roger always came to my rescue. I remember Richard Attenborough had sent him a little note before we started shooting that said, 'Dear Roger: Please look after my daughter-in-law.' So Roger always said, 'Geez, I get to be Bond, and the girl I get to be in bed with is one of my best friends' daughter-in-law!'"

Roger Moore, on any James Bond jitters: "None really . . . probably because I'm a conceited egomaniac! No, it didn't worry me taking over the role. I think the only time I felt nervous about it was when I was on my way to the final press launch just before the opening of *Live and Let Die*. I was driving into London and suddenly got terrible butterflies. I thought, 'Suppose they don't like it? Suppose I fucked up and it's no good?' And I think after a while of thinking this, I then realized, 'Well, it's rather like having a baby; you're on the trolley going into the delivery room, and no matter what you do the baby is going to come out. Good, bad, or indifferent, there's no stopping it.' And so if it's not a pretty baby, then *doodly-doo*! You did your best."

North American Gross: $35.4 million

Overseas: $72.2 million

Duel In The Sun: Francisco Scaramanga (Christopher Lee) and
James Bond (Roger Moore) square off.

THE MAN WITH THE GOLDEN GUN (1974)

Directed By: Guy Hamilton

The Mission: Notorious assassin Francisco Scaramanga (Christopher Lee) — who commands $1 million per hit — sets the sights of his golden pistol on 007 as the two square off in a race for the priceless Solex Agitator energy converter.

Locales: Scaramanga's island inside Red Chinese waters, London, Bangkok, Beirut, Hong Kong, Macao

The Villain and Accomplices: Francisco Scaramanga (Christopher

Lee), Nick Nack (Herve Villechaize), Hai Fat (Richard Loo), Chula (Chan Yiu Lam)

The Bond Girls: Mary Goodnight (Britt Ekland), Andrea Anders (Maud Adams)

Theme Song: Lulu

Score: John Barry

Memorable Lines:

After being presented with a golden bullet inscribed with his number, Bond discounts the obvious threat: "I mean sir, who would pay a million dollars to have me killed?"
M: "Jealous husbands, outraged chefs, humiliated tailors . . . the list is endless."

Bond: "Moneypenny, you are better than a computer."
Moneypenny: "In all sorts of ways . . . but you never take advantage of them."

"He must have found me quite titillating." — *Bond, as he discards his Scaramanga disguise of a fake supercilious papilla* — "a third nipple."

Bond: "You live well, Scaramanga."
Scaramanga: "At a million dollars a contract, I can afford to, Mr. Bond. You work for peanuts: a hearty 'well done' from Her Majesty the Queen and a pittance of a pension. Apart from that, we are the same."

Maud Adams (Andrea Anders): "I had never been in a situation of this scale before. It was pretty nerve-wracking. I really felt the pressure because I had never gotten this amount of attention. I was completely shocked when they had the first press conference before we'd even started shooting. I remember I walked in just expecting a few journalists to talk to me, and it was this giant room crammed full with journalists from around the world. Suddenly, I realized just how big this all was. I was pretty intimidated and beleaguered. But Roger Moore had handled this in the past and was pretty cool about it all. He was very sweet and supportive."

Britt Ekland (left) and Maud Adams (right) give a couple legs up to Hervé Villechaize as Nick Nack in this cheeky publicity shot.

Tom Mankiewicz (Co-Screenwriter): "Harry Saltzman would always pepper you with 10 different ideas, and three of them would be brilliant but seven of them would be terrible and he couldn't distinguish between them. His big thing was he always wanted Bond caught in a giant spin dryer. On every movie, Harry would say 'and here's the spot where you could put him in a giant spin dryer.' Finally, on *The Man with the Golden Gun*, I said, 'Harry, who owns a *giant spin dryer*? Is it the giant from *Jack and the Beanstalk*?' Harry always wanted Bond to spin around to death for some reason. Then when Guy [Hamilton], Cubby, and myself were location scouting in Bangkok, it turned out Harry had earlier gone up north to Ching Mai, where the elephants work the teak forests. He loved the elephants. So he called me up and said, 'There's going to be an elephant stampede in the film! Bond's on the lead elephant!' And I said, '*Oh, boy*!' So I called the people who ran the teak forests, just to get some information. They said to me, 'Well, first

(left) Ian Fleming's cousin Christopher Lee makes his mark on the Bond series, while Roger Moore (right) helps Saida (Carmen Sautoy) lose her charm.

of all, you understand that these elephants don't *stampede*. They just work the forests. You'd have to bring in 50 trained elephants.' Well, it turned out that while Harry was up there he had asked what the elephants were wearing on their feet. It seems the elephants were wearing these canvas-type shoes because it's tough on their feet when they're working the teak forests. So Harry goes and orders 200 pairs of elephant shoes! He told them, 'We've got to have enough shoes for all these elephants.' So flash ahead a few months, Harry is now off the picture, and Cubby and I are in Bangkok, and a guy comes up to us at the Oriental Hotel and says, 'Oh, by the way, Mr. Broccoli, your elephant shoes have arrived.' And Cubby just looks at him and says, '*What?*' And the guy says, 'Yes, 200 elephant shoes ordered by Mr. Saltzman.' And Cubby said, 'What the hell is Harry doing ordering elephant shoes?' And suddenly I remembered from four months earlier and said, 'Oh, Jesus, Cubby — that must be from the elephant stampede Harry wanted to do.' It was so typical Harry. So if you're in the market for elephant shoes, I know where you can get some cheap!"

Maud Adams, on working with Christopher Lee and Roger Moore: "They're very different people. Roger is very happy-go-lucky and loose — he was the real prankster on the set and kept everyone in a good mood. But Christopher is more of a formal kind of actor, a very well-trained and serious person. Very much an intellectual. And I found out he was really sensitive to vampire jokes! As you know, he played Dracula a number of times, and everyone liked to joke around about that, but he didn't view it as a joke. To him, it's a literary person, and it had literary importance to him, so he didn't like the jokes too much. And Roger was always trying to pull his leg."

Tom Mankiewicz: "Roger is most wonderfully self-deprecating. At a press conference for *Man with the Golden Gun*, I remember one of the reporters asked him why he was playing James Bond. And Roger said, 'When I was at RADA [Royal Academy of Dramatic Arts] in London, I played one night in front of Noël Coward, who came backstage afterwards and said to me, 'Young man, with your devastating good looks and your disastrous lack of talent, take any part ever offered you. And in the unlikely occurrence you're offered two simultaneously, take the one that pays the most money!'"

Guy Hamilton (Director), on the 360° barrel roll stunt: "I had seen this stunt in a car show going around the arenas and astrodomes in the U.S. The drivers started out in the parking lot, came racing in and up the ramp, and did a 360° roll. It was pretty spectacular, so I wondered how I could use it in a Bond film. So I thought about a bridge being down, and later in Thailand we found the right place on a river that could work; we measured it and then worked backwards from there as to why they'd be chasing Bond. We designed the takeoff and landing ramps over a *Thai klong* [canal] and then disguised the ramps as a fallen bridge. But it was a stunt that needed a lot of preparation. The car had to be rebalanced, the driver had to sit in the middle, and other technicalities like that. The only thing that ended up being a little hair-raising is that the guy who normally did the 360 couldn't do the stunt on the day we had to shoot. So

Bond makes his escape through the canals of Bangkok

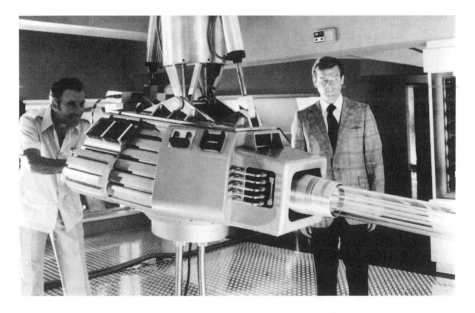

Francisco Scaramanga demonstrates the power of his Solex laser gun on Bond's only means of escape.

one of his assistants did it, who had never done it before. It was a little nerve-wracking, but it was one of those stunts that, if you get up to the right speed, something underneath knocks a piece of the ramp out that falls and that causes the car to start to spin. If you hit the right speed, the stunt basically took care of itself."

Tom Mankiewicz: "It was very much a family. Cubby was the morale builder — 'Don' Cubby I used to call him. And Harry was the guy who was always lighting fires under everybody's ass. But Harry and Cubby were fighting a lot, and I learned very early on that, if I wanted to keep a scene in the film, all I had to do was go to Cubby, show him the scene, and say 'Harry hates this scene.' And Cubby would always say, 'Well, I fuckin' love it! As a matter of fact, it's the fuckin' best scene in the whole movie!' But I never got that close to Harry. On the other hand, I was very close to Cubby and his family. Cubby and Dana were so wonderful to me, and their daughter Barbara was so sweet. She was only 10 or 12 years old at the time, and now her and Michael Wilson are running the show. It's good to see everything has stayed in the family."

Maud Adams, on shooting Scaramanga's island hideaway scenes off the coast of Thailand: "Khow-Ping-Kan was absolutely beautiful. That chain of islands was extraordinary. Absolutely pristine. But I remember we had a long commute to the islands, and we'd have to take a boat out to the location every day. We actually had to live in this small village outside of Phuket — and you can imagine what Roger called Phuket! This little village didn't have accommodations for a crew as large as us, so we had to sort of scramble up in small hotels all over the place. The little hotel I stayed in was where they put all the lead actors, and Cubby stayed there too. But they actually had to send in a painting crew to paint the rooms for us and try to clean them up a bit before we moved in there, because it was pretty primitive. The men were gentlemen and allowed the women to have the rooms with toilets. That was the only luxury we got."

Tom Mankiewicz: "One of my favorite lines I wrote for the Bond films was in *The Man with the Golden Gun*. It's where Bond points the gun at the guy's crotch and says, 'Speak now, or forever hold your piece.'"

North American Gross: $21.0 million

Overseas: $76.6 million

Heating Up The Cold War: Agents Triple X (Barbara Bach) and 007 (Roger Moore) give détente a try.

THE SPY WHO LOVED ME *(1977)*

Directed By: Lewis Gilbert

The Mission: Billionaire shipping magnate Karl Stromberg (Curt Jurgens) uses his massive tanker *The Liparus* to capture two nuclear submarines — one British and one Russian — with plans to launch the nukes at Russia and America in an attempt to provoke a global holocaust. Once accomplished, the survivors will be forced to live underwater, where Stromberg will rule from his amphibious kingdom, Atlantis.

Locales: Austria, Russia, London, Scotland, Egypt, Sardinia

The Villain and Accomplices: Karl Stromberg (Curt Jurgens), Jaws (Richard Kiel), Naomi (Caroline Munro), Sandor (Milton Reid), Aziz Fekkesh (Nadim Sawalha), Max Kalba (Vernon Dobtcheff)

The Bond Girls: Anya Amasova (Barbara Bach), Austrian agent (Sue Vanner), Felicca (Olga Bisera)

Theme Song: Carly Simon

Score: Marvin Hamlisch

Memorable Lines:

When M inquires about Bond's whereabouts, Moneypenny informs him that 007 is on a mission.
M: "Well, tell him to pull out immediately!"
Cut to Bond's "mission" — in passionate embrace with an Austrian beauty on a bearskin rug.

Felicca: "You are very suspicious, Mister Bond."
Bond: "Oh, I find I live much longer that way."

Bond, dismissing Q's precautions on the new Lotus Esprit: "Q, have I ever let you down?"
Q: "Frequently!"

After plucking the escape capsule from the sea, KGB *General Gogol, M, Q, and the British Minister of Defense are aghast to catch Bond atop Anya. Minister of Defense:* "Bond, what do you think you're doing?"
Bond: "Keeping the British end up, sir!"

Michael Wilson (Special Assistant to Producer): "Harry Saltzman was a super salesman. He could really get people motivated, that was very much his ability. But he got financially overextended, and it kind of blew up in his face. The bank started to foreclose on him and get involved in his Danjaq stock. It was a bad financial situation, and consequently the company got kind of paralyzed after *The Man with the Golden Gun*."

John Glen (Editor/Second Unit Director): "*The Spy Who Loved Me* was the first Bond that Cubby produced alone. Harry Saltzman had always been the coproducer, and, now that he was gone and the legal problems had all been sorted out, Cubby came back after three years, and it was like a fresh beginning for him. And I think the film looks and feels that way too."

(left to right) Barbara Bach, Cubby Broccoli, and Roger Moore in a candid moment on the Liparus supertanker set at Pinewood Studios.

Roger of Arabia

Roger Moore: "*The Spy Who Loved Me* is my personal favorite. It became a slightly different type of Bond at that point. Although I didn't really change the character, we tried to inject a little more humor. I think it had all the right ingredients, the right locations, and [director] Lewis Gilbert and I shared the same sense of humor. Guy [Hamilton] could be very funny and very sardonic, and John Glen would sort of laugh politely at my jokes and think, 'I wish the son of a bitch would stop clowning around so we can get on

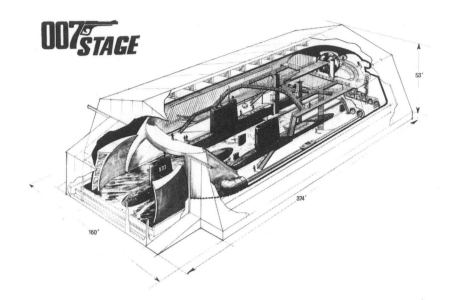

Schematic of the Ken Adam-designed 007 stage at Pinewood Studios, the largest soundstage in the world. It was built in under 13 weeks.

The fully-dressed set of Stromberg's Liparus supertanker. The enormity and complexity of the set brought forth famed director Stanley Kubrick at the behest of Production Designer Ken Adam.

Up In Smoke: The set helped win Ken Adam an Academy Award nomination for Best Art Direction. Star Wars wound up taking the prize.

Captains of the Ship: Production Designer Ken Adam, Producer Cubby Broccoli, and Director Lewis Gilbert at the helm of The Spy Who Loved Me.

with the shoot,' but Lewis Gilbert and I really had a ball. My favorite moment was walking across the desert wearing a black dinner suit with Barbara Bach, and it was this sort of long, romantic *Lawrence of Arabia* shot as we walk over the sand dunes into the setting sun. Then near the end of the scene, I just let my trousers drop down around my ankles. I wanted them to keep it in the film, but they wouldn't go for it!"

Ken Adam (Production Designer), on constructing the enormous 007 soundstage at Pinewood Studios: "It came about because I had made a mistake on *You Only Live Twice*, where I didn't care what the volcano set looked like from the outside. So after we finished shooting this huge structure of hundreds of tons of structural steel, we thought we could just leave the structure up at Pinewood and do something else with it again. But all the locals started complaining that it was a huge eyesore, and so we had to tear it down. I didn't want to make that mistake again, so for *The Spy Who Loved Me* I designed the soundstage around the set. Because at the time there was no stage in the world big enough to serve as a tank and also house three nuclear-powered submarines.

Roger Moore: "Ken Adam is one of the great designers of all time. He is, I think, one of the foremost people responsible for the success of the Bond films. Undeniable genius. Everything was for real in his sets, quite spectacular, and also very expensive. Absolutely beautiful. It was rather sad having to always blow it all up. But everything gets blown up in Bond."

Ken Adam, on building *The Liparus* supertanker: "It was the biggest interior set ever built, and the real design challenge was to give the hold of the supertanker an interesting look. Claude Renoir was our director of photography, and he was a brilliant cameraman. But to be suddenly catapulted into these gigantic sets on the 007 stage was an enormous responsibility for him. He had never dealt with sets these huge before, and I felt he was very nervous. I thought that, the more I could help him with the lighting, the more effective the set would be. So I rang up Stanley

Brilliant visionary Ken Adam, who designed the fantastical world of 007. He's been awarded two Oscars and an Order of the British Empire for his contributions to cinema.

Kubrick and said, 'Stanley, will you come and help me set up the source lighting?' And he said, 'You must be out of your mind! If anybody sees me arriving at Pinewood. . . .' Because by this time he rarely moved out of his house. 'Plus,' he said, 'I can't do that to Claude Renoir — it will be around the industry in no time!' And I said, 'I give you my word of honor, there will be nobody at Pinewood. I've got the keys to the 007 stage. I'll pick you up on a Sunday morning and drive you through security. I guarantee nobody will ever know that you came.' I finally talked him into it. So Stanley and I spent about four hours crawling all over that enormous set, which was quite dangerous. He had great ideas about some natural light sources — because there was no daylight — and where to pinpoint the source lighting, because Kubrick was always very particular on source lighting. It was great of him to do that."

John Glen, on shooting the pretitle ski-parachute jump: "Cubby wanted to open the new film in style. He asked us for something breathtaking. It was the very first thing we shot for *Spy Who Loved Me*, well before filming began. We shot it in June 1976, and the film didn't actually go into production until August 1976. They gave me a budget of $250,000 to do this stunt with Rick Sylvester up in one of the most remote areas on the Arctic Circle. It was like an expedition really, just this small group of guys — mostly mountaineers and skiers. We had to camp at the bottom of Mount Asgard in the middle of Canada's Baffin Island for three weeks, freezing our balls off in tents in order to get that stunt. It was a tough one, but if I had come back empty-handed I think they would've thought up another stunt to put in. But I certainly wouldn't have been doing it; I'd have probably got the sack for having spent a quarter of a million dollars! But I never felt the pressure at the time. I just thought, 'This is my opportunity.' However, because of the adverse weather conditions and the personalities involved, it was a bit of a fight keeping everyone's morale high, overcoming the frustrations of delays. The weather was absolutely terrible and made it impossible to shoot. And after 10 days of waiting around, impatient calls started coming from London wondering what was going on. Finally, one afternoon, the storm clouds suddenly cleared away from the top of the mountain, and we had a brief window of sunshine. We scrambled into position. I was very well prepared, so I knew exactly what we had to do. And because of the extreme danger of the jump, timing was absolutely critical. Plus, the sun was quickly leaving the face. We had three camera positions, and because I didn't trust radios at that time I had this red flag, and I said to Rick, 'Whatever happens, whatever you think you heard on your radio, you don't go until that red flag is buried in the snow!' My last words to Rick were 'Go, go Rick — don't forget *you're James Bond!*' and I shoved the flag in the snow. The last thing I saw was Rick gathering speed as he skied towards the precipice. He shot off the mountain, disengaged his skis, went into freefall, and deployed his parachute. It was a wonderful moment. But then I found out that there had been a problem with a couple of the cameras, and we rushed the film to Montreal for processing. Word came back that just one of the cameras managed to capture it all, but there was a slight focus hiccup. I said, 'Do you think it's acceptable?' And the line producer said, 'I think so.' So I pulled everyone out. We were very lucky; another jump would have been impossible. God was smiling on us, because if you look at that shot you'll see that the sun is not on the mountain, it's only on Rick, and it follows him like a spotlight as he races towards the edge of the mountain. That's one of the reasons why it's such a great shot."

Tom Mankiewicz: "I was at a preview of *The Spy Who Loved Me* with Cubby and Rick Sylvester. I remember the audience absolutely gasped

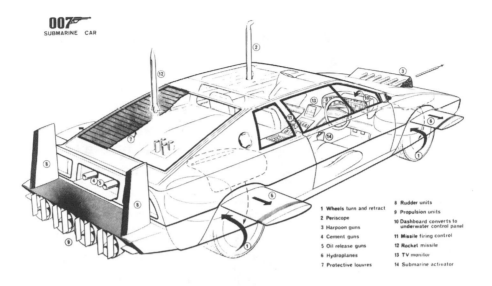

007
SUBMARINE CAR

1 Wheels turn and retract
2 Periscope
3 Harpoon guns
4 Cement guns
5 Oil release guns
6 Hydroplanes
7 Protective louvres

8 Rudder units
9 Propulsion units
10 Dashboard converts to underwater control panel
11 Missile firing control
12 Rocket missile
13 TV monitor
14 Submarine activator

Schematic for the Lotus Esprit submarine car, designed by Ken Adam and special effects supervisor Derek Meddings.

Six different models of the Lotus were constructed, including this fully submersible version for filming in the waters off the Bahamas.

Pyramid Scheme: A silhouetted Roger Moore on location in Cairo.

when Bond went off that cliff. And Rick hadn't seen the film yet, and, watching himself do that stunt, all he could say was 'Holy shit!'"

Ken Adam, on the Lotus Esprit submarine car: "We had built a full-size Lotus to work as a submarine. It could actually drive underwater, but you had to wear a breathing apparatus inside the car because it was filled with water. But because of the louvers over the windshield, you wouldn't be able to see those devices clearly. We shot that down in the Bahamas, and we also modified additional models of the car to perform the other operating effects."

Tom Mankiewicz: "I did a lot of rewriting on the film, stuff with Jaws and also the relationship between Bond and Major Amasova. I wrote this wonderful scene where Bond and Barbara Bach come up to the bar — this is the first time they've seen each other in the flesh — and he orders a drink for her. Then she says, 'And for the gentleman, a vodka martini, shaken, not stirred.' Most of the scene is still the way I wrote it, but they made us cut out the next part, which was Bond says to her, 'You're much more beautiful than you were in your pictures, Major Amasova.' And she says, 'The only picture we have of you, Mr. Bond, was taken in bed with one of our agents, a Miss Tatiana Romanova.' Roger says, 'And was she smiling?' Barbara then says, 'As I recall, her mouth was not immediately visible in the photograph.' Roger says, 'Ah, then I was smiling.' I told them that scene would bring the house down. And Roger, of course, loved it also. But I think it was too risqué for some tastes."

Roger Moore, on James Bond injuries: "They blew three holes in my backside on *The Spy Who Loved Me.* It was the scene near the end of the film when I'm sitting opposite Curt Jurgens at that long table and he tries to shoot me. Well, they blew up the chair under my ass before I could get out of it. I wasn't hospitalized, but I had to have my dressings changed by the nurse at the studio twice a day. The indignity of dropping your trousers twice a day was sufficient punishment."

North American Gross: $46.8 million

Overseas: $138.6 million

Space Cowboys: Lois Chiles and Roger Moore caught between takes on board the Space Station set.

MOONRAKER (1979)

Directed By: Lewis Gilbert

The Mission: French industrialist Hugo Drax (Michel Lonsdale) plots to eliminate all human life by launching globes of toxic gas from his secret space station. Drax will then repopulate the Earth with his genetically perfect specimens, a master race over which he will preside from his heavenly headquarters.

Locales: Yukon, London, California, Venice, Rio de Janeiro, the Amazon, and outer space

The Villain and Accomplices: Hugo Drax (Michel Lonsdale), Jaws (Richard Kiel), Chang (Toshiro Suga)

The Bond Girls: Dr. Holly Goodhead (Lois Chiles), Corinne Dufour (Corinne Clery), Manuela (Emily Bolton)

Theme Song: Shirley Bassey

Score: John Barry

Memorable Lines:

Drax to Bond upon their initial meeting: "You have arrived at a propitious moment, coincident with your country's one indisputable contribution to Western civilization: afternoon tea."

Bond, exposing Holly Goodhead as an undercover CIA agent: "The CIA placed you with Drax, correct?"
Goodhead: "Very astute of you, James."
Bond: "Oh, not really — I have friends in low places."

The Minister of Defense, M, and Bond — mistakenly thinking they're entering a toxic laboratory — confront Hugo Drax wearing gas masks. Drax: "You must excuse me, gentlemen. Not being English, I sometimes find your sense of humor rather difficult to follow."

"Mr. Bond. You defy all my attempts to plan an amusing death for you." Michel Lonsdale as Hugo Drax.

Drax: "James Bond. You appear with the tedious inevitability of an unloved season."

Drax, facing his inevitable demise, holds Bond at gunpoint: "At least I shall have the pleasure of putting you out of my misery . . . desolated, Mister Bond."
"Heartbroken, Mister Drax," *replies Bond, shooting Drax through the heart with a cyanide-tipped dart from his wristwatch.*

A closed-circuit space shuttle camera beams back to the White House and Buckingham Palace a transmission of Bond taking advantage of zero gravity with Holly Goodhead. The Minister of Defense and M look on aghast. Minister of Defense: "My God! What's Bond doing?"
An oblivious Q, studying his instrumentation panel: "I think he's attempting reentry, sir."

Roger Moore: "With *Moonraker*, they were trying to keep up with what was going on around them. You know, in between Bonds, the imitators came along and tried to outdo them. So Bond was sort of forced to do things and go along with the various things that were happening — and

One Giant Leap For Mankind: Roger Moore and Lois Chiles spent weeks suspended on wires to duplicate the zero gravity. (right) Jaws (Richard Kiel) parachutes after 007 in the opening teaser.

space was what was on everyone's mind at the time. But I hated the costumes, and I hated the hats they kept making me wear. They were always doing things to drive me mad! Otherwise, I enjoyed doing *Moonraker* because I enjoyed working with Lewis Gilbert."

John Glen (Editor/Second Unit Director): "After the huge response to the opening teaser in *The Spy Who Loved Me*, I was charged with an even more complex parachute jump for *Moonraker*. Michael Wilson had the idea of Bond being thrown out of an airplane without a parachute, and so we went to California and spoke to world champion skydiver B.J. Worth, Jake Lombard, and aerial cameraman Rande Deluca about the logistics. Normally, aerial photography was shot in 16mm, but we wanted to shoot in 35mm. However, the weight of a 35mm camera could snap your neck when you opened your chute, so we had Continental Systems develop an anemographic 35mm camera with a titanium body that was light enough to mount onto a crash helmet. It weighed just a little over seven pounds, and we stuck that on top of Rande's helmet. Of course, what I didn't realize was that, when he opened his parachute, this extension in terms of weight was more like 50 or 60 pounds. It would break your neck. Rande thought about it and then developed a slower-opening parachute by wrapping rope around it, so when it opened it minimized the upward jolt. But that also meant he was dangerously close to the

The largest set ever built in France: the Drax Space Station, which was partially inspired by Ken Adam's access to NASA's proposed space station.

Hugo Drax's Control Room: Ken Adam nicknamed it the "Mondrian Set," because the colors, black lines, and various screen projections reminded him of a Mondrian painting.

ground when his parachute finally did fully unfurl. But I worked out each shot in advance and figured we would only have three seconds maximum of filming time for each jump. I took an editing machine with me to assemble the little bits of footage, and on the airfield I'd show the boys what we were shooting. On a good day, we could get in eight jumps. By the end of three weeks, we had every shot I needed. It took a total of 88 jumps to shoot enough footage for what was essentially a two-minute sequence. But it was worth the effort."

Ken Adam (Production Designer): "I had enormous responsibilities on *Moonraker*. Lewis, Cubby, and Roger — for tax reasons — didn't want to work in England. So we went to France, and Lewis said, 'Will shooting in France sacrifice the production values?' It was a tall order, but I said, 'No, I could do it. But I'll need every available film studio in France.' I ended up getting every studio in the Paris area, but it put enormous pressure on me, because I could only take certain key people with me. My team was very essential. Peter Lamont had to end up staying at Pinewood to look after the 007 stage where Derek Meddings was doing all the outer space special effects. So my art director, Charlie Bishop, came with me to Paris, and my set decorator, Peter Howitt, came with me, but those were the only ones. I ended up spending some time at NASA doing research, and they showed me their proposed space station. They were very cooperative. But there was a lot of pressure, and it was costing a lot of money because of these such enormous sets: the space station, space corridors, the control room, the great chamber under the waterfalls, the laboratory, the centrifuge — it was all very ambitious, and people were starting to get very worried about the costs. They started saying I was going over budget, and they sent people over to say I wasn't allowed to spend any more money. But France isn't cheap, especially when you're working out of three different film studios and out of your normal surroundings."

Peter Lamont (Visual Effects Art Director): "I stayed here at Pinewood with Derek Meddings, as supervising art director in charge of special effects. *Moonraker* was a very difficult Bond because we'd just

Moonraker's elaborate sets helped propel the budget to over $32 million —the highest of any Bond to that point.

returned from the Academy Awards, where *The Spy Who Loved Me* had been nominated alongside *Star Wars*. Well, *Star Wars* was the most successful film that had ever been made at that time and of course won all the art direction awards. But I felt like we had given a lot and that Ken Adam deserved much more recognition because he was the one who put this whole style on the map."

Ken Adam: "By the time of *The Spy Who Loved Me* and then *Moonraker*, we had established a real formula for the Bonds. It was important that we had someone like Lewis Gilbert directing, who had also directed *You Only Live Twice*. It was the same team, and for me that was very important. Unfortunately, after *Moonraker*, I felt the team was disintegrating. Lewis wasn't going to do the next one, and it became a different feel. That was partly why I left. I was also exhausted after *Moonraker*. It was the toughest Bond I ever made. And after going into outer space, I said, 'Where else can we go?' But I think if the same team was still there I probably would have carried on."

John Glen: "Richard Kiel created such a wonderful character in Jaws. He was such a success that we were tempted to use him again; why throw that away? So I think that caused the problem with *Moonraker* in a sense was that we used Jaws again. Though it was a great idea, the stuff with him finding a girlfriend and being up in space and what have you probably was going a bit too far for a Bond movie. I think that one can get carried

"I was petrified I was going to hit somebody because I didn't have that much control of it," said Roger Moore of driving the gondola hovercraft through throngs of tourists in St. Marks Square.

away. Bond is half fantasy, but I think there's a limit. When you get outside of realism too far, you're in dangerous territory. Hindsight is a wonderful thing. But I must say that *Moonraker* was a very pleasant film to work on, and I think we accomplished some really wonderful stuff."

North American Gross: $62.7 million

Overseas: $140.0 million

Under the direction of John Glen, For Your Eyes Only made a return to the harder edge of Fleming's Bond novels.

FOR YOUR EYES ONLY *(1981)*

Directed By: John Glen

The Mission: When a British spy ship sinks in the Ionian Sea, Greek shipping tycoon Aris Kristatos (Julian Glover) gets hold of the vessel's top-secret ATAC device — a communications control of Polaris submarines — which he plans to sell for top dollar to the Russians.

Locales: London, the Ionian Sea, Madrid, Cortina, Corfu

The Villain and Accomplices: Aris Kristatos (Julian Glover), Emile Leopold Locque (Michael Gothard), Eric Kriegler (John Wyman), Hector Gonzales (Stefan Kalipha)

The Bond Girls: Melina Havelock (Carole Bouquet), Countess Lisl (Cassandra Harris), Bibi Dahl (Lynn-Holly Johnson)

Theme Song: Sheena Easton

Score: Bill Conti

Memorable Lines:

Blofeld, on intercom to Bond's sabotaged helicopter: "Good-bye, Mister Bond. I trust you had a pleasant . . . *fright.*"

Minister of Defense: "We'll have to tell the Prime Minister that Operation Undertow is dead in the water. She'll have our guts for garters!"

In Greece, Bond slips into a church confessional for a covert briefing. Bond: "Forgive me Father, for I have sinned."
Q, removing his disguise as a Greek priest: "That's putting it *mildly,* 007."

Between A Rock And A Hard Place: Roger Moore had to battle his fear of heights to scale the Monastery cliffs. "They were always doing things to drive me mad," grinned Moore. (right) Visiting the grave of wife Tracy in the opening teaser.

John Glen (Director): "At an early point, there was some talk that Roger wouldn't do *For Your Eyes Only*, so we had to be prepared — in case negotiations broke down — to break in a new Bond. So the opening in the churchyard, with Bond visiting the grave of his deceased wife, Tracy, was my idea of introducing the new Bond and keeping the continuity of the character. Roger came back, and since we couldn't come up with a better opening teaser, we left it in. That helicopter chase was our way of getting back to the previous style of Bonds. On *For Your Eyes Only*, we wanted to get away from the lavish sets, spaceships, and push-button technology. Just real people, good motives, good characterizations, and gritty action scenes. And since it was my first Bond at the helm, I'm glad I got to do it with Roger, because he was already established in the role. He knew what to do, he knew the character, and I was able to bring to that a new style and a harder edge."

John Glen, on Roger Moore's reluctance to indulge the cold-hearted side of Bond: "Roger is a personality actor, really. He put his personality into the Bond role and respected a lot of the Fleming criteria.

French actress and Chanel model Carole Bouquet shares a laugh with Roger Moore on location in Cortina. (right) Dragged through the coral reef in a scene taken from the Live and Let Die novel.

But he was also very mindful of how children saw Bond as a hero. So when we had to shoot the scene where Bond kicks over Locque's car as it sits teetering on the edge of the cliff, there was a lot of *discussion*. Locque was a ruthless killer who murdered Bond's friend — I wanted Bond to act in a similarly ruthless way. But Roger was adamant that he wouldn't do it, that something so cold-blooded wasn't in his character. Instead, he wanted to send the car over the edge by just flicking Locque's dove-emblem pin inside, with that slight extra weight enough to send the car crashing. Well, to me that was a little bit like *Moonraker*, a little bit too fanciful. So that's why I said no, you have to take it all very calmly, and then suddenly up comes the leg, and you kick the car over. To me, that was the turning point in his style. You suddenly realize how ruthless he can be, and it gave him a much harder edge. It also gave him a real strength of character that I was looking for. I think it helped the film."

Roger Moore: "Oh, we *discussed* that scene at great length! I said, 'I don't think this is very nice of Bond — the poor bastard is already on his way out. It's pretty vicious.' Although it was Bond, I thought it wasn't very

I Think He Got The Point: Bond disposes of a Gonzales henchman before making a Mary Poppins-esque escape.

Greek marine archaeologist Melina Havelock (Carole Bouquet) is captured by a Kristatos thug.

Roger Moore Bond to be that vicious. But really what I was worried about was that, if I kick that car over, I might bloody well fall over the cliff with him!"

John Glen: "All the time I was editing the earlier Bonds, all I remember thinking is that, if I ever get a chance to direct, let it be a Bond film, because it was my forte. I have that enthusiasm and the knowledge of the characters and the instincts for what it takes to pull one off. And I developed a technique where I always put the audience in the driver's seat. The way you shoot it, it's from the point of view of the audience, to let them experience it themselves. It's a technique that you can't do with multi cameras. You have to plan it very, very carefully. But the audience really gets into it that way. Because you can only watch car chases for so long; it gets pretty boring just seeing cars screech back and forth unless you get inside the car and see it from that perspective. The chase in *For Your Eyes Only*, where Bond escapes in Melina's little yellow Citröen Bug, was my first real opportunity to do that on a Bond movie."

Roger Moore, on the worldwide media attention: "I think on one of the Bonds the PR fellow in charge said, 'So far, we've had 191 reporters visit the set.' And 189 of those all wanted to do an in-depth, one-on-one interview with me, which is bloody impossible. I'd say, 'I don't mind — we can do publicity all day. But we won't have a film to sell at the end of it because I won't be available to actually *shoot* the film!' You had to draw the line somewhere!"

John Glen, on Bond being dragged underwater through the coral reef: "That scene came straight out of Ian Fleming's novel *Live and Let Die* and which had been in and out of Bond scripts for years. It was a sequence that no one really wanted to shoot, except for Cubby. The reason it wasn't used in the film *Live and Let Die* and was rejected by most directors for the subsequent Bonds was because it was such a complex sequence to shoot. There were no guarantees you were going to get it, because it was a mixture of underwater and above water. It involved four

Topol was suggested for the role of Greek smuggler Milos Columbo by Cubby Broccoli's wife Dana after she spotted him at a social event.

Surprise ATAC: Bond and Melina swipe the prized ATAC system from under Kristatos' nose.

to five units shooting the material. It was very difficult to control, and the cost of that part of the operation was very high. In fact, it was the highest of the Bahamas operation, running something like $2,700 per foot. But it was an important sequence because it allowed us to show Bond getting out of extreme danger by relying on his wits rather than gadgets."

North American Gross: $62.3 million

Overseas: $132.6 million

Octopussy wound up in competition with Sean Connery's rival Bond production Never Say Never Again in 1983. Octopussy won the box office battle.

OCTOPUSSY (1983)

Directed By: John Glen

The Mission: Renowned gem smuggler Kamal Khan is used by rogue Soviet General Orlov (Steven Berkoff) to detonate a nuclear bomb on a U.S. military base in West Germany. Furious with the Kremlin's growing détente with the West, Orlov hopes the nuclear disaster will pressure U.S. withdrawal, leaving Western Europe wide open for Soviet attack.

Locales: Central America, East Berlin, London, India, East Germany, West Germany

The Villain and Accomplices: Kamal Khan (Louis Jordan), Gobinda (Kabir Bedi), General Orlov (Steven Berkoff), Mischka (David Meyer), Grischka (Anthony Meyer)

The Bond Girls: Octopussy (Maud Adams), Magda (Kristina Wayborn), Bianca (Tina Hudson)

Theme Song: Rita Coolidge

Score: John Barry

Memorable Lines:

"Fill 'er up, please!" — *Bond, after landing his Acrostar Mini Jet at a roadside gas station.*

Bond, handing his dinner jacket to Q for mending: "You wouldn't have a small piece of thread, would you, Q? Someone seems to have stuck a knife in my wallet."
Snaps Q: "Ah, they missed you. What a *pity.*"

"Having problems keeping it up, Q?" — *Bond, after Q's rising Indian Rope gadget falls flat.*

After surviving Kamal Khan's jungle manhunt, Bond is rescued from a river by a passing tourist boat. "Are you with our group?" *asks a perplexed tourist.*
Groans Bond: "No, ma'am, I'm with the economy tour."

Kamal Khan: "Mister Bond is indeed a very rare breed . . . soon to be made extinct."

Two-Timer: Sultry Maud Adams returns for her second Bond Girl role.

Maud Adams (Octopussy), on her return to Bond: "I was shocked when they asked me back for another Bond film. It had never happened before. I had no idea what was in the back of their minds, and I still really don't. I've speculated that maybe because it's such a family operation and they have a great deal of loyalty to the people they've liked over the years. I've always felt a lot of goodwill coming from the family. But how it happened was they asked me to come to London to screen-test with James Brolin, whom they were considering for the role of Bond. It was a secret at the time, and I think they needed someone they could trust, or to rely on, to test with him. James Brolin was very good, and certainly looks-wise he was very well suited for the role. But they had never cast an American as Bond before, and also I found out they were renegotiating with Roger

The view from Goldeneye

The living room at Goldeneye

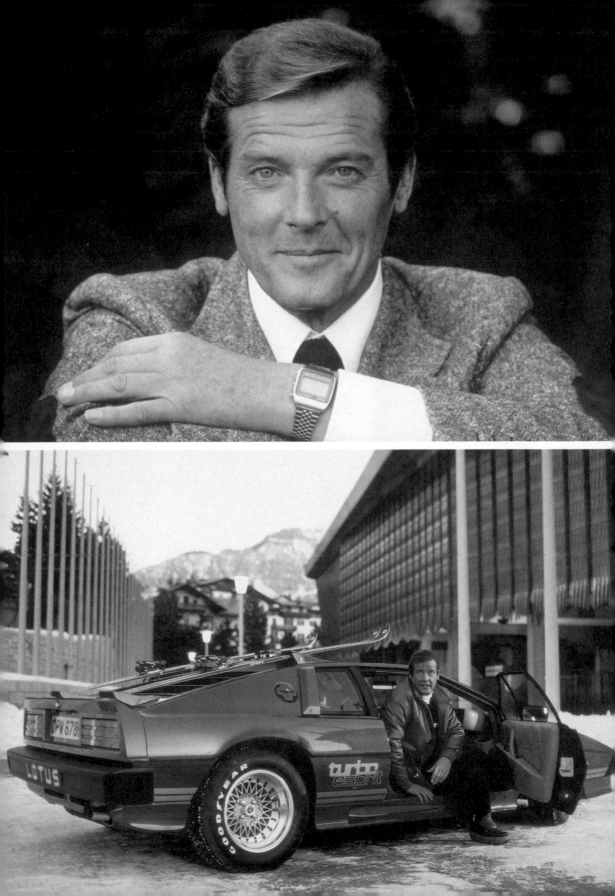

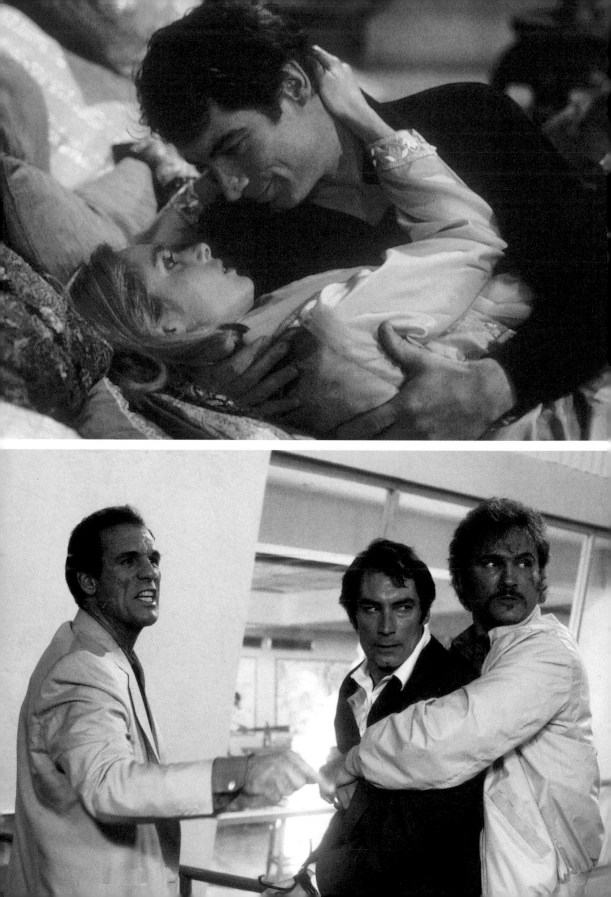

at the time. So I think this was one of their kind of negotiating tools, that if there was someone else who was possibly going to be doing the part he'd sign. I think it was part of their poker game. But when I was there, I started wondering why they were going to all the trouble of dying my hair dark to see what it would look like. Because in my mind, I was convinced I was just there to *help out*. But I didn't mind, because I've always liked them and didn't have a problem doing them that favor. So I was very surprised when they suddenly asked me to do the part."

John Glen (Director): "In the background, there was always this sort of poker game that Cubby would play, where we were spending quite a few hundred thousand dollars testing various actors for the role. But I always used to wonder how serious Cubby was and if it wasn't just a ploy to keep Roger's money in bounds, you know? But Cubby was such a good poker player that you never knew it. It was only afterwards that you realized what had happened. But he wouldn't confide in you, even being the director, about the financial side of it. And that was why Cubby was such a brilliant producer, because he never bothered me with all the stress and strain of the financial stuff. I had a budget, and as long as I kept to the budget Cubby would make sure the money was forthcoming."

Roger Moore: "Cubby and I were great mates, and we played backgammon endlessly on the set. We never paid one another until the last day of shooting. And when Cubby was losing, the assistants would try to call me into work, but he wouldn't let me go. He'd say, 'The son of a bitch is not getting up until he loses!'"

Maud Adams, on learning of her character's name: "I said, 'Oh, my God! Not that! *Octopussy??*' Of course, by then, you knew the characters always had double entendre names, and they never gave me one in *The Man with the Golden Gun*, so I guess I always felt cheated that I didn't get one before. Then when I realized that *Octopussy* was part of Ian Fleming's short story collection, I sort of thought, 'Well, times have changed, and maybe it will be acceptable.' I was a little leery in the

Pair-A-Dice: Bond outwits Kamal Khan (Louis Jordan) by appropriating his loaded dice in a high-stakes game of backgammon.

Mid-Fright Train From Georgia: Bond hitches a ride on a departing Soviet train.

Bond makes a smooth entrance into Kamal Khan's palace. "Roger was always very keen on doing a lot of his stunts," says director John Glen.

Bond takes a flying leap from Gobinda (Kabir Bedi) on the Octopussy Circus train.

"Oh, James!": 007 and Octopussy in passionate embrace. (right) Bond smokes out an assailant on the streets of Udaipur.

beginning but not so leery that I wouldn't take the part. Now, I don't even react. But at the time, I had some reservations about the name. . . . It was a little controversial."

John Glen: "Roger was always very keen on doing a lot of his stunts. All that stuff with Roger fighting with Kabir Bedi under the train was for real. I remember Roger said to me, 'What's that you've got under the train?' I said, 'It's a rig.' He said, 'You're not expecting me to go under there, are you?' I said, 'Absolutely.' And he said, 'Well, where are you going to be?' I said, 'Well, I don't want to put any more weight on it, so I thought I'd watch from here.' And he said, 'Well, if you don't go, I don't go.' So I had to get underneath as well. But when you see Kabir Bedi slashing away with his sword, that was Roger under there. And he was bloody gutsy, I'll tell you, because those bloody trains are pretty unforgiving."

Maud Adams: "Roger always loved to pull these elaborate practical jokes. He would tell the entire set, and everyone would be in on it except you. And, of course, you're in the middle of a take, and all of a sudden you realize everyone is sitting there on the edge of their seats waiting for Roger's punchline. They were always pretty risqué, and he would always do them to me! Probably because I was so gullible and would always choke and blush and not know what to do with myself. But Roger has a great sense of humor and was always ad-libbing lines, quite a few of which made it into the finished film."

Roger Moore: "We used to come up with like four or five different lines for a scene. I'd always ad-lib things, and it was up to the director to decide what to use. But Bond should be fun. It's entertainment. It shouldn't be taken too seriously. You have to be relaxed in the role. Because the minute the acting shows, you should get out of it. You can get away with it as a villain, you can act, but heroes can't. They've gotta be flip, charming, and look as though they don't give a damn. When, in reality, you're actually a seething mass of nerves underneath."

Maud Adams: "I remember one mishap with Roger. I unfortunately knocked him in a very *sensitive* area. It was the scene in front of Octopussy's bed, where he sort of turns me around and kisses me fiercely. Well, when I turned around, I hit him by accident in the groin. It's these long legs — I don't know where to put them. It took him a while to recover. I felt so bad."

North American Gross: $67.9 million

Overseas: $115.8 million

One Moore For The Road: At 58, Roger Moore makes his seventh – and final – film as James Bond in A View To A Kill.

A VIEW TO A KILL (1985)

Directed By: John Glen

The Mission: Wealthy industrialist Max Zorin (Christopher Walken) conspires to seize control of the world microchip industry by destroying Silicon Valley with a man-made earthquake along the San Andreas fault.

Locales: Siberia, England, France, San Francisco

The Villain and Accomplices: Max Zorin (Christopher Walken), May Day (Grace Jones), Dr. Carl Mortner (Willoughby Gray), Scarpine (Patrick Bauchau)

The Bond Girls: Stacey Sutton (Tanya Roberts), Pola Ivanova (Fiona Fullerton), Kimberly Jones (Mary Stavin)

Theme Song: Duran Duran

Score: John Barry

Memorable Lines:

"Taxi! Follow that parachute!" — *Bond, in pursuit of May Day.*

"Well, my dear, I take it you spend quite a lot of time in the saddle."
Jenny Flex: "Yes, I love an early morning ride."
Bond: "Ah, I'm an early riser myself."

"You slept well?" *Zorin asks Bond, after 007's night spent with May Day.*
Bond: "A little restless, but I got off eventually."

"So, does anyone else want to drop out?" — *Zorin, after ejecting a disgruntled business partner from his airship.*

John Glen, on shooting the Eiffel Tower parachute jump: "As you can imagine, they're very touchy in France about people doing stunts on the Eiffel Tower. The tourist trade there is enormous, and obviously the police were very nervous about bodies falling on tourists. But we also needed one of the main roads along the Seine cut off for our exclusive use for two or three hours a day. It took a lot of negotiations with the French officials to let us do that. But James Bond opens a lot of doors. I think it was good publicity. However, we ended up having to do all our stunt work very early in the morning when photographic conditions were less than ideal, because you can't stop the tourists from going there. B.J. Worth was doubling for Grace Jones, and we got that stunt in one take. It looked absolutely beautiful."

Christopher Walken and Grace Jones discuss a scene with director John Glen on the streets of Paris as producer Michael Wilson looks on.

Watch Your Step: B.J. Worth, doubling for Grace Jones, prepares to parachute off the Eiffel Tower.

Half-Off Sale: Bond's severed car takes to the Champs Élysées in hot pursuit of May Day

Production Designer Peter Lamont constructed this full-scale set of the Golden Gate Bridge on the Pinewood backlot for the climactic battle between Bond and Zorin.

Roger Moore, on shooting atop the Eiffel Tower: "I remember we were taken up in the morning to the halfway station, the service station of the Eiffel Tower. But elevators don't stop there on the way down, they never stop. So it meant having to walk down every day, which was about 2,000 steps. Let me tell you, that is a long, long walk!"

Peter Lamont (Production Designer), on re-creating the Golden Gate Bridge at Pinewood: "We went to the top of the Golden Gate Bridge, and it was quite a scary experience. We rode up in a claustro-phobic elevator, complete with three guards and their guns, that stops at a very narrow platform inside the tower. A fellow pointed and said, 'Right up that ladder, and be very careful when you get to the top.' He went first, and I'm carrying all these cameras and a bag of measuring equipment. Suddenly, he opened a hatch, and there we were, right at the very top.

Christopher Walken and Tanya Roberts in a candid moment on the Chantilly, France set.

Then my assistant came up, and we had to measure it all. We were all absolutely astounded by the view up there. We then had to construct three identical sections of the bridge back at Pinewood, one of which was a full-scale portion of the tower."

Christopher Walken (Max Zorin): "There is a quality of theater about the James Bond films: all the people in them are larger than life. So to be able to do one was a very seductive offer. I was raised on the Bond movies, and they are just so big and theatrical. To get to play a Bond villain was quite amazing. It's interesting, but I think there's an element of jealousy for James Bond inherent in every Bond villain. When I saw my first Bond film as a kid, I saw it all in very romantic terms: James Bond was very real, and he was the man you wanted to grow up to *be*. And I think the villains, in a strange way, also admire Bond and want to be him. But they can't, so they must destroy him. *A View to a Kill* was a long shoot because of all the huge stunts, but I had fun. Roger and I got along really well. He's a very nice man and quite funny. We had some good times."

Maud Adams, on her surprise cameo: "I flew up to San Francisco to visit with Roger and Luisa, and while I was on set at Fisherman's Wharf Roger and John [Glen] suggested putting me in the background for a fun little in-joke. So if you look closely, you'll see me walk by in the crowd. I have the distinction of actually being in *three* James Bond films!"

Grace Jones (May Day): "I remember doing a scene with Tanya Roberts where she's escaping from the collapsing mine, and I grab onto her, and I'm not letting go, ever. It was like either she falls or she comes out of her clothes. And I'm still holding on, but she was kicking, and there was a very, very high precipice behind me. I mean, if I fell, that was it. I would die. And I have to hold onto her leg while she was kicking, and believe me she was kicking like a thoroughbred, and that was very frightening. It's the only part where I scream in the movie, actually *scream*. I actually got very scared."

Fall From Grace: May Day prepares to toss a Russian bodyguard.

Bond skis across Siberian glaciars in the opening teaser. (right) Lois Maxwell makes her 14th — and final — appearance as Miss Moneypenny, alongside Roger Moore, Desmond Llewelyn, Patrick Macnee, and Robert Brown at the Royal Ascot Racecourse.

Dolph Lundgren (Venz): "I was probably only 23 years old at the time, and I was hanging out on the set with my then girlfriend Grace Jones. Then one day director John Glen said he needed a bad guy to point a gun at Christopher Walken for the scene at the racetrack. So John took a look at me and said, 'Do you think you can do that?' and I said, 'Ummm . . . I don't know.' And then he said, 'No, you can do it — you'll be fine.' So I walked out there, did it, and *A View to a Kill* ended up becoming my first acting job. I mean, if you blink, you'll miss my part. But after we shot the scene, John said, 'You know, kid, I think you have some talent. You hit your mark, you got it on the first take . . . maybe there's a future for you in films.' And of course, at the time, I didn't know what I was going to do for a career. We shot it in '84, and by the time it came out in '85, I had started shooting *Rocky IV*. But I was just a kid at the time, and I remember being extremely star struck by Roger Moore. He was a very funny, very pleasant guy. The first time I met him I was in the commissary at Pinewood, and Roger walked in, took one look at me, and said, 'Wow, he's bigger than Denmark . . . in fact, he *is* Denmark!'"

John Glen, on Roger Moore's farewell to Bond: "I think the time had come. He knew it. He's a clever enough man to know you can push something so far, but you can't push it any further. No, I think we all knew and Roger knew that it was the end of the road for the Bonds as far as he was concerned. I suppose it's remotely possible that, had *View to a Kill* been such a sensational smash that it doubled the box office of the previous one, the guys at MGM would've demanded he do another one. But Roger knew it was time for a change. He had already gone on to do three more Bonds after pretty much saying he was done."

Roger Moore: "I think it was the interminable farewell tour of the variety artists, you know? You can't keep on saying that you're not doing any more and then doing another one. So I just had to say that was it. I had done enough. I mean, for the last three I was getting a little restless. But I had an absolute splendid time doing the Bond films. I played a lot of backgammon, managed to steal a lot of wardrobe, and got well paid. Nothing could beat it."

North American Gross: $50.3 million

Overseas: $102.1 million

6

The Bard's Bond: Timothy Dalton

A bored, bikinied beauty is sunning herself on the deck of her Mediterranean yacht. "If only I could find a *real* man," she sighs hopelessly into her mobile phone. Seconds later, a certain black-clad secret agent parachutes onto the canvas awning and somersaults down into her arms.

It was a most fitting introduction for Timothy Dalton as the new James Bond. Deciding to forgo the more lighthearted tongue-in-cheekiness of Roger Moore's 007, the producers wanted to reestablish Bond as a flesh-and-blood human being for 1987's *The Living Daylights*. Since the departure of Sean Connery, James Bond had become much more an invincible comic book superhero than the dark and damaged killer of Ian Fleming's original text. With his extensive Shakespearean background and acclaimed film and television work, the 40-year-old Timothy Dalton was deemed a perfect choice to make Bond more human. But in the end, perhaps *too* human.

Recalling the initial discussions for *The Living Daylights*, Dalton told me that, before he signed on, he wanted to know their plans for the series. "They said, 'We think it's getting a bit too flippant. . . . People are beginning to not take the movies seriously at all. Maybe people are even beginning

To Be, Or Not To Be Bond: Shakespearean vet Timothy Dalton entertained three previous Bond offers before finally accepting the role in 1986.

to slightly mock them, so we want to get back to something more serious,'" related Dalton of the 1986 meetings with the Broccolis and director John Glen. "And I said, 'Well *I* think that's how they should be too!' So I went back to the books, to Ian Fleming's original conception of the character, and tried to do something like it was originally intended. . . .

"I guess I was being a real purist about it all," added Dalton with a wry grin.

Dalton's efforts, however, did not go unappreciated. Most critics praised his interpretation of the role, welcoming the return to the harder edge of the early Connery films. Audiences were intrigued by the about-face; Dalton's Bond was a more textured, vulnerable, and romantic hero. But moviegoers had also grown accustomed to the languid humor and breezy charm of Roger Moore, which for many was an indelible ingredient in the mix. Dalton's more somber portrayal left little room for the expected throwaway humor. Dalton said he was aware there would be some prob- lems with his choices. "Going into it, I knew some people preferred Sean Connery, and some people preferred Roger Moore, but I thought to myself, 'My God, what if *nobody* likes me?'" Dalton noted with a hearty laugh. "It doesn't even matter if you make a good movie, what if they don't like *you* as Bond? I mean, the results ended up being lots of people really loved what I did, but I guess there were a lot of people wishing it was more like what Roger Moore was doing. But that's one of the perils of stepping into an institution and following in the footsteps of lots of famous people."

It was a dilemma that first troubled Dalton back in 1969 and again in 1971, when he was originally approached by Broccoli and Saltzman to take over the role from the departing Connery. Then in his early 20s, Dalton was a rising young Shakespearean actor with already a number of impressive film credits under his belt, including *The Lion in Winter* (opposite Katherine Hepburn, Peter O'Toole, and Anthony Hopkins), *Cromwell* (with Richard Harris and Alec Guinness), *Wuthering Heights* (opposite Laurence Olivier), and *Mary, Queen of Scots* (with Vanessa Redgrave). Dalton remem- bered declining the initial Bond offer by telling Broccoli and Saltzman that "I was absolutely flattered, but I thought Sean was a tremendous Bond — too good, actually. It would have been a very stupid move to try and take

*"My God, what if nobody likes me,"
Dalton feared after signing on as 007.*

over from him.

"But there was a second, more practical, reason," emphasized Dalton. "I was only about 24 or 25 at the time. And Bond *can't* be that young. He must be a mature man. Basically, I considered myself too young and Connery too good."

Nonetheless, Dalton's dance with Bond would continue on for the next 15 years. In 1980, he again was offered the role when it looked like contract negotiations with Roger Moore had stalled. "It was never quite clear, at that time, if Roger was giving it up," he said. So Dalton signed on for Dino De Laurentis's *Flash Gordon*, and Moore continued on as Bond for three more installments: *For Your Eyes Only* (1981), *Octopussy* (1983), and *A View to a Kill* (1985). But after *A View to a Kill*, Moore felt it was time to quit leaping off buildings and into the beds of twenty-something beauties and officially hang up his holster. The casting search commenced for a new Bond, and among the top contenders were Sam Neill, Trevor Eve, Mel Gibson, and Andrew Clarke. But it was Pierce Brosnan, fresh from a successful stint on TV's *Remington Steele*, who became the clear front runner. Just as the contract was about to be signed, a last-minute glitch with *Steele* sabotaged Brosnan's deal, and the 007 producers were left scratching their heads as to who could fill Bond's shoes. Talk turned to Dalton once more, and this time the Welsh actor with the gray-green eyes, muscular six-foot-two frame, and deep resonant voice accepted the role. He was signed in August 1986, and filming commenced on *The Living Daylights* almost immediately.

Dalton said he made his intentions clear from the outset. "I grew up with Sean Connery's Bonds, and they seemed to be genuinely tough and exciting," he explained. "And then we got into Roger, who was genuinely kind of lighthearted and flippant and funny. And certainly terrific in that style, but it never struck me as being really kind of *James Bondian*. I mean, I liked what I grew up with, which was Sean. The people who grew up with Roger preferred Roger. But to me, Bond is a flawed hero. How does he deal with himself morally when he's on the side of right and his job is to kill people? He's put in the position where he could call someone a friend one day and be asked to kill him the next. . . . I wanted to capture that spirit of the man — the essence of Fleming's work.

"When the Bond films first started," continued Dalton, "I think everyone believed in honor, justice, and truth of our government. People were also fascinated with the Secret Services of the different governments. Now it's different. We all know what our governments get up to, and we haven't a lot of pride in what they do."

Dalton's Bond was certainly the most conflicted. In *The Living Daylights*, when Bond's colleague Saunders — head of Station V (Vienna) — threatens to report his insubordination to M, Bond couldn't care less. "If he fires me," he sneers, "I'll thank him for it."

Maryam D'Abo and Timothy Dalton on location in Vienna.

Living Daylights costar Maryam D'Abo, who played Czechoslovakian cellist Kara Milovy, who falls in love with Bond, described Dalton's portrayal as "a more thoughtful Bond. . . . I felt he was taking it back to more of what Ian Fleming originally wrote," D'Abo told me. "The man was not a glamorous, cocktail-sipping, flippantly going from girl-to-girl kind of guy. He was actually quite a peculiar guy and quite a loner. And quite a workaholic for his country. And I think Tim succeeded in bringing that side of the man to the role. He became more of a man than this glittering facade.

It was much more credible."

But credible is not what most moviegoers want in escapist entertainment, especially when it comes to James Bond. And the decision to push an even tougher edge in 1989's *Licence to Kill* met with mixed reactions from audiences. It was the first Bond film to receive an R rating for excessive violence, and the plot involving a vicious drug lord and Bond resigning from the Secret Service to exact revenge left audiences slightly dumbfounded, wondering why the fun had disappeared from Bond.

"We took a big leap," conceded Dalton on *Licence to Kill*. "I think a lot of people had loved the idea that they could go and watch a lighthearted and flippant film, take the kids, have a nice time, and not be sort of threatened in any way . . . and didn't like a much more serious approach. But then there were all these people that said, 'Great, you've revitalized it — it's back on the right track.' Everyone had an opinion."

Up against blockbusters like *Indiana Jones and the Last Crusade, Lethal Weapon 2*, and *Batman* in the summer of 1989, *Licence to Kill* had a less than enthusiastic response at the North American box office. Director John Glen, who marked his fifth consecutive time at the 007 helm with *Licence to Kill*, realizes now that they perhaps made some judgment errors. "Michael [Wilson] and I talked about it with Cubby endlessly about how we wanted to take everything a step further and try to get back to the Connery Bonds," explained Glen. "But I think on *The Living Daylights* we succeeded better in a sense with his character than on *Licence to Kill*. Timothy played it very well, but I think it was the nature of the stories that we developed. They involved the drug trade . . . I mean, these guys are nasty people. They play for keeps. You play it any other way, and the film is going to be all wrong. . . . Our humor was more of a black humor, more in a Dalton way.

"And on *Licence to Kill*, we did exclude — unwittingly — the younger audience," admitted Glen. "It was something we didn't think about enough."

But Glen remains extremely proud of *Licence to Kill*, citing it as the finest film he's ever made. "The Timothy Dalton Bonds stand up very well today," offered Glen. "I think that, in a way, they were almost ahead of their time."

Born in Colwyn Bay — a seaside town in northern Wales — of English parents, Dalton himself always seemed ahead of his time. The oldest of five children, Dalton decided upon an acting career at age 16 after attending his first play — a production of *Macbeth* at the Old Vic. Dalton's father was a successful advertising executive, and both of Dalton's grandfathers had worked in showbusiness as vaudevillians before his maternal grandfather became a theatrical agent. Dalton's grandmother had also played English music halls with a young up and comer named Charles Chaplin.

In 1964, after attending school in Manchester and Belper, Dalton joined the National Youth Theatre and made his stage debut that summer in Shakespeare's *Coriolanus* at the Queen's Theatre. Dalton continued his training at London's prestigious Royal Academy of Dramatic Art for two years, where, according to fellow RADA classmate John Rhys-Davies, Dalton was an immediate sensation.

"It was my second job at RADA, and I remember when Timothy opened the second act of this play he would be wearing a long black wig, a loin-cloth, and covered in black paint," recalled Davies. "And this 2,200-seat theater would be just packed with women every night. And I remember we all used to say that, when Timothy made his entrance on stage, every woman in the audience took in a deep intake of breath. . . .

"And not through their mouth or nose," added Davies with a grin.

Davies, who went on to a successful film career, is perhaps most famous to audiences as Indiana Jones's stoic yet befuddled sidekick Sallah in the *Raiders of the Lost Ark* movies, as well as for *The Lord of the Rings* trilogy and on TV in the series *The Untouchables* and *Sliders*. Davies was reunited with Dalton in 1987 on *The Living Daylights*, where Davies

John Rhys-Davies: "I've never seen such a sexual ruckus going on."

played the imposing Soviet General Leonid Pushkin. The affable Davies, a fellow Welshman, remembered Dalton's stage presence as inciting "pure animal sexuality.

"There would be two or three hundred women outside the stage door every night literally *begging* for him," Davies told me with a chuckle. "I've never seen such a sexual ruckus going on. Basically, it was 300 women saying 'Fuck me, fuck me,' every night. It was an extraordinary sight to witness."

But the young Bond-in-waiting refused to cash in on his roguish good looks. Instead, Dalton continued to focus on his stage work, appearing in *Richard III, As You Like It, Love's Labor Lost, Romeo and Juliet,* and *The Merchant of Venice.* And even though he launched a promising film career in 1968 with *The Lion in Winter,* Dalton continued to return to the theater. "Several actors I knew had become movie stars and then quickly disappeared," explained Dalton. "I was influenced by them and consequently turned down films for a long time while I went back to theater . . . I wanted to improve, to learn. I know I'm a better actor because I stayed in the theater."

Eclectic film choices did follow, as did numerous TV appearances, from the acclaimed BBC dramatization of *Jane Eyre* to *Mistral's Daughter* to *Sins* with Joan Collins. But Dalton was always considered one of the mainstays of the Royal Shakespeare Company and a shining jewel of London's West End. And yet he admitted he was puzzled by the reactions when he took over the role of James Bond. "My career had always been a mixture of stage, screen, and television," he said with a shrug. "There are some roles *no* actor can resist. I think it's every kid's dream to play James Bond." And Dalton had already essayed practically every classic romantic hero from English literature, so James Bond seemed a natural progression in, if not a glaring omission from, his pantheon of portrayals. Only Dalton didn't expect Bond to overtake his life.

"Maybe I was dumb, or maybe I was arrogant, but the first questions I got from journalists were 'Yeah, it's great, but aren't you frightened of being typecast? Aren't you afraid of what this image will do to your career? From now on, you *are* James Bond for the world!' And this is what I mean by being naive or dumb, but I said, 'Come on, guys — I've been a working actor all my life. I've done lots of different things. Okay, so most of the work one does as an actor doesn't reach as wide or as public as Bond. But I'm in my 30s, I've been around. . . . I'm now the fourth person to play Bond, so surely an audience is getting used to the idea of actors coming in and doing Bond and then other actors coming in and doing Bond. It's an ongoing thing.'

"They didn't like that," continued Dalton. "Even though it's true, you suddenly become JAMES BOND for the entire world. Everyone suddenly looks at you as James Bond." Dalton revealed the moment that the global impact of Bond finally hit home. "It quite frankly shocked the shit out of me," he explained, shaking his head in disbelief. "I happened to be doing this little documentary about wolves, and I was spending some time up in northern Canada and also northern Alaska. I went to live with the Eskimos while we were making it. And it was as far away from human civilization as you could probably get" — Dalton couldn't help but chuckle recalling the memory — "so here we were, skidding in on this ice runway near this remote village in the middle of nowhere. And suddenly, all these Eskimos came out, and when they saw me get off the plane they started pointing and shouting, 'It's JAMES BOND! It's JAMES BOND!'" Dalton couldn't hold back the laughter. "I was just so completely *floored*! I mean the influence of these movies is completely *total*. It's just such a strange feeling that absolutely seizes you."

But Dalton still continued to indulge in a diverse array of projects between and after the Bonds, including *Hawks, The Rocketeer, Salt Water Moose, Scarlett*, and the comedy *Beautician and the Beast*. "I had longed for years to do an out-and-out comedy," he said, "but no one had ever asked me to do one. . . . To some extent in our life, we become victims of what everyone else thinks we are." However, as much as he tried to distance himself from the Bond image, Dalton was forever branded. "I just think of myself as Tim Dalton, the actor, but the rest of the world doesn't. And I think that can limit you very much in this world," he admitted. "No one wants you to play, say, a Toronto advertising executive, or an Idaho cop, or let's say just a regular British guy. Because they know the minute you walk onto the screen, all the audience is going to say, 'Hey, it's James Bond.' So there is that downside. And I realize now that all the journalists were right about image. . . ."

Timothy Dalton with author David Giammarco in Los Angeles.

Dalton then elaborated on the dilemma facing any actor stepping into the Bond role. "It's a fame through notoriety, I think, rather than a fame through recognition of acting work. It's a double-edged sword." Dalton was quick to point out the advantages as well. "It definitely did help me make some films that maybe would never have been made . . . and I can always get a table in a restaurant now," he laughed. "But I am very, very surprised by it all. I mean, it's been over 10 years now. *Ten years!* That's a long time. But it is lovely when people come up to me — and even though it's still shocking to me — and say, 'I really loved what you did with Bond, and I wish you were doing more.'

"So I am glad that I did it," he added, "but I'm also glad I'm not doing it. Because it's not James Bond who *happens* to be called Timothy Dalton today. It's back, I think, to Timothy Dalton, the actor, who *played* James Bond."

Dalton was, admittedly, never comfortable with the intense publicity surrounding the Bond films. He shied away from interviews, especially when the press started dissecting his private life and reporting his romantic liaisons over the years with various women. Old pal Davies said he was disappointed by Dalton's reticence with the media. "I love Timothy immensely, but I think he thought himself more important than Bond, and I think that showed in the amount of time he was prepared to spend promoting it," explained Davies. "I think he regarded himself as a more serious actor. But when you've got a three-picture deal, and with something as huge as Bond, you've really got to get out there and help promote. It's not enough to just *do* them, you have to get out there and *sell* them too. And I always felt that he shortchanged them."

Dalton loathed the media intrusion, and his disdain for the Fleet Street press hounds was profound. D'Abo, who spent nearly five months globe-trotting with Dalton while shooting *The Living Daylights* in Morocco, Vienna, London, and Tangiers, described Dalton as "the most professional actor I've ever worked with," she said, "and a great team actor. But he is also a very reserved and private person. He's a very quiet man, actually. He's not an extrovert by any means."

In fact, Dalton's favorite pastime is fishing, which he pursues with the same intensity and dedication as his acting. His favorite locales are the rivers in western Ireland and in the north and west of Scotland, and he's pulled sharks out of the Pacific and put down lines in Mexico and Alaska. It's a solitary diversion which Dalton enjoys "mostly because it's just completely and wonderfully different from the world that I work and live in," he said. "And I suppose there's also an element of the natural hunting instinct."

But the predatory and prying eyes of the worldwide press weren't about to deter Dalton from continuing on as Bond for a third film. "The last one I made was in '88 and came out in '89, and we were starting to do a third, which would've been the end of my contract," Dalton explained. "I originally thought it would be a nice idea if a different guy took over the game each time. I thought, if there was going to be a series of actors playing James Bond, then why not do it that way? I'll do one and then let someone else do one and keep an interest going. And also you don't run the danger of getting too typecast. But they wouldn't let me do that. They said, 'No, no, no — you've got to do three.' So I said, 'Okay.' We started the third, we were in preproduction on it, and talking about the script, meeting directors. But then the lawsuit came down between the Broccolis and MGM/UA, which was then under one of its many different phases of ownership during that period of time.

"It was obviously a very big lawsuit, and it stopped everything," continued Dalton. "And that effectively ended my contract, because they couldn't make another one at that time. My contract had basically run out. And they

Desmond Llewelyn instructs Carey Lowell and Timothy Dalton in Licence To Kill.

said to me, 'Well, would you do another one?' And I said, 'I can't say no, and I can't say I will either, because we don't know when we're going to do it.' But we decided we weren't going to say anything about that, because with no Bond movies getting made the last thing we wanted was publicity about me leaving.

"When it finally became possible to make one again, the question was asked again. They said, 'We'd love you to come to do more — how do you feel?' But by then, after a four-year break, I found it was intellectually easy to say, 'I'm done!' By then, I knew how fixed the image was in people's minds, and I wanted to get back to being Timothy Dalton the *actor*, not *James Bond*."

Still, when it was officially announced that *Goldeneye* was going into production in 1994 and Pierce Brosnan had been named as the new 007, Dalton couldn't help but feel some regret about his decision. "Emotionally, I think it was probably a little more difficult because, in all honesty, I felt I did it right, and nobody was going to stand in my box," Dalton confessed. "I guess I probably thought of it territorially, being a little bit possessive. So intellectually it was an easy decision, but emotionally. . . ."

Dalton's voice trailed off, but he then smiled wistfully. "You just have to move on," he shrugged. "The safe road is to say it's a lifetime franchise, they're going to do them forever, and that's the rest of my life. But the more risky thing to do is say, 'No, go on — you've done it already. Be happy. Get on and rediscover being yourself and do different things.' So that was the choice I took."

But it wasn't until *Goldeneye* was before the cameras and advance teaser posters of Brosnan's Bond started appearing that Dalton says he finally felt a sense of closure. "When I saw those posters of Pierce standing there," laughed Dalton, who then stood up from his chair and demonstrated the classic Bond position, left arm crossed and right hand holding an imaginary gun by his head, "I suddenly thought to myself, '*Jesus*, I don't have to stand there with a gun to the side of my head anymore!' I suddenly found the most tremendous sense of liberation, and I started feeling more like myself than I'd ever felt in years! I suddenly felt *free*."

Dalton continued: "The minute the attention shifted from me to Pierce, I started getting (a) more scripts sent to me, and (b), this was really interesting, I started getting scripts of a completely different kind. The focus had shifted, and I was suddenly out of that mold. Though it will never shift entirely, because I realize the five of us are members of this strange silhouette — it's a club, really."

Even after his departure, Dalton remained close with the Bond family. "Cubby had particularly become a very good friend," he explained, "and certainly his daughter Barbara, who is now producing, is one of my best female friends that I've got." So what did Dalton think of the Pierce Brosnan Bond films? "Well, they are all friends of mine, and I'd be a very unobjective critic," he smiled. "But I'm glad it's there, and I'm glad they've been so successful. And I hope they all will be.

"It truly is one of the oddest phenomenons in movie history," Dalton reflected. "*I* saw them as a kid, *you* saw them as a kid . . . so maybe everyone's kids should go and see Bond movies and grow up with them."

Rock 'N Roll: When a "00" training mission on Gibraltar goes awry, Bond takes matters into his own hands.

THE LIVING DAYLIGHTS *(1987)*

Directed By: John Glen

The Mission: At the height of the Afghanistan war, Soviet General Koskov (Jeroen Krabbé) and international arms dealer Brad Whitaker (Joe

Bond and Kara pilot a Russian cargo plane out of an Afghani–Russian battle.

Bridge Work: An optical effect involving a real bridge, foreground miniatures, and live action: "An incredible achievement using old-fashioned techniques," said director John Glen.

Don Baker) scheme to utilize KGB funds intended for an arms deal to instead finance a massive opium purchase for distribution in America.

Locales: Gibraltar, London, Bratislava, Blayden, Vienna, Tangiers, Afghanistan

The Villain and Accomplices: General Georgi Koskov (Jeroen Krabbé), Brad Whitaker (Joe Don Baker), Necros (Andreas Wisniewski)

The Bond Girl: Kara Milovy (Maryam d'Abo)

Theme Song: a-ha

Score: John Barry

Memorable Lines:
Saunders to Bond: "You're bloody late! This is a mission, not a fancy dress ball!"

"We're free!" *exclaims Kara after Bond springs them from their jail cell. Bond winces:* "Kara, we're inside a Russian airbase in the middle of Afghanistan!"

Bond parachutes a jeep from the rear hold of a cargo plane, landing him and Kara in the Pakistani desert. Bond: "I know a great restaurant in Karachi . . . we can just make dinner!"

Tom Mankiewicz: "After Roger said he wouldn't be returning, the search was on for a new Bond. They tried for Pierce and couldn't get him because of *Remington Steele*. But they really wanted to get back to a harder-edged Bond, and I remember the guy who was running UA at the time called me and said, 'Would you phone Cubby and lobby for Mel Gibson? I know you're still close to him, and just remind him what an opportunity this is.' It turns out Mel Gibson had apparently agreed to do one James

Bond film. And if the film grossed over a hundred million domestically, he'd do another. But Cubby didn't want Bond to be played by a major star. Because it then becomes a *Mel Gibson* movie, as opposed to a *Bond* movie. Plus, height was a big thing for Cubby. He didn't ever want a short Bond. And he thought Mel was too short to play Bond. But they were very close to making a deal with him."

Timothy Dalton: "What I found so appealing about Bond was that Ian Fleming had tapped into a sort of mythological figure — a *George and the Dragon* type of hero who single-handedly takes on the forces of evil. I really wanted to capture the spirit of the man and the essence of Ian Fleming."

Tom Mankiewicz: "I remember Cubby called me one day and asked me what I thought of Timothy Dalton. And I said, 'I think he'd make a great Bond villain.' There is something ubiquitous about him on screen, quite omnivorous. Cubby said, 'No, for Bond.' And, as I later found out, because I would meet him over at Cubby's all the time, a really lovely guy. I liked him a lot. He's such a wonderful actor, and I think he was the best all-round choice to play Bond at the time."

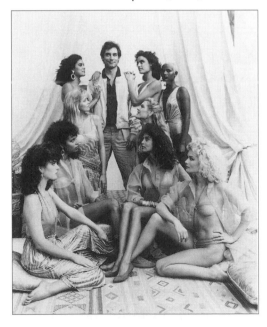

Bond with his hands full.

Timothy Dalton: "*The Living Daylights* had already started filming before I arrived — which was right at the very last minute. I had been shooting *Brenda Starr* in America on Saturday, then flew back to London on Sunday, and started work on the Bond film first thing on the Monday."

John Glen (Director): "There are certain criteria you never change with the Fleming character. Roger was certainly one of the most handsome men ever, and certainly one of the most well-dressed men, with impeccable manners, and knew everything about everything — which is a real criteria for the Bond/Fleming character. But Timothy brought out a much rougher side closer to Connery. Timothy is a very ballsy, gutsy guy. He did most of his own stunts, like the scene on the tops of the speeding trucks in the opening teaser, which was very, very dangerous. I was pretty keen on getting him involved as much as possible. Timothy was game for anything; he really wanted to get his hands dirty. In fact, I had to stop him from doing things which I felt were just too big of a risk."

Maryam d'Abo, on being cast as leading lady Kara Milovy: "There was more of a part written for me. I think a lot of the 'Bond Girls' didn't really have substantial parts written for them, and consequently they could appear very wooden. But the whole approach for *The Living Daylights* was to get more credible and more natural people. I think I fit into that much more."

Lois Maxwell (Miss Moneypenny): "When they were going into production on *The Living Daylights*, Cubby rang me at my house in Toronto and said, 'I want you to hear this from me before you hear it from anyone else, but we're not going to use you in the next film with Timothy Dalton.' And I said, 'Oh, well, I can understand that. It would look silly for me making goo-goo eyes at Timothy Dalton.' And then I said, 'But I want to play M.' And Cubby said, 'I have an M.' And I said, 'Yes, but nobody's terribly interested in your M!' So I said to Cubby, 'Picture this: the new Bond comes in, and there is another face at Miss Moneypenny's desk. She says, "You're 20 minutes late — go into M's office immediately." So he goes in, and that high-backed armchair swings around, and there's Moneypenny. And she says, "Synchronize your watch with me, Commander . . . and never be late again." She never calls him James again.' I said, 'The public would love it, Cubby. It would be such a classic moment.' So he said, 'Hmmm . . . well, I'll talk to MGM about it and get back to you.' So two or three days later he called back and said, 'I'm afraid it won't work, Lois.' And I said, 'Why not?' And he said, 'Because traditionally the head of MI5 has always been a man.' And I said, 'Well traditionally, the prime minister of England has always been a man too. But Mrs. Thatcher is in office.' But he didn't go for it. Then, of course, Stella Remington was made head of MI5 not too long after! So, had they used my idea, they would have been ahead of the curve. And then they did finally end up making M a woman with Judi Dench. But I consider myself very lucky to have been part of this remarkable series. I was sorry I had to leave."

Cello-Feign: Maryam d'Abo fakes it as a Russian cellist.

Maryam d'Abo: "I spent two months learning how to fake play a cello so audiences would believe my performance; got calluses on my fingers from playing it morning to night. It wasn't pretty. I also spent five weeks learning to ride horses in Morocco, going off from dawn to dusk with the stuntmen into the desert. But I have to say the best part of doing *The Living Daylights* was the camaraderie among the cast and crew. We all ate together and hung out together. There was a great sense of family on the Bond film."

John Rhys-Davies (General Leonid Pushkin): "The great joy of *The Living Daylights* for me was the incomparable experience of working with Cubby Broccoli, who was a great prince of a filmmaker. He'd seen everything; he'd done everything. He'd been dissatisfied with much of what he'd seen in life and had enormous standards. And if he liked you, there was nothing he would not do to make his actors happy. I'm sure that

Ice Scream: "It was pretty terrifying," says d'Abo of shooting the toboggan snow chase.

every actor felt the same thing, but I felt that I had a very special bond with Cubby. He would always sit with me and tell me these wonderful tales, some of which are so sad in their own way."

Maryam d'Abo on the cello-case-as-toboggan stunt: "It was quite frightening to shoot that. It took us three days in minus 20° freezing cold. They built this little steering mechanism into the cello case, and I was the one who had to control it because Timothy was holding the cello. It was pretty scary because we were going down that mountain pretty fast, and I had to make sure we didn't crash into the crew on our right or the trees on our left and just keep going straight. And because Timothy is heavier than me, the case was off balance and kept trying to spin around. Plus, there were all these little explosions going off in the snow around us. So it was pretty terrifying for me, actually. At the end of the day, we would all laugh and get drunk to alleviate the stress."

John Rhys-Davies: "To do a Bond film is to do an old-fashioned film in style. There is the money to do it right. They go out of their way to make sure the actors are comfortable and happy. There's a real touch of the old-fashioned Hollywood still there, something which isn't present with these unimaginative suits in Hollywood today. And Barbara [Broccoli] has become such a breathtakingly beautiful woman. She's also inherited all her dad's skill and shrewdness. I saw her recently at a premiere in London, and it's funny 'cause I remembered her as this slightly gawky young girl that her dad brought on like a son. And as I was talking to her, I couldn't help thinking how proud Cubby would be to see her now. She's such a lovely woman. And Michael Wilson was also very kind to me. Top-quality people. I have absolutely golden memories of the Bond experience."

North American Gross: $51.2 million

Overseas: $140.0 million

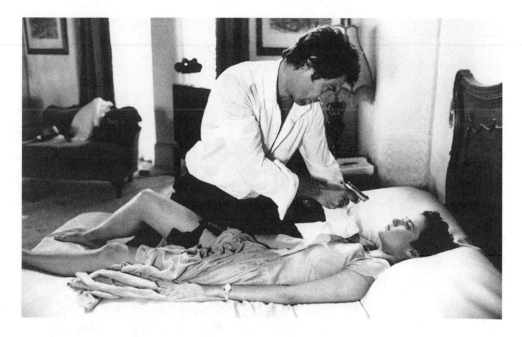

James Bond (Timothy Dalton) questions the true motives of Pam Bouvier (Carey Lowell) in a pivotal scene from Licence To Kill.

LICENCE TO KILL (1989)

Directed By: John Glen

The Mission: The goals of South American drug czar Franz Sanchez (Robert Davi) for an international cartel — bolstered by his unique methods of cocaine smuggling — attract a lot of attention when Bond's CIA pal Felix Leiter (David Hedison) and his new bride (Priscilla Barnes) are targeted for death.

Locales: Florida, England, South America

The Villain and Accomplices: Franz Sanchez (Robert Davi), Milton Krest (Anthony Zerbe), Killifer (Everett McGill), Truman-Lodge (Anthony Starke), Heller (Don Stroud), Professor Joe Butcher (Wayne Newton),

Dario (Benicio Del Toro)

The Bond Girls: Pam Bouvier (Carey Lowell), Lupe Lamora (Talisa Soto)

Theme Song: Gladys Knight

Score: Michael Kamen

Memorable Lines:

Sanchez (Robert Davi) teaches Lupe (Talisa Soto) a lesson in Licence To Kill.

"What did he promise you, *his heart? Give her his heart!*" — *Sanchez, after he and his henchmen catch Lupe in bed with another man.*

"He disagreed with something that ate him" — *note pinned to a barely alive Felix Leiter, after Sanchez dunks him in a shark tank.*

M to Bond: "This private vendetta of yours could easily compromise Her Majesty's government. You have an assignment, and I expect you to carry it out objectively and professionally."
Fumes Bond: "Then you have my resignation, sir."
Snaps M: "We're not a country club, 007!"

John Glen (Director): "Timothy wanted to go even harder, a much more realistic Bond. If you give Timothy a scene, and because he is who he is — a trained classical actor — he can do it 100 different ways. So

Sanchez puts the squeeze on Bond. (right) Burning rubber on the Rumarosa Pass in Mexicali for the final confrontation between Sanchez and Bond.

there was a lot more to discuss with him on this picture, a lot more to thrash out."

Timothy Dalton: "To me, Bond was not Superman. He's rather an ordinary man, but with some very special qualities. He lives in a world that brings danger to him and to those he loves. He's also a real paradox. He's a killer, but he's on the side of good. It was that real conflict that I wanted to tap into. As well, Fleming wrote him as someone who smokes up to 60 cigarettes a day, drives fast cars, gambles . . . these are often perceived as vices but are easy to understand when you are living on the edge. So, of all the things Bond does, you get the strong feeling that, while he has his life, he wants to live it to the full — not for ostentation or snobbery, but because he needs to touch life in all its forms."

John Glen: "Things started getting a bit rough when the studio went into some financial straits under their transitional management. They started exercising more budgetary control. Suddenly, we were being told to cut down on this, cut down on that. We were under severe pressure to keep the budget down. That was why we had to shoot *Licence to Kill* down at the Churubusco Studios in Mexico City and not at Pinewood. Of course, the whole essence of Bond is that you are extravagant on the screen. It

(left to right) Latin beauty Talisa Soto, stunner Carey Lowell as Pam Bouvier (a role Sharon Stone originally auditioned for), and Timothy Dalton.

doesn't mean to say you're throwing money away; what you are doing is presenting to the audience what they expect. And they expect luxury, and we're going to provide it. When you think about it, my five Bonds only increased in budget from $27 million in 1980 to $33 million in 1989. The budgets since *Moonraker* a decade earlier had not really increased at all. So we were making first-rate action films on a fraction of the budget available to our competitors in America. It's actually really amazing that we were able to retain such high standards. Now, of course, the budgets are well over the hundred-million-dollar mark."

Timothy Dalton, on Bond comparisons: "That's the problem of doing a revival. It's something you get in the theater all the time. Whatever you play, well, you get compared to someone in the past. It's like playing Hamlet, you know? But if you do a new play, or like most movies, no one has anything to compare you to. They have to take you at face value. If there had never been a James Bond movie before, no one had heard of Bond, and *The Living Daylights* or *Licence to Kill* or any of the others had just been released as a movie in its own right, the reaction and appreciation would be completely different. You really have a heavy legacy on your shoulders doing Bond."

Mexican Stand Off: This brutal battle between Bond and Sanchez fired up U.K. and U.S. film censors.

John Glen: "If there was a fault with the film, I think it was our choice of subject, because there is no compromise with the drug world. These drug guys aren't comical villains by any means. The plot was very much up to the minute, as it seemed at the time that the world was being run by the drug barons. We played it straight up, how they are in the real world. It was also much truer to the characters in Ian Fleming's original novels. It was really a more adult film than the more recent Bonds had been. Quite a departure. Consequently, we had a lot of problems with the censors, and we had to make numerous cuts. The reviews were pretty good generally, but the fact that a lot of kids couldn't get in to see the movie affected the box office. Plus, that summer we had a lot of heavy competition: *Batman, Indiana Jones and the Last Crusade, Lethal Weapon 2*. And, in a sense, we were a foreign movie. Bond has always worked better in the rest of the world than it has in the United States, which is 50% of the business at least. But I remain pretty proud of *Licence to Kill* — I think it was the best Bond I did. And if you look at it today, it stands up extremely well. I think it's a fantastic movie."

North American Gross: $34.7 million

Overseas: $121.5 million

Billion Dollar Bond: Pierce Brosnan's first three Bonds have earned over $1 billion. "There was a lot of pressure on me to deliver," says Brosnan of becoming the fifth 007.

Golden Spy:
Pierce Brosnan

If any actor was born to play James Bond, it's Pierce Brosnan. No other actor around today more naturally embodies the essence of the role than Brosnan, who has proved a winning balance between the brutality of Sean Connery and the wit and suavity of Roger Moore. Along with that, Brosnan has managed to inject a humanity into the character, something which stems directly from Ian Fleming's text but had been mostly neglected in previous Bonds.

In fact, Brosnan has displayed an uncanny knack for filling the void left by cinema icons. He single-handedly resuscitated the James Bond series, restoring a luster and audience enthusiasm for 007 not seen since the Bondmania heyday of Sean Connery. *Goldeneye* (1995), *Tomorrow Never Dies* (1997), and *The World Is Not Enough* (1999) consecutively topped each other as the highest-grossing Bond films in the history of the franchise. Then Brosnan took a gamble and reprised the role of big-screen tough guy Steve McQueen for the remake of the 1968 thriller *The Thomas Crown Affair*, which, produced by Brosnan, went on to gross over $100 million at the worldwide box office.

Pierce Brosnan and author David Giammarco clown around on the set of Goldeneye in 1995.

It seemed that on the set of *The World Is Not Enough* in the spring of 1999 that Brosnan was finally at peace — both with himself and his life — after years of well-documented heartache and disappointment, both professionally and personally. At the age of 46, Brosnan had finally achieved a sense of calm, due in part to his five-year relationship with TV journalist and environmentalist Keely Shaye Smith and their two-year-old son, Dylan Thomas, but also an A-List career stability after toiling for almost 10 years in mostly little-seen movies and straight-to-video projects.

"I have much more confidence now . . . more assuredness," acknowledged Brosnan, now sporting strands of gray at the temples of his healthy head of jet-black hair and a few more creases and lines around his famously chiseled features. "I mean, I was *terrified* playing Bond. It was a long way to fall if you screwed it up. . . .

"But now," he continued, "I don't feel that terrible 'Are they going to like me? Am I going to succeed?' I can stand there, as the man, with the knowledge that I've made two fine films and they've worked, and audiences have come back, and a whole new generation is discovering Bond films. That's an enormous satisfaction, pride, and accomplishment to have."

Brosnan paused to reflect and then added, "You know, if I did nothing else in my acting life, at least I've done that," he mused. "Bond has been a golden opportunity that I knew, if I got it right, it would allow me to take care of my family and hopefully have a few years of a healthy career and sock some money away . . . it allows you, hopefully, longevity as an actor in this business. That's what you always want."

But it also bestowed upon Brosnan a newfound clout as producer, which the actor was undeniably relishing. Through his Irish Dreamtime production company, Brosnan was able to shepherd smaller, more personal films like *The Nephew* — about a unique love affair set in Ireland — as well as a kid's film entitled *Mr. Softee.* But it was the big-budget, major studio *The Thomas Crown Affair* which garnered both critical praise and

Pierce Brosnan in a scene from The Nephew – his first producing effort under Irish Dreamtime.

healthy box office, that proved to be the acid test of Brosnan's producing prowess.

Directed by Brosnan pal John McTiernan (*Die Hard, The Hunt for Red October*), *The Thomas Crown Affair* pitted Brosnan as a millionaire art thief (updated from McQueen's bank robber) who, after stealing a Monet from the Metropolitan Museum, succumbs to the charms of a savvy insurance investigator (played by Rene Russo), who wants to first bed and then bust the debonair playboy. "I wanted to explore the love story much more than the original," reasoned Brosnan on his remake-of-choice. "I wanted to make an adult, romantic film, wrapped up in a caper that was absolutely glamorous and sophisticated."

If Brosnan's Crown seemed a little similar to a certain secret agent, he was admittedly aware of the inevitable comparisons. "I think it goes without saying, but Crown's much more of a bruised character, really," conceded Brosnan, who cast original star Faye Dunaway in a cameo as Crown's psychiatrist. "It does have Bond overtones to it, which there's nothing wrong with. And that was one of the reasons for picking the film. The idea was that it would dovetail well into that persona and carry the audience that has found me in Bond into another movie. And I think there's something to be said for that, in keeping your audience with you as much as possible."

But audiences didn't follow him as faithfully in his much more radical

departure as Archie Belaney — a.k.a. Grey Owl — the famous Brit who passed himself off as a Native Canadian environmentalist in the early 1900s. Directed by Sir Richard Attenborough in the hinterlands of northern Quebec, *Grey Owl* saw Brosnan sporting braided hair extensions and buckskin. "I know I've put my neck out there on the line going into such a characterization as this, but you have to break away and challenge yourself," he said of *Grey Owl*. "If it works and it's entertaining and it's brilliant, then great. But if you fail, then so what? You just go on. Hopefully, you don't get burned too badly with it."

Braids & Buckskin: Brosnan shakes things up for Grey Owl.

Despite the lukewarm reception to the film, Brosnan was taking it all in stride when I spoke to him in Los Angeles the following year. "You can be as hot as you've ever been and still have a movie that doesn't connect, that doesn't kind of turn people on," he shrugged. "I remain very proud of the movie, and I love the movie. . . . I just think it had flaws. . . . I wanted more in certain respects." But Brosnan's next outing, as the ruthless and dastardly spy in *The Tailor Of Panama*, proved to be an overwhelming critical success and generated a healthy box office in the spring of 2001. Based on John le Carré's controversial novel and directed by John Boorman, *The Tailor of Panama* allowed Brosnan to delve into a darker arena as a seductive scoundrel — sort of a nastier, edgier version of James Bond. *The Tailor of Panama* not only served to remind audiences of Brosnan's acting range but also reinforced his box office appeal even in a non-Bond film.

Actually, Brosnan has been the only Bond actor who's managed to sustain an equally successful film career between 007 outings; Sean Connery's post-Bond success came only after years of struggling after giving up the role, and Roger Moore and Timothy Dalton never really overcame the Bond typecasting. Brosnan, on the other hand, has been able to escape being eclipsed by his world-famous alter ego with starring roles in such

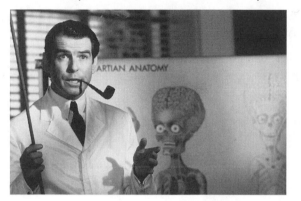

Alien Instructee: Brosnan briefs the White House in Martian etiquette for the comedy Mars Attacks!

other diverse projects as *Dante's Peak, The Mirror Has Two Faces,* Tim Burton's sci-fi spoof *Mars Attacks!*, and *Evelyn.*

"I do think the climate is a lot different now than in Connery's day," surmised Brosnan on the Bond typecasting. "Sean did make movies between Bonds, but they didn't have the same profile. It must have been so intense for him back then in the '60s, doing these films. To step into such an arena that everything else in your life got swamped out. It took him a long time to get away from the character, and I know he's always hated that.

"But it was a different planet then," he continued. "It wasn't as easy for actors to go off and make their own films and start their own companies. Any kid on American TV has his own company now. They're born with them over there. But I've lived in L.A. for 18 years now, and I've had a career before James Bond, whether TV or some of the films I've done, so it's just a lot different now, I think. Audiences are more sophisticated nowadays.

Going into this, I knew I was going to get the label of Bond and that he will be with me for life. But I'm an actor, and I also want to do as many different roles as possible. And Bond has allowed me to do that."

Yet reports in the British press that Brosnan would be ripping up his license to kill after *The World Is Not Enough* and exiting the series were completely unfounded. Brosnan was contractually committed to three Bonds — which he had made — and had the option for a fourth. It was never in doubt that Brosnan would be back for another go 'round in *Die Another Day*. The role in his fourth Bond picture fits him like a glove. He knows it, the producers know it, and, more importantly, the world's Bond fans know it. The character and the legacy mean too much to Brosnan to simply toss away. In fact, James Bond has been an indelible, almost cosmic thread through the tapestry of his entire life. Brosnan was born in 1953 — the same year that 007 made his literary debut in Ian Fleming's *Casino Royale*. Eleven years later, Brosnan ventured into a movie house for the first time and saw *Goldfinger*, an experience he that says set him on course as an actor.

"There was this gold lady, naked," he smiled, remembering that pivotal cinema experience. "A man with a hat that decapitated people and statues and this amazingly cool dude who just kind of strutted through the world, beat the shit out of anybody who got in his way, and got the girl. It really grabbed my attention. I remember walking out of the theater wanting so badly to do what he did."

Almost two decades after that, Brosnan's wife, Cassandra Harris, would end up being cast as Countess Lisl in the 1981 Roger Moore entry *For Your Eyes Only*. And it was while visiting Harris on location in Corfu that Brosnan met Cubby Broccoli for the first time. Brosnan never guessed that five years later he himself would be offered the chance to be Bond . . . *James* Bond. But according to *For Your Eyes Only* director John Glen, they quickly spotted Brosnan's potential. "I remember Julian Glover [who played Soviet agent Aris Kristatos in *For Your Eyes Only*] turned to me at one point and said, 'Pierce is a fantastic actor; you know, he would make a wonderful Bond,' and it was really after that conversation that I took a second look at Pierce," recalled Glen. "I realized he had everything: he's a good-looking

Brosnan's late wife Cassandra Harris, alongside Roger Moore, in 1981's For Your Eyes Only.

guy, he's young, good actor, athletic. So I suggested to Cubby on several occasions that we should consider him.

"But I think the *Remington Steele* character he was playing influenced their thinking a bit that maybe he didn't have enough venom, if you like, for the Bond character," continued Glen. "But I kept coming back and saying, 'What about Pierce?' Eventually, we ended up testing him at Pinewood, using scenes from *From Russia with Love* and some of the best scenes from other Bond films. It was a three-day testing process, and he was absolutely fantastic. He was wonderful. I mean, you knew he really wanted to do this part. And then we sent the test over to the studio in America, and everyone agreed with us. So we announced we were about to sign him for *The Living Daylights*."

Brosnan was to be the fourth 007, picking up the mantle of Sean Connery, George Lazenby, and Roger Moore. But then it seemed the stars suddenly realigned, and James Bond was removed from the actor's orbit. NBC, which had cancelled Brosnan's detective series *Remington Steele* shortly before the actor was tagged as Her Majesty's next superspy, decided to take advantage of the Bond publicity and renewed Brosnan's contract. "Their interest was suddenly rekindled after our announcement," sniffed Glen, "and Cubby found that unacceptable. He wouldn't have Remington Steele playing James Bond simultaneously."

Glen is still in disbelief at how quickly everything fell apart. "We were all literally celebrating that he got the job over a special dinner at the White Elephant restaurant," recalled Glen. "The deal was done. All that was left to do was just put the pen to the paper. But that evening was when the news broke, and it changed everything. We were so absolutely frustrated, and Pierce was shattered."

Brosnan would be forced to abandon his hopes for Bondage to the subsequently named Timothy Dalton. Amid the ensuing media frenzy, Brosnan did his best to put on a brave face. "I was really, really angry," recalled Brosnan, "because the whole thing was all played out in the press. And this production always comes with such a high profile of publicity to begin with. But I didn't speak publicly about it. I just wanted to have dignity through it all.

"Of course," added Brosnan with a grin, "it didn't help that, wherever I went in the world, people who recognized me always said, '*You're the guy that was going to be,*' '*should've been,*' '*could've been,*' '*might've been.*' And I always felt, 'When is this going to stop?' I didn't do the damn thing — I got it, and I lost it."

Brosnan admitted that he was even tempted by producer Kevin McClory to star in his rival Bond production — *Warhead 2000* — in order to chase away some of the demons. "When Tim Dalton's second Bond came out, I just remember quietly thinking to myself, 'Shit, I could've been doing this movie myself,'" related Brosnan. "And, oddly enough, Kevin McClory found me in Dublin one day and pitched the idea of me doing his Bond film. There was a Japanese outfit that had lots of money to back it. But there was so much litigation and paperwork attached to the project. Essentially, *Warhead 2000* was a remake of a remake. It's *Thunderball,* and it's *Never Say Never Again.*"

So Brosnan decided to opt out of the project and instead bide his time. If Bond was meant to be, it would come around again, he figured. He put it out of his mind and delved into more varied projects. Brosnan followed the brief resuscitation of *Remington Steele* with the two miniseries *Noble House* and *Around the World in 80 Days* and a series of feature star turns in films like *The Fourth Protocol, The Deceivers, Mister Johnson, Lawnmower Man, Mrs. Doubtfire,* and *Robinson Crusoe.*

Meanwhile, Timothy Dalton's somber interpretation of Bond in *The Living Daylights* (1987) and *Licence to Kill* (1989) received a mixed reaction from audiences. After a six-year absence of Bond due to studio legal wrangling, the producers were anxious for a fresh start, and Brosnan once again got that fateful phone call. In retrospect, Brosnan is relieved it took nine years for him to assume the role that everyone knew was rightfully his.

"When I was 33, I looked like such a boy, such a *dweeb*," he laughed. "Now there's a lot more age on the face, and the heart and the soul, and a deepening of the self somewhat. And to be honest, I feel I have more courage now that I've got more life behind me. I think there's a maturity and a steadiness as a performer. It takes a real courage to play the role, to stand there with the shooters. And of course, when I look back to Sean now, I'm not intimidated by his performance, and I'm not intimidated by the role. But I was a little intimidated back when I was 33. It just all feels very right that it's happened now in my life."

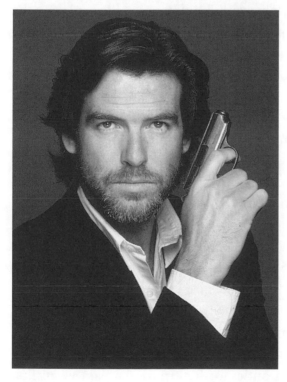

An early publicity shot of Brosnan as Bond from 1994.

But being suddenly thrust in the white-hot media spotlight quickly left Brosnan second-guessing his decision. When he was announced to the world as the new Bond at a London press conference attended by over 800 members of the world media, he realized his life had "literally turned 180 degrees."

He said he remembered arriving home after the press conference and "just lying on the bed and feeling terrible . . . just fucking depressed, like a vacuum had sucked everything out of me by this prying world," he sighed. "They wanted to know everything about me and my life. And when I woke up the next morning and read the newspapers — I got every newspaper, and I was on the front page of every one — there were suddenly photographs of people from my past, photos of me as a child, and photos of old girlfriends. They literally dug everything up about me, and I just looked at all this and said to myself, 'What the hell have I let myself in for?'

"I then had to catch a flight to New Guinea that day, and when I landed I thought I would get some clarity and perspective. So I went jogging through the jungle and happened to pass this isolated little village. Suddenly, these little kids came running out shouting '*James Bond! James Bond!*' I thought I was hearing things, so I stopped and said, 'What did you say?' And they pointed at me and said it again: '*James Bond*!!' I just shook my head and thought, 'My God — this is *insane*!'"

Brosnan is now much more at ease with the worldwide attention — and the role itself. "I feel very comfortable with Bond now. . . . I love playing the role, and I actually feel like I'm just getting the hang of it," he admitted on the set of *The World Is Not Enough*. Which means that he will not be quitting the Bond series anytime soon. "Although," he added, "I'd like to have a bit of a breather between Bonds, more like three years instead of two. After shooting for nearly six months and then doing months and months of promotion, it seems like I just finish one Bond, and then we start shooting another one."

Brosnan's spacious dressing room — really more of an apartment — on the Pinewood Studios lot is filled with photos of his three children from his first marriage, as well as snapshots of current love Keely and their infant children. But the most distinguishing feature is the abundance of canvas paintings — some half-finished and some framed — spread throughout the room. Brushes and oil paints are perched below a couple of easels, and Brosnan proudly — albeit rather shyly — explains his inspirations. His works are figurative, and all feature bold colors. Brosnan originally worked as a commercial artist as a lad growing up in London but only began indulging his talents as an outlet for his emotional pain when first wife Cassandra Harris was dying of ovarian cancer during the late '80s. Devastated by the loss of his wife of 14 years in 1991, Brosnan soon took his fight against the disease from black-tie dinner charities to congressional appeals and has donated earnings from the sale of his paintings to ovarian cancer research. "Painting is probably the only thing that truly relaxes me," he explained with a wistful smile. "When the paint flows, then I know I am truly relaxed."

Brosnan's turbulent life has left him with a certain gravity, betrayed by a slight melancholy that creeps into his conversations. His eyes belie an icy-calm exterior. They offer the hint of sadness, of someone who has endured great emotional pain but who has managed to survive. He admits he always felt like a loner, an outsider growing up in rural County Meath, Ireland. It was a solitary childhood which saw his father abandon the family early on, never to be seen again until much later in Pierce's life. Then Pierce's mother moved away to England, leaving him behind to be raised by various relatives. She went to London to study nursing and only saw young Pierce once or twice a year.

"You learn to be happy within all of that; you learn to create your own happiness," reflected Brosnan on his unsettled upbringing. "And you learn to forgive. You learn to rise above it. And you learn to view people with a different kind of clarity, because they've hurt you and because there was no one there for you to go to. There was not this symbol, the father figure or the mother. So you learned to find your own independence and survive. If you didn't know, you acted as if you did know."

In 1964, he followed his mother to London — coincidentally on the very day Ian Fleming died — and only a few days later the two saw their first movie together: *Goldfinger*. Brosnan soon drifted into acting, first through secondary school and then the Group 64 theater troupe. However, it was while working as a commercial artist in London that a fellow artist urged him to join the Oval House Theatre Club. Suddenly, Brosnan felt liberated. "It was a stepping stone into another life, away from a life that I had, and acting was something I was good at, something which was appreciated," he recalled. "That was a great satisfaction in my life."

Brosnan would later study at the Drama Centre in London for three years, eventually being picked by Tennessee Williams himself to star in the playwright's *The Red Devil Battery Sign*. The reviews of Brosnan's performance were exceptional, "and from then on I was never out of work," he said.

A series of challenging stage assignments followed before director Franco Zeffirelli cast him in *Filumena* opposite Joan Plowright, marking Brosnan's West End debut. It was during this time that Brosnan met Cassandra Harris, and soon they were inseparable, marrying in December 1977. Their early years were marked by career struggles as they both tried to forge names for themselves as actors while caring for her two children (Charlotte and Christopher) and eventually Sean, the son they had together in 1983.

Soon after Harris shot 1981's *For Your Eyes Only* and Brosnan filmed the TV miniseries *The Manions of America*, the couple decided to take the big leap across the Atlantic to the United States. Within two weeks of relocating to Los Angeles, Brosnan was interviewed for the role of Remington Steele, a suave but bumbling character who would serve as a more macho "front" for a one-woman detective agency in the comedy-adventure series. The producers, however, had not intended on casting a British actor but were so impressed with Brosnan that they altered the character and hired him to star opposite Stephanie Zimbalist as the brainy Laura Holt. *Remington Steele* would end up launching Brosnan's U.S. career and made him a star, running from 1982 until 1987. But that same year *Steele* was finally canceled, Cassandra Harris was diagnosed with ovarian cancer, and "life turned around on a dime," explained Brosnan. They spent the next four years fighting the disease and "cherishing every single moment together. . . .

"Going through an illness like cancer is dark and cruel, watching someone's life dwindle away," he said softly. "And yet at the same time it is intoxicating because every second is so precious." When she finally succumbed to the disease at age 39, Brosnan found himself alone for the first time in 17 years and a single father of three. It was during this time that Brosnan soared professionally, with roles in such high-profile films as *The Lawnmower Man* and *Mrs. Doubtfire*, culminating in his lauded return to Bond in 1994 with the offer for *Goldeneye*. But he certainly never imagined he'd be changing diapers all over again.

That's exactly what happened with the unexpected pregnancy of girlfriend Keely Shaye-Smith, whom Brosnan met on a trip to Mexico in 1994 for an environmental fundraiser. Dylan Thomas was born in January 1997. "The baby is definitely meant to be in my life, in our lives. No question

A candid shot of Brosnan hitting the links during The Thomas Crown Affair.
In Summer 2002, Brosnan was planning a sequel to his 1999 hit.

about it," Brosnan said a few months later on the set of *Tomorrow Never Dies*. "Before I met Keely, I remember aching for an infant, aching for life, new life. I thought, 'No, no, no — men surely don't go through this.' But then I'd think, 'Oh, it would be lovely to have a child.'"

But plans to marry in May 2000 were unexpectedly halted when Brosnan's 17-year-old son Sean was rushed to intensive care after a tragic car accident in Malibu, where the car Sean was riding in with his friends plunged 130 feet down a ravine. Pierce and Keely were adamant about postponing their nuptials until Sean had made a complete recovery from his injuries. Then shortly after the accident, Keely discovered she was pregnant once again, and the couple decided to wait until after the baby was born before finally tying the knot. Their second son — Paris Beckett Brosnan — was born in February 2001, and Keely and Pierce finally exchanged their vows in August 2001, throwing an extravagant wedding celebration on the grounds of 13th-century Ashford Castle in Cong, County Mayo, Ireland.

Pierce, Keely, and the Brosnan brood live in the actor's Spanish-style Malibu estate — at least when Brosnan isn't working. During the fall of 2001, the family was staying in Dublin while Brosnan shot *Evelyn*, the next film he produced under his Irish Dreamtime banner, and then in January 2002 the actor was back in Bondage in London on the set of *Die Another Day*. But after working virtually nonstop the past few years, Brosnan is adamant about stopping to smell the flowers now. He says he wants to take more time off to spend with his ever-growing family. "Right now, life couldn't be sweeter," smiled Brosnan. "Our little boys are healthy, and we're very, very happy. And that's all that matters in my book."

And with that, Brosnan reaches out to his wooden coffee table and knocks on it three times. Just to make sure.

It seems the world is much more than enough for Pierce Brosnan.

Golden Gals: Pierce Brosnan with Izabella Scorupco and Famke Janssen

GOLDENEYE *(1995)*

Directed By: Martin Campbell

The Mission: A secret Russian satellite weapon called GoldenEye has been compromised by former 006 agent Alec Trevelyan (Sean Bean) in partnership with Soviet General Ourumov (Gottfried John). The two conspire to electronically defraud billions from the Bank of England and then cover their tracks by firing GoldenEye's powerful electromagnetic pulse directly at London, obliterating all computer and electronic circuits.

Locales: Russia, the Caribbean, French Riviera, London, Cuba

The Villain and Accomplices: Alec Trevelyan (Sean Bean), General Ourumov (Gottfried John), Xenia Onatopp (Famke Janssen), Boris Grishenko (Alan Cumming)

The Bond Girls: Natalya Simonova (Izabella Scorupco), Xenia Onatopp (Famke Janssen), Caroline (Serena Gordon)

Theme Song: Tina Turner

Score: Eric Serra

Memorable Lines:

A camera rig catches the chase between Xenia's Ferrari and Bond's Aston Martin.

Nervous MI6 evaluator Caroline, during Bond's Aston Martin road test: "I enjoy a spirited ride as much as the next girl, but . . . who's that?" *Bond, suddenly giving chase to Xenia's Ferrari:* "The next girl."

"I like a woman who enjoys pulling rank." — *Commander Bond, after being snubbed by Xenia for a Canadian admiral.*

New M (Judi Dench) lecturing Bond: "I think you're a sexist, misogynist dinosaur — a relic of the Cold War, whose boyish charms wasted on me obviously appealed to that young woman I sent out to evaluate you."
Bond: "Point taken."
M: "Not quite, 007."

Bond, after Q demonstrates his new grenade pen: "They always said the pen was mightier than the sword."
Q: "Thanks to me, they were right."

Natalya to Bond: "You think I'm impressed? All of you, with your guns, your killing . . . for what? So you can be a hero? All the heroes I know are

(left to right) Robbie Coltrane as Valentin Zukovsky, Sean Bean as 006, and Joe Don Baker as Jack Wade.

dead. How can you act like this, how can you be so cold?"

Bond: "It's what keeps me alive."

Natalya: "No, it's what keeps you alone."

Valentin Zukovsky, hearing the click of Bond's gun cocking behind his head: "Walther PPK, 7.65mm. Only three men I know use such a gun: I believe I've killed two of them."

Robbie Coltrane (Valentin Zukovsky): "It's every boy's dream, really, to be in a Bond film. Especially if you're British. When you get your call sheets and it's got '007' stamped on the front, you really do get quite excited. And, of course, getting to say that immortal line when he puts the gun to my head was terrific. I would've paid them to get to say a line like that!"

Sean Bean (Alec Trevelyan/006): "I love playing a villain, especially if it's a strong, meaty part like this was. The villain has always been an integral ingredient to the success of the Bond films, and I felt Alec Trevelyan was a very good adversary to Bond, being a former '00' agent himself. It was a superb match — each with the same training and same razor-sharp instincts, and each knowing that the other is a totally professional, ruthless killer."

Dame Judi Dench (M): "I was thrilled when I got the phone call to play M, because I had been a huge fan of the Bond films for years, and Bernard Lee, who had played the part for so many years, was actually a great friend of mine. I played her very tough, but how could you become head of MI6 by being anything but tough?"

Joe Don Baker (CIA operative Jack Wade): "I think I'm only one of a couple actors asked to play two different parts in the Bond movies. I played the villain in *The Living Daylights*, and in *Goldeneye* I became the hero. It's difficult to say which is more fun, but as an actor you generally have more fun playing the bad guy. However, Jack Wade is such a colorful character, and there are so many levels to him, that he is a pretty interesting role to play."

Peter Lamont (Production Designer): "On *Goldeneye*, my biggest coup was in building the Arecibo dish. It cost a lot of money, but I think the results were sensational. However, I'm probably most proud of building the city streets of St. Petersburg. From getting the permission to do it, to designing it and building it, to filming the very first shot on that set was a period of exactly six weeks and four days. That was quite an achievement for me. It's quite remarkable how we pulled it off so quickly."

Chris Corbould (Special Effects Supervisor): "*Goldeneye* was a particular challenge because it was almost a reinvention of Bond after a long layoff. People hadn't seen Bond for a long time, so it was a real mission to bring it into the '90s and make sure it was still a viable franchise. I have a real fondness for *Goldeneye* because it was my first Bond totally in charge after working on seven previous Bond films. It was also Pierce's first Bond, so we had quite a close relationship from the word *go*. We both had to really prove ourselves on *Goldeneye*."

North American Gross: $106.4 million

Overseas: $244.9 million

Tanks For The Memories: Bond's visit to St. Petersburg leaves the city in ruins.

Russian concerns about damage to their streets forced Peter Lamont to rebuild St. Petersburg from the ground up back in England.

"I wanted to bring more edge to this," says Brosnan about Tomorrow Never Dies.

TOMORROW NEVER DIES
(1997)

Directed By: Roger Spottiswoode

The Mission: British media baron Elliot Carver (Jonathan Pryce) provokes a war between the U.K. and China to secure the worldwide broadcast and print domination of the Carver Media Group.

Locales: The Khyber Pass, the South China Sea, London, Oxford, Hamburg, Saigon

The Villain and Accomplices: Elliot Carver (Jonathan Pryce), Henry Gupta (Ricky Jay), Stamper (Götz Otto), Dr. Kaufman (Vincent Schiavelli)

The Bond Girls: Wai Lin (Michelle Yeoh), Paris Carver (Teri Hatcher)

Theme Song: Sheryl Crow

Score: David Arnold

Memorable Lines:

Moneypenny's phone call to Bond — requesting his whereabouts — interrupts his language "tutoring" with a voluptuous Danish professor.
Bond: "Umm, I'm just up here at Oxford . . . brushing up on a little Danish."
Moneypenny: "You always were a cunning linguist, James."

"You know, this job of yours is murder on relationships." — *Paris to Bond.*

Dr. Kaufman, boasting about his assassination techniques as he prepares to execute Bond and disguise it as a suicide: "I am a professor of forensic medicine. Believe me, Mister Bond, I could shoot you from Stuttgart and still create the proper effect."

Bond to Carver: "You really are quite insane."
Carver: "The distance between insanity and genius is measured only by success."

Sheryl Crow (Singer/ Songwriter): "There's just such a legacy with the Bond songs, and it was an honor to be part of all that. I really enjoyed the process, because it was like I had carte blanche to just go out on a limb and do something totally camp and fun and experimental. It's kind of an interesting process writing the title song for a Bond film, because they can't give you the script,

Something To Crow About: "I think I would've made a fantastic Bond Girl," says Sheryl Crow.

and they can't tell you what the movie is about. So you're kind of going at it blind, which actually adds to the fun of it in a way. I've loved the Bond films since I was a kid, so shooting the *Tomorrow Never Dies* video was also a real blast too, doing that sort of 'Bond Girl' homage. I really like that video a lot. . . . I think I would've made a fantastic Bond Girl in the film!"

Teri Hatcher (Paris Carver): "I think it was one of the few times in a Bond film that showed a real emotional relationship between Bond and a woman. *Tomorrow Never Dies* was unique in that way, and it made Paris quite different from other Bond girls because of their past. It was a small role, but it motivated Bond's actions and was an integral part of the film."

Bond and former flame Paris (Teri Hatcher) take care of unfinished business.

Pierce Brosnan, on Bond kicking the habit: "I just didn't think it was cool to see him smoking. I mean, the doors were open: Roger [Spottiswoode] said, 'Light up if you want to. Go ahead.' But it just didn't feel right, because the great joy and surprise was that kids go to see these movies too. There's a whole generation of kids growing up with Brosnan as Bond. And as cool as it would have looked for Bond to light up a cigarette and pour a large vodka as he puts the silencer on the PPK, it just didn't feel right. . . . I guess it's still okay for Bond to drink and have a variety of different women, but apparently the message is 'Kids, Don't Smoke.'"

Vic Armstrong (Second Unit Director/ Stunt Coordinator): "*Tomorrow Never Dies* is probably my proudest achievement because we kept the flag of Bond flying high, bringing them into the 21st century. I mean, they edged into it on *Goldeneye*, but I still thought there was room for improvement. The bike chase in *Tomorrow Never Dies* is super value for the money when you look at it. You get a real bang for your buck on that film. And the car chase through the car park is something everybody still talks about. . . . I like *Tomorrow Never Dies* a lot — I think it was a pretty hefty Bond."

Bond's nerve-shredding motorbike chase over helicopters, rooftops, and under whirling blades on the streets of Saigon.

North American Gross: $125.3 million

Overseas: $221.3 million

Take The Money And Run: Bond makes an unconventional escape near the Guggenheim Museum in Spain.

THE WORLD IS NOT ENOUGH (1999)

Directed By: Michael Apted

The Mission: Duplicitous oil heiress Elektra King (Sophie Marceau) is in league with ruthless anarchist Renard (Robert Carlyle) to nuke the oil pipeline running through the Strait of Bosphorous, leaving her in control of all oil supplies from Eastern Europe.

Locales: Spain, London, Scotland, Azerbaijan, Turkey, Kazakhstan

The Villain and Accomplices: Elektra King (Sophie Marceau), Renard (Robert Carlyle), Gabor (John Seru), Sasha Davidov (Ulrich Thomsen), The Bull (Goldie), The Cigar Girl (Maria Grazia Cucinotta)

The Bond Girls: Dr. Christmas Jones (Denise Richards), Elektra King (Sophie Marceau), Dr. Molly Warmflash (Serena Scott-Thomas)

Theme Song: Garbage

Score: David Arnold

R You Listening? John Cleese makes his debut as Q's assistant "R."

Memorable Lines:

"If you can't trust a Swiss banker, what's the world come to?" — *Bond, in negotiations at the La Banque Suisse de L'Industrie.*

R (John Cleese), being introduced by Q to Bond: "Ah yes, the legendary 007 wit . . . or at least *half* of it."

Christmas to Bond: "Do you want to put that in English for those of us who don't speak *spy*?"

Christmas: "The world's greatest terrorist running around with six kilos of weapons-grade plutonium can't be good. I have to get it back, or somebody's going to have my ass."
Bond: "First things first."

Zukovsky, on Bond's surprise appearance: "Can't you just say hello like a normal person?"

Elektra to the captured Bond: "I could have given you the world."
Bond: "The world is not enough."

Elektra: "Foolish sentiment."
Bond: "Family motto."

With a gun to her head, Elektra taunts Bond: "You wouldn't kill me. . . .
You'd miss me."
Bond, after shooting Elektra: "I never *miss*."

Bond, in bed with Christmas: "I thought Christmas only comes once a
year."

Neal Purvis (Co-Screenwriter): "That line 'Christmas only comes
once a year' at the end of the
film got such a collective groan
from the audience. It's such a
bad joke, but it works, and
people left the cinema with a
smile. People think we gave
her the name Christmas just
so we could use that joke, but
in fact that name came from
a man who was named
Christmas Humphries. He was
a leading lawyer here in Britain
in the '50s, and I always
thought it was an interesting
name but an even better name
for a girl. And the character
was originally going to be
from Christmas Island, so it
wasn't as ludicrous a setup.
We had about five different
lines, like 'Christmas is
coming early' There were

*A Leg Up: Christmas Jones (Denise Richards) and
Bond make a quick exit out of a nuclear test facility.*

about five variations, but that was the one that caught people on the day of shooting."

Michael Wilson (Producer), on cultural differences:
"Bond is an international character and therefore calls for locations that are exotic. Not always beautiful but exotic. But American films do tend to focus only on America. I remember an early conversation I had about *The World Is Not Enough* with one of the L.A. script people at the studio. They said, 'Nothing's at stake in this film.' And I said, 'Well, there's *eight and a half million people* living in Istanbul.' But that's the kind of thinking: unless it's Los Angeles or New York City, nothing is really at stake in the world."

Playing His Cards Right: Robbie Coltrane returns as Zukovsky.

Robbie Coltrane, on his return as Russian enemy-turned-reluctant-ally Valentin Zukovsky:
"I was surprised that they asked me back, but I guess I slept with all the right people! Valentin Zukovsky is still the same character from *Goldeneye*, but he's moved on now. He's gone semi-legit. It's kind of realistic, really. That's what those guys in the mob do — they make all their money from prostitution and then buy a couple of launderettes. Next thing you know, they're sending their kids to Harvard."

Desmond Llewelyn (Q): "I was lucky with *The World Is Not Enough* because I got three days' worth of work out of it. It's really quite remarkable because I've only ever had tiny little bits to do in the films, yet people think I'm this big movie star with huge masses of money. They never

"Pierce understands the true value of doing his own stunts," says Vic Armstrong.

think I should be riding the Underground. Whenever I'm on the cross-channel ferry going over to Ireland, someone will always say to me, 'Has anyone ever told you that you look exactly like the man in the Bond films?' They never believe it's actually me and are quite shocked to see me in everyday situations. It's funny, but I went to my grandson's school play a couple months ago, and a little boy came up to me and said, 'Are you Q?' And I said, 'Yes, I am.' And he said, 'Where do you live?' And I said, 'I live here in Bexhill.' And he just looked at me in absolute horror. He said, 'You live in *Bexhill?* Why don't you live in *Hollywood?*' So that's the attitude I always encounter."

Vic Armstrong (Second Unit Director), on the pretitles sequence: "There's a lot of guts in *The World Is Not Enough*, and I think the boat chase was a fantastic opening. It was originally going to be a different sequence, but then they said to me, 'Look, we want a chase from MI6 at Vauxhall Bridge to the Millennium Dome, and we want to finish on a hot air balloon.' That was it. So it was my job to fill everything in. I was doing *Entrapment* at the time, so every Sunday I would go down to the Thames with [stunt coordinator] Simon Crane, and we'd start dreaming up ideas and writing them down and deleting ideas and balancing them. There has to be a real rhythm to an action sequence and a lot of preparation. Eventually, we came up with that layout along the Thames. And having Pierce doing the stunt was a real bonus. When you see him in that boat, where there's hundreds of gallons of water smacking him in the face, you know that ain't no CGI. He's out in the river at top speed, and the wake coming off the boat was just tremendous. Pierce is a real pro. He really understands the true value of doing stunts. He knows the audience relates to him being in those sequences."

North American Gross: $126.9 million

Overseas: $225.1 million

Die Harder: The costliest Bond film in history packs quite a wallop in celebration of the 40th anniversary. Here Bond hijacks a hovercraft from the opening teaser of Die Another Day.

DIE ANOTHER DAY (2002)

Directed By: Lee Tamahori

The Mission: A power-crazed North Korean colonel (Will Yun Lee) is determined to reunite North and South Korea in order to wage an international war.

Locales: North Korea, South Korea, Hong Kong, Cuba, London

The Villain and Accomplices: Gustav Graves (Toby Stephens), Colonel Moon (Will Yun Lee), Zao (Rick Yune)

The Bond Girls: Jinx (Halle Berry), Miranda (Rosamund Pike)

Theme Song: Madonna

Score: David Arnold

Neal Purvis (Co-Screenwriter): "*The World Is Not Enough* was a little over the top but was still fairly real. For *Die Another Day*, we wanted the universe to not cross over into the universe of all the other action movies. We went for a bit more of the fantastical, bit more of the glamor, kind of like the tone of *The Spy Who Loved Me*."

Robert Wade (Co-Screenwriter): "As a springboard for *Die Another Day*, we looked at Ian Fleming's novel *Moonraker*, which has never been done as a film. That book was really used in title only and the name of the villain, Hugo Drax, for the film. So the idea of a villain hiding in plain sight and living amongst the good guys — where he purports to be a sort of benefactor to the world, but he's actually the opposite — was a basic element directly inspired by Fleming's book."

Jinxed: I always loved the women in the Bond films — they were images of such beauty and sexuality to me," says Halle Berry.

Michael Wilson (Producer), on the settings of North Korea and Cuba: "North Korea is an intriguing, exotic place. I think everyone's wondering about it — it's still kind of mysterious. We decided upon it well before President Bush got around to calling it part of the 'Axis of Evil.' That happened afterwards. And Cuba is another kind of Stalinesque state where the creeping liberalization seems to be. It's another cult figure personality holding onto power and oppressing a lot of people. Yet the Cubans themselves are quite open and fun loving. So it's a very odd situation down there."

Neal Purvis: "We wanted to use Cuba in the last picture. The opening titles were going to start there, but then the idea sort of slipped through the cracks. We just think Cuba is a really interesting place at this particular moment in time. And in some ways, North Korea does have some links to Cuba. Dictators often see eye to eye on certain matters. But when we started work on *Die Another Day* in July 2000, Bill Clinton was still in power. And the tricky thing is when you're writing a film and choose a place like Korea; you do slightly run the risk that world events might blow up in your face by the time the film is released. However, if you're dealing with what is sort of a Cold War now, then North Korea is the last great communist cut-off world. Cuba is more an in-between ground, the fact that people visit it for vacations. We have a little joke in the film about Castro. He's not in it, obviously, but he's referred to in a line that references him."

Halle Berry (Jinx): "Getting to play in the Bond universe is just so surreal, so cool. Many of the images that are presented in these movies are tremendously innovative with all the gadgets and all the tricks and all the stunts — that's been so much fun to see firsthand how it's all done."

Rosamund Pike (Miranda Frost): "The ante has certainly been upped for this film. I think Michael and Barbara are doing a fantastic job of making sure that it really sets the pace for the next however many years. It's a big event, this commemoration. And it's so good that Michael and Barbara have been recognized by BAFTA for their contributions to cinema. Bond is such a phenomenon — I keep finding myself saying, 'My God, I can't believe I'm now part of all this.' It's very exciting but also a huge responsibility to make another fantastic Bond character and sort of live up to all the expectations. I mean, I don't think there are many actresses who wouldn't love the chance to create one of these women. I'm always going to be thrilled to have played Miranda; she's a pretty tough cookie. Plus, I'm the first English woman that Pierce Brosnan has come up against since he's been doing the films, which is a big kick for me."

Vic Armstrong (Action Unit Director), on topping himself: "Each time out, you have to go through a mental checklist of what stunts you've done before, what Bond has done before. Sometimes I throw a little spike in there as an homage to an old Bond film and things like that.

But basically, you have to come up with something original, something exciting, and something the audience won't be disappointed with. But I don't like to blow things up just for the sake of it; it has to be story driven. Having said that, however, I do like to push as much as I can into Bond — you do owe your audience an awful lot with these films."

Neal Purvis: "We had a different ending for *Die Another Day* that got chucked a few weeks before we started shooting. So over Christmas, we rewrote this whole thing on the cargo plane. It was a major thing for Peter Lamont to achieve so quickly. And it was so weird because, shortly after we wrote the new set piece, we happened to look out our office window and suddenly saw this huge nose cone of an airplane coming by. They cut the front off a cargo jet, and it was being brought into Pinewood on the back of a lorry. It was very surreal. But with Bond, you can suggest anything, the most ludicrous ideas, and there is machinery in place here at Eon to facilitate whatever you imagine. Like on the last film, we had an idea come up one morning about whether we could do a scene on a ship. And by the afternoon, they had already secured the *Art Royal*. Stuff like that is pretty mind-blowing. On this one, we got Buckingham Palace to put the flag up early for the scene where Gustav Graves parachutes down outside Buckingham Palace. It had to be shot early in the morning, but the palace doesn't put the Union Jack up until 8 a.m., and we needed the flag in the shot for 5 a.m. So they asked the palace if they could break protocol and put it up early for us. That was pretty amazing, getting permission to do all that at Buckingham Palace."

Toby Stephens (Gustav Graves), on essaying a James Bond villain: "Bond is a genre where the dialogue is quite big, and yet you have to deliver it in a way where people don't roll in the aisles laughing. It's a very delicate balance. And you have to find where that balance is. So sometimes they'll shoot it different ways, and in the editing room they'll find out where it is. Yet in one's own head, you have to believe somehow what you're saying. If you don't believe it, then it's inevitably going to fail. My favorite Bond film is *From Russia with Love* because I loved Robert

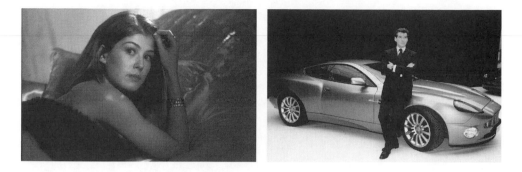

"It was the biggest adrenaline rush I've ever had getting a job," says Rosamund Pike of her role as MI6 agent Miranda Frost. (right) Pierce displays his new Aston Martin Vanquish.

Shaw's performance. His scenes with Connery were so gritty, there was so much tension in there, that you really thought Bond had had it. And that's the trick: if you can make the audience believe, for one second, that Bond has had it — even though you know he's going to win in the end — then you're on a winning streak."

Chris Corbould (Special Effects Supervisor): "The ante has really gone up on *Die Another Day* because it is the 20th Bond and also the 40th anniversary. I mean, you always have that whole 'I've got to do better than the last one,' but particularly on this film they've really gone to town trying to make it spectacular. Like normally, I usually have a 60- or 70-man crew, but on this one our crew has reached 110 people. Everything has been taken a notch upwards."

Goldeneye

Driving onto the *Goldeneye* set (a former Rolls Royce aircraft factory an hour's drive from London at Leavesden in Hertfordshire), you're immediately struck by the enormity of the temporary home to the 007 crew: 1.25 million square feet of interior space and the biggest back lot in the world, accommodating an airfield, control tower, and entire city streets. When *Goldeneye* went into preproduction in late 1994, with principal photography due to start January 16, 1995, it was suddenly discovered that the usual home to Bond — Pinewood Studios and the infamous 007 soundstage — didn't have enough available space to house the mammoth production. An alternative venue had to be immediately found, and it was decided that the sprawling hangars of the Rolls Royce factory afforded a large enough space fitting for the return of the larger-than-life secret agent.

Entering the cavernous Soundstage A, I spied Brosnan fully immersed in the role that had eluded him for years but was now finally his. Dressed in army fatigues and camouflage vest, Brosnan was in full-bore Bond mode as he threw punches and pummeled a stuntman into submission before tossing him off a railing as part of the film's climax atop the giant satellite dish,

EON PRODUCTIONS LTD.
GOLDENEYE
Leavesden Airfield, Hill Farm Avenue, Leavesden, Herts. WD2 7RR   Tel: 01923 68   Fax: 01923 68

1st UNIT

PRODUCERS:	Michael Wilson	CALLSHEET NO: 94
	Barbara Broccoli	
		DATE: Wednesday 17 May '95
DIRECTOR:	Martin Campbell	

UNIT CALL: **08.00 ON SET**
Breakfast available from **07.30**
on Backlot near Reception

LOCATION

1) Backlot, near Reception Leavesden Airfield	2) Backlot Runway opposite Reception, Leavesden Airfield	3) Factory 1 (outside canteen), Leavesden Airfield

Loc.	I/E Set Synopsis	Sc.	D/N	S/Bd	Pgs	Cast
Loc. 1	EXT. SUMP	351Ept	Day	Arecibo I 50pt, 52, 53, 54	1/8	1. 3
Loc. 2	EXT. CABLE CAR ARRIVAL/ TRANSMITTER CRADLE	410pt,412pt, 413pt	Day	Arecibo II 38, 40, 41, 43	3/8	1. 2
Weather Cover Loc.3	INT. CHAIN / ENGINE ROOM	413pt, 414A, 415AB, 415AD to complete	Day	Arecibo II 46,48,49,50,54,60,61, 62,63,64,65,67,69	3/8	1. 2

I.D.	Artiste	Character	D/R	P/Up	M/Up	L/Up	On Set
1.	Pierce Brosnan	BOND	1	07.00	07.30		08.30
2.	Sean Bean	TREVELYAN	2	06.00	06.45		08.30
3.	Izabella Scorupco	NATALYA	3	06.30	07.00		08.30

STUNT CO-ORDINATOR
Simon Crane   08.00

STUNTS

Jamie Edgell	Bond Double		07.00	08.00
Sean McCabe	Trevelyan Double		07.00	08.00

STAND-INS

Adrian Bell	Bond		08.00
Julian Barsham	Trevelyan		08.00
A N Other	Natalya		08.00

REQUIREMENTS

Art Dept / Props	As per script to include all artiste personal props: crowbar
Armourer	As per Charlie Bodycomb: Trevelyan's machine pistol & blanks and hand gun
Camera	As per Phil Meheux BSC.
Costume	As per Lindy Hemming. Body pads req'd for artiste

Original cast and crew call sheets from the 1995 production of Goldeneye.

Electrical	As per Terry Potter.
Make-Up/ Hair	As per Linda DeVetta & Colin Jamison. Trevelyan's scar req'd. Blood.
Medical	As per Paul Cooke. Unit Nurse s/by 08.00 on set
Publicity	David Giamarco (Canada) on set
Sound	As per David John.
Sp/Fx	As per Chris Corbould: bullet hits req'd, slime on surface of dish, chain and cogs to be practical for engine room, cable car to be practical
Catering	Breakfast at 07.30. Lunch available from 13.00. PM break 16.30 for 75 people please
Rushes	To Production Office for collection by Rank Labs.

Gerry Gavigan, 1st Assistant Director

TRANSPORT

Car 1. Brian Brookner	0831 24	P/Up Mr Campbell from home (time t.b.a.) and convey to Leavesden
Car 2. Colin Morris	0836 21	P/Up Mr Brosnan from home at 07.00 and convey to Leavesden
Car 3. Mike Smith	0973 55	P/Up Mr Bean at 06.00 and convey to Leavesden
Car 4. Len Furssedonn	0956 24	P/Up Ms Scorupco at 06.30 and convey to Leavesden
Car 5. Edward Anderson	0831 61	Work to Production Office instructions

ADVANCED SCHEDULE

SET	SCENE	D/N	Pgs	S/Bds	Cast	Location
Thursday 18 May 1995				Arecibo II		
INT. CHAIN / ENGINE ROOM	413pt, 414A, 415AB, 415AD to complete	Day	3/8	46,48,49,50,54,60,61, 62,63,64,65,67,69	1. 2	Factory 1.
INT. TRANSMISSION CRADLE SKY BACKING	415B	Day	1/8	Arecibo II 73, 75, 77	1	B Stage
Friday 19 May 1995				Arecibo 1		
EXT. DISH/FENCE/SUMP	351C, 351E	Day	4/8	25,27,29,30,31,32,33, 37,38,40,42,43,44,46 47,49,50pt,51	1. 3	B Stage
Saturday 20 May 1995				Arecibo 1		
EXT. DISH/FENCE/SUMP	351C, 351E to continue	Day	4/8	25,27,29,30,31,32,33, 37,38,40,42,43,44,46 47,49,50pt,51	1. 3	B Stage
Sunday 21 May 1995 REST DAY						
Monday 22 May 1995				Arecibo I		
EXT. DISH/FENCE/SUMP	351C, 351E to complete	Day	4/8	25,27,29,30,31,32,33, 37,38,40,42,43,44,46 47,49,50pt,51	1. 3	B Stage
EXT. DISH - vertical	453, 453C, 462	Day	3/8	Arecibo II 183A, 185, 200, 202	2	A Stage

Exterior of Leavesdon's Rolls Royce factory that became production site of Goldeneye when Pinewood's available space proved limited.

Interior stages before getting the Bond treatment by production desinger Peter Lamont.

The Bond makeover of Leavesden proved attractive to George Lucas, who subsequently shot The Phantom Menace there.

re-created in part here to match footage already shot on the Arecibo dish in Puerto Rico. It's the last week of production, and this blowout has been taking weeks to shoot.

After the umpteenth take, director Martin Campbell is satisfied, and Brosnan strides over, sweat-drenched and adrenaline pumping, and introduces himself. He explains that he's been engaged in the "*War and Peace* of fight scenes" and suggests I join him for his much-needed break. "We'll drive over to my dressing room," he says.

Drive? Great! I immediately entertain thoughts of cruising in Bond's new Aston Martin DB-5 — or at least the $150,000 BMW Roadster — for a spin around the lot. Visions of smoke screens, oil slicks, machine-gun headlights, and ejector seats quickly spring to mind.

But as we round the corner, Brosnan says, "Hop in," and I look down to see not the DB-5, or the BMW, not even the Lotus Esprit . . . but a battery-operated *golf cart*. Not exactly what I had in mind. He starts the ignition and turns to me with a grin, "Fasten your seat belt, David — we're going to be hitting speeds in excess of three miles an hour!" And with that, the new 007 puts the pedal to the fiberglass and recklessly swerves and screeches the golf cart around the soundstages, dodging production assistants and the occasional pigeon, finally skidding to a halt . . . well, okay, *slowing down slightly to a halt* at the doorstep of his dressing room. It was like something out of not so much a James Bond movie as the Bob Hope Golf Desert Classic.

Resurrecting 007

Six years is a long time for a licensed-to-kill secret agent to go without a mission. And a lot had changed. The Cold War had completely defrosted, the KGB was kaput, and threats from SMERSH and SPECTRE were no more. Even the seemingly indestructible Ernst Stavro Blofeld — Bond's once arch-nemesis, who killed his wife — hadn't been heard from in years.

So it was decided to take Bond back to where it all began for his seventeenth adventure. The title came from the Jamaican estate of author Ian Fleming — nicknamed Goldeneye — where between 1952 and 1964 he wrote many of his Bond novels and short stories at the beachfront vacation

"It was a long way to fall if I screwed it up," admitted Brosnan about his first 007 outing.

home. A vintage 1962 Aston Martin DB-5 — made famous in *Goldfinger* — once again became Bond's mode of transportation for *Goldeneye*. The locales of Monte Carlo, the Caribbean, Switzerland, and St. Petersburg evoked the Bondian globetrotting glamor of yesteryear, and the Bond beauties — Famke Janssen and Izabella Scorupco — were sultry European exotics in the tradition of Ursula Andress and Claudine Auger.

And though Bond himself had a new and much younger face, the man assuming the myth echoed the unmistakable style, grace, and charisma from Hollywood's Golden Age. Without question, Pierce Brosnan looked the look, talked the talk, and walked the walk, while effortlessly balancing the irony, brutality, and sophistication needed to portray the world-famous superspy in the employ of Her Majesty's Secret Service.

"Pierce brings a real humor and touch of class to the role, as well as being very good at action," was how New Zealand-born Martin Campbell described the new 007 during his directing duties on *Goldeneye*. "He brings a real depth to the role too, although I'm always wary of saying things like 'depth' and 'Bond' in the same sentence. Bond isn't about any deep meaning or any subtext underneath it all. What you're looking for is a damn good ride and a damn good piece of entertainment — and that's what *Goldeneye* is, pure and simple."

Timothy Dalton had sipped his last vodka martini as Bond in 1989's *Licence to Kill*, which disappointed at the box office in America and forced the producers to rethink the series. Unfortunately, due in large part to legal wranglings between Danjaq (the company of Albert Broccoli) and MGM/UA over television and video rights to the films, producers Michael Wilson and

Barbara Broccoli weren't able to commence work on another Bond until those legal issues were resolved. They wound up with a lot more time to retool the series than originally imagined.

"It was very frustrating for everyone," recalled Wilson in his Eon office during production of *Goldeneye.* "We weren't in the business of lawsuits, we were in the business of making movies. But in retrospect, I think it was the best situation we could have had if we were going to have a hiatus. We got a new Bond; we have a lot of new faces — director, cameramen. It's a different look and a fresh approach."

Wilson also shook things up by bringing in a new team of writers, who had no previous experience on a Bond film. Longtime Bond writer Richard Maibaum had died in 1991, so Wilson took a chance on screenwriters Michael France (whose only previous big-screen credit was the Sylvester Stallone actioner *Cliffhanger*), Jeffrey Caine (*The Cold Room*), Kevin Wade, and finally Bruce Feirstein to give a final polish to *Goldeneye.* "There is a feeling that, if you bring in young people and it's a contemporary film, they will bring to it contemporary ideas," explained Wilson. "We had a lot of ideas pitched to us by writers, agents, and the studio, but Michael France came up with what we thought was a very good idea. It had some pretty interesting plot twists and some interesting characters. It was all there, and it worked its way through the three other writers, and it was still intact. Jeffrey Caine had come in and worked a lot on the script and made some real strong contributions."

"What I tried to do was bring Bond back out of all the excesses of the last few films," noted screenwriter Caine. "Bond tended to become just a little too cartoonlike. There were things that didn't fit reality. Bond isn't about realism anyway. The British Secret Service doesn't really run that way. I wanted to go back to the classics like *From Russia with Love* and *Goldfinger.*

"I sought to give Bond more to do that was maybe smarter and more witty and to cut down a little on the stunt work and high-action stuff," added Caine. "However, that can be an uphill battle because the studio wants lots and lots of action . . . so you just pile it on. But I find it a little tedious after a while, if you have too much of it. So I tried to level that stuff, which you have to have, with some quieter scenes showing character and wit — things that have been neglected in the last few movies. . . . I really yearned for the intelligence of those early Bonds."

The Story

Goldeneye's teaser begins as a flashback inside a top-secret Soviet nerve gas facility — a seemingly impenetrable fortress carved out of solid rock — hidden beneath a huge dam wedged deep in mountainous terrain. The intricate assignment demands a two-man operation, and Bond is teamed with his friend and Secret Service contemporary, Alexander Trevelyan 006 (Sean Bean). Their relationship is close and trusting, two men working with one mind — the very definition of the grace under pressure required by those select oo agents.

Double 00's: Sean Bean as 006 and Pierce Brosnan as 007 launch a blind assault in Goldeneye's opening teaser.

But in midmission, their presence is exposed, and 006 is trapped. For once, Bond hesitates. Aborting the operation will certainly save his partner's life; otherwise, he will be haunted by the consequences forever.

But now it's the present, and the death throes of hard-line Communism have given birth to something far more sinister. The hammer and sickle have quickly and quietly been replaced by organized crime — with Russia serving as the epicenter of a new European mafia whose tentacles are spreading across the globe, bringing social, economic, and violent repercussions in its wake. The swiftly changing political alliances made former enemies friends and old friends deadly adversaries.

Bristling with advanced firepower and featuring self-defense systems against every known form of electronic battlefield threat, a supersecret NATO Tiger helicopter is skyjacked. It's poised to become a tug-of-peace prize between the great powers and a vicious new strain of criminal mind — code-named Janus.

Bond's briefing from M is simple. He is ordered to Russia to penetrate the local arms mafia, seek out Janus, reassure the current Kremlin leadership, and somehow bring the perpetrator to justice for his part in the Trevelyan/006 affair. But on one point M is adamant: there is to be no vendetta. Avenging 006 will not bring him back, and Bond is dutifully reminded that a license to kill can also be a death certificate.

Bond tracks the shadowy Janus and his cohorts from St. Petersburg to the south Atlantic, and the climax of the story is played out in a race against time on the surface of the world's largest radio telescope, where Bond finally comes face to face with his past.

The 1,000-foot-diameter parabolic dish concealed in a remote region of Cuba is the only transmitter capable of allowing Goldeneye — an orbiting space satellite — to activate the one remaining rogue satellite that has the distinction of being able to paralyze the entire international community by knocking out its technological capacity with a powerful electromagnetic pulse. Within minutes, the United Kingdom would quite literally return to the Stone Age, followed swiftly by Tokyo, Frankfurt, New York, and Hong Kong.

Once again, 007 is forced to break all the rules. Blind frontal assault. Zero backup except for the untrained Natalya. No preplanned escape route. It's Bond at his most brutal and resourceful best.

In the original treatment for *Goldeneye*, Bond became involved with the case by following a trail of dead scientists and while trying to decipher what was going on. However, screenwriter Jeffrey Caine didn't see this as true to Bond's legacy. "It was like detective puzzle stuff at the beginning. I argued that what Bond typically did was to throw himself into a dangerous situation and see what happened, rather than cerebrally follow a trail of clues. We put in a whole new first act, and I said that what we needed to do was to show Trevelyan/006 [Sean Bean] and Bond in action in the beginning, to establish who they were. And then cut from titles to where Bond is now, and something has to happen which puts him on the trail of Trevelyan without knowing it's Trevelyan."

Brosnan . . . Pierce Brosnan

"The question the press were asking me at the beginning is 'Is there still an audience out there for James Bond?'" related Brosnan, relaxing in his spacious apartment-sized dressing room on the set of *Goldeneye*. "And the answer is 'Yeah, you better believe there is!' There's a big audience waiting . . . it's been six years."

The groundswell leading up to *Goldeneye*'s release was enormous, fueled by a kick-ass movie trailer that had been unspooling in theaters for months, resulting in excited cheers and applause from eager audiences. "The warmth from the public has been very supportive," confessed Brosnan, during his prerelease jitters. "I feel a great responsibility to the role and to the film to make it successful — and, hopefully, make it stand on its own feet again. There's a real richness right now, certainly of achievement, having done it, wanting it, being scared of it, and having been excited by it."

"So when what happened with Timothy Dalton happened, I knew I was going to be on some short list," admitted Brosnan. "And I just said to my agents, 'Look, let's sort out whether it's going to happen or not.' I did want to do it, but I didn't want a long, protracted flirtation — either use me or not, but let's not fuck around. And then it happened."

Reflecting back on the failed first go-round with Bond, Brosnan figured it was actually for the best. Had he acquired the license to kill nine years earlier, he didn't think he would've done the role justice. "I have kind of a youngish face," offered Brosnan, chuckling and rubbing his jaw.

"It just feels right that it's happened now in my life," he surmised. "It's been such a thread through the tapestry of my life. My late wife was in a Bond movie, and that I should get offered the role in '86 and then lose it, never expecting it or seeking it out in the first place, and for it to come back into my life again, it carries a certain significance."

"There's definitely an element of pro-Pierce about this project . . . it's palpable," noted director Campbell between takes of the satellite dish fight scene. "And justifiably so. It's a role he's wanted to do, he missed out last time, and I think people perceive him as the perfect Bond. I mean, who else in the world could do it? When we were originally casting, we didn't just consider Pierce, we were considering an opening casting call, right from the word *go*. And you'd be amazed at how many people *aren't* right for this role. It's a very difficult character to nail."

Producer Michael Wilson echoed that sentiment. "All the actors who have played Bond are leading men and not character actors," he explains. "So what they have to do is find something within themselves, to put themselves somehow in this role. And I think, when you write the script, you have to think of the person playing the role as a very important element.

"And with Pierce," continued Wilson, "I think he had to really dig down and find the character. It was a process he worked on with Martin Campbell. Long before shooting started, Barbara [Broccoli] and I spent a lot of time with Martin, discussing our view of the character, so the director had all our thoughts in mind when he was dealing with Pierce. He's really managed to bring out of Pierce this character. I think audiences will find him surprisingly good, because it's not a Pierce Brosnan they've seen before. He plays Bond in a very different, very unique way. He doesn't try to imitate any of the former Bonds."

To define who Bond is, Brosnan said he "looked at what Fleming put down, and then really you just look at the text and at the script. You read it over and over again. . . .

"When it comes down to it," surmised Brosnan, "Bond is a *killer*, plain and simple. He's ruthless; he's a commander. He's very, very sophisticated. He has a stillness to him. He's funny, ironic . . . he's a loner. He's somebody who I think has a vulnerability too, which he masks within all these things. And hopefully, for a moment, you get to see a little bit behind the curtain, as it were."

Brosnan said that he bought all the Fleming Bond books back in 1986 and had read them all during the ensuing years, even going so far as to keep an old first-edition copy of *Goldfinger* with him in his *Goldeneye* dressing room. "Just because of the significance of it," he explained, pointing out the good-luck charm poised on a nearby shelf. "As a boy in 1964, just over from Ireland, *Goldfinger* was the first film I ever saw, and that was the touchstone . . . . Little did I think that I would be playing the role someday."

Though Brosnan was determined to make the character his own, he did figure his frame of reference couldn't help but be influenced by Sean

Connery and Roger Moore. "Sean's performance in the Bond films is indelible in my history as an actor and as a man. His film was the first film I ever saw. You have to take that into account, but you can't be intimidated by it. You use it, you make peace with it, and you accept your fear of the role. . . .

"Then you *embrace* it," he added.

With Brosnan on board for *Goldeneye*, writer Jeffrey Caine said he saw a chance to vanquish the improbable fight scenes and cartoon villains that inhabited many of the previous Bond films. "What we had, not so much with Dalton, but with Roger Moore, was a guy fighting Jaws and these mountain-sized men, doing these roundhouse kicks that are so slow in coming that you can actually eat breakfast while you're waiting for them to connect," Caine chuckled. "The bad guy kind of stands there waiting, and then they do connect, and the villain staggers back, and you're saying, 'Oh, *come on!*'

"But," added Caine, "Martin Campbell won't do that. When Pierce Brosnan hits somebody you're going to believe they've been hit!"

Izabella Scorupco, who as *Goldeneye*'s Russian computer programmer Natalya Simonova helped 007 with his hard drive problems, enthused that Brosnan was the Bond of her dreams. "I know this sounds very diplomatic," she giggled, "but I wasn't very stuck on any of those other Bonds before. I really think Pierce is the best — from his body language to his expressions. And he knows exactly what to do with the character. You know, he's had a lot of time to think about it . . . and he's done such a fantastic job. I just think he's the best person they could have chosen."

Famke Janssen, who played *Goldeneye*'s lethal-legged Xenia Onatopp, offered similar praise for her on-screen adversary. "I think he's about as perfect of a Bond as you can imagine," she enthused. "Of course, he's very handsome, which is very important for James Bond. But he's smart, and he has a wit, and he doesn't take himself too seriously. . . . It's actually *strange* how much he looks and acts the part."

Rehearsing the Big Day

If you've just been named the new James Bond, what's the first thing you do? When Brosnan finally got the word in 1994, he did what pretty much every guy in the world had been doing the previous 32 years. He looked in the bathroom mirror and said those immortal words: "My name is Bond . . . James Bond," Brosnan confessed with a somewhat sheepish laugh. "Yes, I admit that I did that. Actually, I even tried it once when I was brushing my teeth too! And believe me, you look pretty stupid with a mouthful of toothpaste running down your chin."

But he didn't stop there. "Yeah, I did the pose too," he revealed, grinning with slight embarrassment. "I did the gun barrel walk across the room and then turned and shot. And actually, when we filmed that little sequence for real . . . I have to admit, it was a pretty big thrill."

A P.C. James Bond?

From the outset of the $50 million production, a lot was being made in the media as to whether *Goldeneye* would adhere to the tenets of '90s political correctness. Would Bond — the very poster boy for political incorrectness three decades running — suddenly succumb to the sweeping wave of moral regeneration? "It's a lot of bullshit," said Brosnan, addressing the charges. "I think the whole P.C. thing in our society is really a big yawn, quite frankly. We should all just use common sense and treat each other with respect. Not being P.C., however, is what made Bond 'Bond' in the first place. You take that away, like with what happened to Dalton, and he was a prig. I smoke occasionally, I like cigars. But I'm not going to smoke as Bond. I do drink the vodka martinis, though, and I whack a woman [Xenia Onatopp]. . . . She's a killer, and she tries to fuck with Bond, so I whack her."

As for Bond's other legendary whacking abilities, it was full steam ahead. "Yeah, there's quite a lot of that 'whacking' going on too," laughed Brosnan. "I think it's about four . . . or is it three? I don't remember. They tried to take that out in the last two, but that's not Bond. Where's the fun in life? We all know about AIDS, every child knows about it. They know you can't just fuck around anymore. But damnit, we've got to have fun! We want to see *The Man*! It's a fantasy."

And Martin Campbell was the strongest proponent of bringing that fun back to Bond. "For some bizarre reason, 'politically correct' is the clichéd term for the '90s, and I think it's bullshit," sniffed Campbell. "And so does Bond. The truth of the matter is he is not politically correct. He is still a sexist chauvinist. We're not making statements about anything. We're dealing with a romantic hero here, which is a rarity these days."

And Famke Janssen added that, the day Bond succumbs to political correctness, the series would most assuredly die. "He is a politically incorrect character, which is what makes him so much fun and is why people pay the $7.50 to sit there for two hours and go 'wow! This guy can get away with this kind of stuff, and I can't,'" she explained. "There are women in the movie that give him a hard time, but that doesn't mean he's not trying to get away with the things he's always tried to get away with."

"We have a lot of intelligence and some pretty interesting characters," offered Caine of *Goldeneye*'s then unknown prospects in the movie marketplace. "The idea that Bond's nemesis in this film should be 006, an agent trained to the same degree of skills as himself, was very appealing to me and, I think, will be for the audience as well. It gives Bond a worthy and believable adversary. To see the battle of the 'oo' minds is terribly intriguing."

Brosnan, admittedly unsure of how *Goldeneye* would be received, summed up the film this way: "You put your money down, and you sit back, and you want to be entertained and feel great with a fair amount of escapism. The guys want to come out of the theater feeling like James Bond, and the girls want to go to bed with him. . . .

"And in between," added Brosnan with a proud smile, "is one heck of a wild ride."

Necking: "I don't think you should ever change Bond — he should always be the tough guy, flirting with everyone," says Izabella Scorupco, seen here in passionate embrace with 007.

DIRECTING BOND: MARTIN CAMPBELL

"I've grown up on the Bonds since 1962, so I had no worries I could direct it as well as anyone previous," said Martin Campbell.

"Bond films have always been successful to varying degrees," noted director Martin Campbell, who was selected to helm 007's return in *Goldeneye* after his previous efforts *No Escape*, *Criminal Law*, and the acclaimed BBC production of *Edge of Darkness* caught the eyes of Michael Wilson and Barbara Broccoli. "And the truth of the matter is that the essential difference from Bond film to Bond film is going to be certain ingredients in the mix. Bond will always be Bond — he hasn't changed one iota. You know, it's Pierce Brosnan this time, and, when you think of Roger Moore or Sean Connery, they brought their own personalities and their abilities and their trepidations to the part, and Pierce has done the same thing."

But Campbell definitely knew going in that he had to shake — not stir — the contents of the last two Bond films in order to save the series. "To be honest, I didn't like the Tim Dalton films," Campbell admitted. "For me, Tim wasn't a good Bond. Not that he's not a fine actor, 'cause he is. But I thought he was too angry and too aggressive about the whole thing. And we didn't have the humor, which is absolutely essential. It's got to not quite take itself so seriously. And that never worked on the last two Bond films. I felt they were past their 'sell by' date, to be quite honest with you. Apart from a new Bond, we needed a better cast, better acting, and a better story. And that's what we've done."

Added Campbell, relaxing momentarily in his director's chair between camera setups on *Goldeneye*, "This film moves much faster than other Bonds. It's funny, but you look at some of the old Bonds, and it's just amazing how slow they seem now. They wait a lot longer before there's another piece of action.

"But I tend to direct at a fair pace anyway," added Campbell, nodding in the direction of the bustling crew members. "And the truth is that in the '90s people get bored very quickly, so you've got to keep the whole thing moving. From that point of view, I think *Goldeneye* is going to be faster paced than any previous Bond."

So did Campbell feel pressure to top previous Bond escapades, especially the now expected take-your-breath-away opening sequences, which had become a hallmark of the series since *Goldfinger*?

"If you look at hugely expensive films like *True Lies*, which had some tremendous stuff in there, you can't say, 'Oh God, how am I going to top that?' Because you can't," he explained. "You'll end up with something like *The Last Action Hero*, where the action is meaningless, and nobody gives a shit. If they don't want to see the movie, no amount of action or spectacle is going to drag them to the cinema. It's all got to be part of the story. Sure, we've got some good stunts, but I never really see it in terms of 'God, what do we have to do different?' What I'm aware of is that the opening sequence has to get one big gasp out of the audience.

"I mean, Bond did that in one, and only one, film, and that was when he skis over the cliff with the parachute in *The Spy Who Loved Me*. That scene really grabbed you by the balls. And, fortunately, I think we've got a kind of similar moment."

GLOBETROTTING IN STYLE: GOLDENEYE'S LOCALES

Bond commandeers a launch in Monte Carlo

Casino Royale: Bond is given the royal treatment at the Monte Carlo casino.

Monte Carlo, eight miles from the Italian border, occupies less than three-quarters of a square mile of land but is perhaps the most luxurious resort center on Earth, and its residents enjoy the highest per capita income in the world. A highly popular tax haven, Monte Carlo and its casinos are a magnet for top racing drivers and international high rollers . . . and, of course, James Bond, who engages in a little game of chemin de fer with Xenia Onatopp for his grand return in *Goldeneye*.

"I think shooting in Monte Carlo really helped bring it home for me that this is a James Bond movie," related Brosnan. "You can't help but feel full-throttle Bond in Monte Carlo. There were hundreds of people watching, and you're there in the tux, driving the DB-5 outside the Monte Carlo casino, and it seems like the whole world is there. The set is lit, and you're on center stage as this legendary figure. . . . It really was quite extraordinary."

St. Petersburg

A number of key locations in Russia had to be duplicated on the back lot at Leavesden when startled Russian authorities suddenly realized the *Goldeneye* crew intended on staging a tank chase scene and shoot-out on the decrepit city streets of St. Petersburg. "They were concerned that a 36-ton tank roaring all over the place could destroy the streets and the sewers below," explained production designer Peter Lamont, who marked his 15th 007 assignment with *Goldeneye*. "So I just said one day, 'Look, this may sound stupid, but why don't we build the Russian street, with cross streets, here [in England]? We'll put in a bridge for the military vehicles to travel across, and we'll bring all the tanks here for the shots.' Well, everyone thought it was a good idea, and we had money in the budget that I could pinch from other things, and, quite miraculously, within seven weeks we were shooting on the street. That was quite an achievement."

Lamont began his Bond association on *Goldfinger* as a draftsman in the art department and has worked on every 007 outing since, progressing through chief draftsman, assistant art director, set decorator, and art director. His first Bond film as production designer was *For Your Eyes Only*, and he has continued in that capacity ever since. He received an Oscar nomination, alongside longtime production designer Ken Adam, for *The Spy Who Loved Me* in 1977. He has also received British and American Academy Award nominations for his work on James Cameron's *Aliens* and *True Lies* and a win for *Titanic*.

Lamont's St. Petersburg street creations were indeed impressive, with proper perspective from every vantage point on the sprawling outdoor set. "It might seem a bit ridiculous, but it was never thought that we'd be shooting St. Petersburg here," said Lamont as he gave me a walking tour of the intricately detailed replica. "It's going to be a little disheartening having to tear it all down, especially after you put so much work into it."

But for *Goldeneye* director Martin Campbell, *not* shooting in St. Petersburg allowed him to breathe a sigh of relief. "It meant getting more time here and more control," explained Campbell. "I mean, who knows what can happen over there. The thing is, when you see the film, it'll be pretty seamless. A fair amount takes place in St. Petersburg, but it's not the most important aspect of the story. I must say, though, the London locations will look seamless against the St. Petersburg location, because the architecture of St. Petersburg is very much Italian."

Puerto Rico

Another substitution occurred for *Goldeneye*'s fiery climax on and around the Arecibo satellite dish, where Puerto Rico had to double for Cuba as Bond infiltrates enemy headquarters. Brosnan recalled the three-week location shoot as being a "nice tropical break from England," he said. "I like Puerto Rico a lot. . . . It's a funky place. It was extremely, extremely hot the whole time we were there, especially in the jungle.

"It's a tough place to live, though," he added. "I've been there a couple of times before and have always been very impressed by the will of the people. They have a really poor life there, and yet their spirits are so strong. . . . It's quite humbling to be with them, especially when you're part of this gigantic, multi-million-dollar production."

✿

M & M'S: BOND'S NEW BOSS

Up until his death in 1981, British character actor Bernard Lee was James Bond's crusty superior, forever admonishing 007 for his cavalier attitude towards bureaucratic authority and regulations but tolerant because Bond was his ace agent. With shooting under way on *For Your*

Gentleman's Club: Dame Judi Dench shakes up MI6.

Eyes Only when Lee passed away on January 17, 1981, at age 73 — and having not yet shot his scenes — Albert Broccoli was forced at the last minute to fill M's vacant chair with actor James Villiers. And then in 1983's *Octopussy*, Robert Brown was introduced as the new head of MI6, a role that would continue through to *Licence to Kill*. But by 1995's *Goldeneye*, the changing times had impacted Bond as well, and, in a reflection of '90s events within the real British Secret Service, Dame Judi Dench was brought in as Bond's superior. 007 was now having to answer to a woman.

"She calls him a sexist, chauvinist dinosaur, and he replies, 'Point taken', at which she says, 'Not quite,'" explained director Martin Campbell on the set of *Goldeneye*. "But there's a reason she says that — it doesn't just come out of the blue.

"This M is very much a person who is into statistics and analysis — much more political than previous M's," continued Campbell. "The old M was always Bond's boss but very much one-on-one. But this M is someone very different. She sees the '00' section as perhaps having seen its day and not required anymore.

"Of course, it is still required," added Campbell with a smile, "or otherwise we wouldn't have a story."

Dame Judi Dench is the multi-award-winning actress who received the Order of the British Empire in 1986 and an Academy Award in 2000 for her supporting role in *Shakespeare in Love*. The distinguished actress has starred on stage, screen, and television and has won five British Academy Awards.

"And I don't like her," said Brosnan of his new female boss. "And she doesn't like me. We tolerate each other because we're thrown into the same circle of business; she really sticks in my craw, but we have to get on."

Personally, however, Brosnan admitted that he was quite pleased with M's gender change. "It just makes sense because Stella Rimington was the head of MI5, so it seems appropriate. But I suppose, in the tradition of Bond, it's quite significant. In fact, Cubby's favorite scene in *Goldeneye* so far is the one between Judi Dench and myself."

Consistent throughout the years, however, was M's office; it was a nostalgic trip through England's glorious gentlemen's club Intelligence past: the dark, wood-paneled walls, those leather double doors, the red and green warning lights, the naval decor of the room — it was a link to the early days when, smoking his pipe, the low-key, no-nonsense M would brief 007 on the intricacies of his next mission.

"Ken Adam designed the first set for *Dr. No,*" explains Bond production designer Peter Lamont, "and when I joined him on *Goldfinger* we refurbished the office with real wood rather than paper. And over a period of time, it's had little knick-knacks (not to be confused with Herve Villechaize's Nic-Nac character in 1974's *The Man with the Golden Gun*) put into it. But it pretty much always stayed the same all these years."

However, with a new M on board, it was decided to revamp M's staid digs accordingly. "The only person who is old now is Q, and so with a new, younger M we wanted to shake it up," explained Lamont, who sent a letter to MI6 headquarters requesting permission to look around for ideas. "They were very polite, but they said they didn't allow visitors. But I did have a book of the exteriors of the place, so I sort of decided where M's office would be located geographically. And then we totally rebuilt the office, and it looks quite different now. It's very modern."

MODEL BEHAVIOR: DEREK MEDDINGS

Miniature Giant: Derek Meddings takes five on his Siberian terrain during Goldeneye.

If you never noticed Derek Meddings's work, then you were paying him a compliment.

That's because for 40 years — and for six of the James Bond films — Meddings was the mastermind behind some of the cinema's most impressive miniature special effects, earning him an Academy Award and a BAFTA for the 1978 film *Superman: The Movie* as well as an Oscar nomination for his work on *Moonraker* in 1979.

Meddings pioneered the use of miniatures through the 007 films but actually got his training with the puppet master himself — Gerry Anderson — on the classic television series *Thunderbirds*. "Back then I had this marvelous opportunity to try things," explained Meddings, who also created miniature model effects for *Stingray, Fireball, XL5, Captain Scarlet, Joe 90*, and *UFO*. "There were just so many special effects in each episode. I had to create all kinds of situations. Everything on *Thunderbirds* and the other shows had to be done in miniature. If a car drove or a plane flew, they were models.

"And now, in retrospect, it really gave me the kind of training that you just can't get anywhere nowadays," he added. "We used to have something like 200 special effects miniatures in a one-hour program."

When Meddings became miniatures supervisor in 1973 for his first Bond outing, *Live and Let Die*, he was already a master at model deception. For that film, he created and exploded Dr. Kananga's poppy fields as well as the human explosion in the film's underwater scuffle, when Bond forces drug kingpin Mr. Big to swallow a compressed air bullet, blowing actor Yaphet Kotto to smithereens. Meddings created the body, and then novice makeup effects genius Rick Baker — who would go on to earn six Academy Awards for his work in such films as *An American Werewolf in London, Men in Black, Ed Wood,* and *The Nutty Professor,* as well as *Star Wars* — was charged with creating the replica head of Yaphet Kotto.

Meddings's model work so impressed Bond producers Broccoli and Saltzman that he was asked back for *The Man with the Golden Gun* (1974) to create and then explode Francisco Scaramanga's solar reactor and island headquarters. But it was in *The Spy Who Loved Me* (1977) that Meddings hit new heights for the series, with some truly spectacular — and seamless — model work on an immense scale, most notably *The Liparus* supertanker, which swallows entire nuclear submarines and was, in fact, a 63-foot-long "miniature."

"We built *The Liparus* at Pinewood and then shipped it to the Bahamas, where we could shoot at sea," noted Meddings. "From my experience, you can't miss shooting models in the ocean. You've got the biggest background in the world and the largest tank in the world, and you don't have to worry about whether the lighting is realistic or whether the water looks like real water. And since we were working with a 63-foot-long tanker, we needed a vast work area, and it really paid off."

When Meddings blew up *The Liparus* for the film's climax, the 63-foot model sank to a watery grave — despite Meddings's best efforts to retrieve it. "We were supposed to get it out, so I figured we could just put cables on it and pull it up with a crane," he laughed, "but I forgot that it was 10 tons of concrete. I heard it ended up washing away within a very short period of time. One of the divers went down a month later, and it was completely gone."

Meddings also worked on the miniature Atlantis undersea city as well as James Bond's Lotus Esprit submarine car, which was a clever combination of miniatures, half-scale, and full-size models and remains one of the dramatic highlights of the Bond series.

"Lotus supplied me with six or seven cars, and each one had to do something different," remembered Meddings. "To give the car the underwater, streamlined effect, we created wheels that disappeared inside the body and wheel arches that came down and filled that space. We also built louvers that would go over the windshield to give the impression of strengthening the glass. Actually, only one car could work underwater — it had an engine, and you could actually drive it underwater like an airplane, diving and climbing and that sort of thing. . . . It was quite ingenious, I must say."

Meddings's next Bond film, *Moonraker*, proved his most complicated, using by today's standards a primitive method of inserting FX shots, but *Moonraker* also remained his proudest moment, he said.

"Sometimes I look back at *Moonraker* and wonder how we pulled it off," Meddings said of his Oscar-nominated effects work. "It was difficult because we were working with outer space, and it was all done by winding back the camera. We didn't do any opticals on it at all. Everything was windbacks. There was only one optical with a laser beam, but all the rest of it — all the shuttles taking off, the shots of shuttles flying over Earth, the space station — was all done by winding back film in the camera, where, each time you inserted a new element into the shot, you then had to matte out that part of the screen, so you don't print over that again, wind back, and do it all over again. In one shot alone, we did 48 passes on one piece of negative."

Meddings recalled that perhaps the most difficult scene involved the fleet of Hugo Drax's space shuttles docking on his radar-proof space station in orbit above the Earth. "That space station was 12 feet across, and I had to shoot that and then put a big sheet of glass in front of the camera and matte out, in black paint, the space station and then do all the shuttles docking," said Meddings, shaking his

"Sometimes I wonder how we pulled it off," said Meddings of his Oscar-nominated FX work for Moonraker.

Drax's Space Station: A ' miniature' 12-foot long model.

Derek Meddings airbrushes finishing touches on an Earth matte painting.

Moonraker Shuttle Lift-Off: A combination of miniatures, foreground plates and magnesium flares.

head in disbelief. "It was very tedious. . . . I don't know how we did it, actually."

However, his return to the Bond series in 1995 for *Goldeneye* proved to be Meddings's most extensive and painstaking Bond undertaking. For one scene, Meddings was required to scale down and stage a battle between a moving train, a Soviet tank, the Arecibo satellite dish and control room, and Russian MIG fighters — each costing thousands of dollars. In fact, Meddings's miniature Siberia set, covering all of Stage 3 of the Bond production studios, was over 150 feet wide and 100 feet in length. Miniature in name only, this proved the only effective way of shooting the Russian sequences and was truly one of the most impressive, intricately detailed sets ever built.

"This plays such a major part in the film," said Meddings as he walked around the scaled-down, snow-capped Russian terrain on the cavernous *Goldeneye* soundstage. "It had to establish where we were in the film, and there was no way we could go and do this abroad because it means you have to build a radar station somewhere out in the wild. It would've been far too expensive and problematic. And the beauty of doing it this way, of course, is the production designer can come up with any crazy idea, and we can build it as a miniature."

Preparing a shot on the Siberian terrain for Goldeneye.

Meddings and his team built the radar station, helicopter, and helipad, and his greatest accomplishment, he felt — the Russian MIG 29s — all in miniature. "We built the jets to be seven feet long, and they had two inducted engines so that they were sucking in air and blowing it out the back. They were absolutely incredible. We had all the lights on the undercarriage just like the real Russian jets, which, as you know, are unbelievable state-of-the-art weapons."

Medding's radio-controlled MIGS take flight on the backlot.

A larger scale MIG used for the close shoots.

That scene from *Goldeneye* required three Russian jets taking off from a remote airbase, so Meddings utilized the studio's own back lot airfield and control tower. "What I did was build a miniature runway on the existing runway in scale with the seven-foot Russian jet," explained Meddings. "And then I used the control tower as the background. We were able to do something that has never been done before in that we had three radio-controlled airplanes taking off in formation. And it looked totally believable. In the background was the control tower, which we stuck a big red star on. And we had three Russian vehicles which drove in the background that gave the scene movement. You end up with this great perspective in the shot.

"The jets are just so perfect," added Meddings with an enthusiastic smile, "that you can actually shoot them in extreme close-up. The miniature pilots moved inside, and you can't tell them from the real thing."

To replicate the Russian MIGs, Meddings assumed he'd have to undertake his own covert spy operation to steal the blueprints. Fortunately, *perestroika* made the task considerably easier than James Bond stealing a Russian Lektor. "We actually got permission from the Russian embassy," marveled Meddings. "We said we wanted to use Russian jets in the film, and they allowed me and the entire art department to go climb all over their jets at an air show. So there we were, with measuring sticks and cameras, walking all over their fighter planes. It's very funny because everyone in the crowd was wondering what was going on, and some clever so-and-so in the crowd said, *'Looks like a little bit of industrial espionage going on here!'*"

Footage shot in Switzerland was duplicated exactly for another miniature set, where in the opening sequence a plane careens off a cliff followed closely by a free-falling Bond astride a motorcycle. "Every rock and tree is identical on the miniature set to match the footage shot in Switzerland. It's an exact copy," Meddings proudly explained.

For the film's climax, Meddings created a fiery explosion collapsing the Arecibo dish where Bond and Trevelyan do battle. The miniature set was rigged with explosives so the radio telescope and dish came crashing down to destroy the headquarters below, with the roof, girders, and rubble raining down. "We shot it at 120 frames a second, so everything is a bit slow," says Meddings. "We shot three camera angles to capture the action — a very low camera, one up above, and one on eye level."

Meddings admitted that, although he was extremely pleased with the take, he's always a little sad to see his sets destroyed or "have them put out for rubbish because of lack of space — especially the Russian tank which was struck by a train.

"A real train couldn't travel fast enough and couldn't hit a tank, so we built it all from scratch and shot this tank coming out of a tunnel in close-ups, and no one knew it wasn't one of the real ones," he said. "It was just such a spectacular destruction. I don't think you can do that with a computer. And it was all done with spectacular miniatures which had to be destroyed."

CGI effects were a bit of a sore spot with Meddings, who felt films had become too reliant on computer-generated effects. The Bond films have always accomplished their inspired stunts and action sequences the old-fashioned way, and that added sense of realism always made them all the more thrilling. CGI shots can never quite capture the look and feel of tangible objects — whether miniature or full-scale — being photographed with natural lighting, shadows, and perspective. Real stuntmen parachuting out of a real plane at 15,000 feet is far more convincing than cheating it on a computer, and Meddings lamented the hold CGI had taken on FX shots. "Producers have gotten into a situation now where they ask you to do a film, and then they ask if you have access to a computer," noted Meddings with a wry grin. "And then I say, 'Why?' And they'll say, 'Well, we've got a lot of computer stuff to do in the film.' They give you the script, you read it, and you realize they haven't got a lot to do at all. Now they've all gotten this strange idea that, if you haven't got a computer, you can't make a film. . . . It's completely ridiculous.

"I look to the early Bonds and to the Bonds I did, and we never had a computer," Meddings added, "and the films have never suffered for it. They've always been exciting, and I think what people have to realize is that it's just another tool — like blue screen, front projection, and other systems that we have."

Meddings, who also worked on such films as *Krull, Spies like Us, Hudson Hawk, Neverending Story II* and *III, Cape Fear*, and Tim Burton's *Batman*, said that, "if you go back to *Superman*, a lot of the shots with wires were taken out when we were actually shooting film. We did it in such a way that we made sure the wires didn't show. Yes, there were occasions when we did have to take it out, and it was done optically, which was sometimes a struggle. Now, of course, with computers it's so easy. But I think people are too quick to say, 'We'll do it CGI.' They're forgetting that, until the film is cut, they can't have it done because it costs so much money. But if you're doing it optically, you'd have that shot done already. Every time you put the scissors to a CGI shot, you've just lost $5,000 for two frames of footage. So you have to wait until the film is completed and then work out how long that shot should be. Then it's given to the people to work on."

For *Goldeneye*, Meddings admitted there were some computer effects, including compositing green screens together on a computer instead of blue-screen shots on an optical printer. "But we've done a lot of flying shots and things on wires, and we don't have to take them out by computer because we've already made certain that we didn't see them when we were shooting," he explained. "I've painted them, puffed them down with dust, and shot in a situation where the lighting is right. That's how I want to do shots. I don't want to do half a shot and then have it taken away for four weeks to be worked on by a computer. I don't want my work repaired by a computer. There's got to be a human element."

Sadly, cancer claimed Meddings shortly after he completed his work on *Goldeneye*. He was an indispensable part of the Bond team and a true optical-effects genius. Even after more than four decades in the business, Meddings still had a boyish enthusiasm for his work, which to him wasn't work at all. *Goldeneye* was dedicated to the memory of Derek Meddings.

*

GOLDEN THIGHS: FAMKE JANSSEN

Dutch born but living in America for the past decade, Famke Janssen played the luscious but lethal post-Soviet assassin Xenia Onatopp in *Goldeneye*, possessing a most unique way of killing her victims:

crushing them to death with her thighs during the peak of sexual ecstasy.

"I had a heart attack when I read the script," laughed Janssen on her villainous thighmaster role. "You should have seen me when I read it for the first time. I yelled, 'Oh, my God, I can't believe I have to do this!'"

Janssen described the character as being quite a challenge, "mostly because Xenia is such a sexual character. . . . To put your sexuality out there on the screen for the world to see is not easy.

ThighMaster: Famke Janssen as the lethal-legged assassin.

"And this is not a movie that just a few people will see," grinned the then-27-year-old former model and Columbia Univer-sity graduate. "Everyone is going to see this movie. And, of course, we got into a lot of trouble with those scenes because we're dealing with a PG-13 rating, and it had to be tame enough to get through. And this character is defi-nitely not tame. Especially when you get a close-up on my thigh, squeezing a guy's ribcage, you're already getting into trouble. I'm really curious to see how those scenes are going to work."

Janssen began her professional modeling career in Holland before mov-ing to New York, where she majored in writing and literature at Columbia while studying stagecraft with Harold Guskin. She then moved to Los Angeles, where she continued to develop her acting skills under the tutelage of renowned acting coach Roy London. After appearing in episodes of *Melrose Place* and *The Untouchables* and the *Star Trek: The Next Generation* episode "The Perfect Mate" (as Kamala, the most beautiful woman in the galaxy), Janssen made her film debut opposite Jeff Goldblum in *Fathers and Sons.* She then landed the starring role alongside Scott Bakula in Clive Barker's *Lord of Illusions*. It was during the early stages of that film that the *Goldeneye* producers asked to see footage of her at work and soon screen-tested her in London for *Goldeneye*'s voluptuous viper.

"I just felt it was really important to be a character that the audience can really have fun with" was Janssen's take on Xenia Onatopp. "Not that Bond movies are very serious, but I think you need a scapegoat or somebody you can laugh at. And that's what I tried to do with this character, but it wasn't always easy."

Under Onatopp: Taking Bond's breath away in Goldeneye.

She admitted she got carried away during her sex-as-a-weapon scenes and had to be somewhat . . . restrained. "I guess I was getting *too* into it," she laughed. "But when your character loves to kill men, and when you like to do it between your thighs, it's a very sexual thing. There should be a lot of pain involved. It's a real S&M thing. So it soon became a decision of how much *pleasure* I could take in the act. The fact that I was enjoying it so much was difficult to contain. . . . I don't think too much of it made it past the censors."

Janssen joked at the time that she wasn't too worried about frightening away prospective dates after her man-killing Bond debut, "because I'm married," she said, "but I am worried that my husband will run away after he sees this movie," she laughed. But Janssen was quick to shrug off any possible "Bond Girl" career stigma. "I know it's something that people will try to do, but, as much as they've tried in the past to label me as a model-turned-actress or as a person in a horror movie, it just doesn't stick," she said. "Because I just want to keep working and keep finding a new stigma to overcome.

"And, to be honest, I think there were many reasons in the past why these women didn't go on to do other movies after Bond. I think a lot of them weren't actresses. And maybe a lot of them didn't have the aspirations that I have. And certainly the roles weren't that well written, and there wasn't as much that you could do with them. They were very much props, not meant to do anything much but be pleasing to the eye." And to the thighs.

✪

HEATING UP THE COLD WAR: IZABELLA SCORUPCO

"I'm not opposed to being labeled a 'Bond Girl' because I'm not a feminist," said Polish-born Izabella Scorupco of the so-called stigma attached to her role as the sexy Russian computer operator Natalya Simonova in *Goldeneye*. "But it's up to the individual. You can never blame it on the Bond Girl, you just blame it on the actor and what she does with the part. To be honest, I don't really think it was Bond being chauvinist, it was the women in bikinis being stupid. Personally, I don't want to watch a Bond movie if the women are going to walk around in business suits or work clothes. It's silly."

Pole Vaulting: Izabella Scorupco as Bond Girl Natalya.

Born in the village of Byalystok near the Russian border, Scorupco lived with her mother, a doctor, until they moved in 1978 to a Swedish suburb outside Stockholm. "In Poland and Sweden, the Bond films were very big," she said, adding that *Goldfinger* remained her favorite. "You're automatically a fan because everyone knows him. But we girls watched the Bond films because of all those beautiful clothes. I never looked at the cars, or the gadgets, or what was going to explode."

At school, Scorupco studied drama and music until, at age 17, she was discovered by a Swedish film director who cast her in a movie called *No One Can Love like Us*, which made her an instant teenage idol in Sweden. After working as a model, she decided to pursue a singing career, which led to her first single, "Substitute," in 1989. It was a big success, reaching gold status in Sweden, as did an album released shortly after called *IZA*. The hit release was followed by another number-one single, "Shame, Shame, Shame," in 1991, but Scorupco admitted it was all a sham. "You just realize how easy it is to become popular," she said of her all-girl, Bangles-flavored band. "I was really *acting* as a singer more than being a singer. But if you pretend for too long, then your responsibility becomes too big."

Three's Company: Bond with matters in hand.

So she quit singing and concentrated instead on her acting career, landing the lead role in a medieval drama, *Petri Tears*, and then her big break in 1995's *Goldeneye*. "I laugh to think of myself as an action hero," laughed Scorupco between takes of a stunt sequence with Brosnan — where the two tumble down the inside shell of the Arecibo satellite dish — on the set of *Goldeneye*. "It's quite funny to come in at six in the morning and your first scene is to kick open a door and look like you're going to kill someone!"

As for the supposed PC updating of Bond, Scorupco remained adamantly opposed. "That's why everyone loves him, because of who he is," she said. "I don't think you should ever change Bond. He should always be the tough guy, flirting with everyone. It's up to the females to really be strong and independent."

Tomorrow Never Dies

Deep inside the cavernous soundstages of Frogmore Studios — actually a converted supermarket warehouse an hour north of London in St. Albans — the world's most indestructible secret agent is having a little trouble disposing of the bad guys on the closed set of *Tomorrow Never Dies*.

Scene 122, Take One, finds a captured Bond inside the broadcasting lair of media mogul Elliot Carver. After being roughed up by four security guards inside a recording studio, Bond quickly turns the tables on his captors in a brutal fight scene filled with fast and furious flying fists.

Pierce Brosnan, clad in the de rigueur black tuxedo and with nary a bead of sweat on his brow, suddenly lurches for a microphone stand and swings a seeming death blow to the remaining guard's skull. But the henchman, clinging to a mixing console, sputters and gasps back to life. So Brosnan calmly picks up a large glass ashtray, nonchalantly walks over to the goon, and with the equivalent of an ironic Bond aside smashes it over his wobbling head . . . only the candy-glass prop ashtray fails to break.

"Cut!" yells Roger Spottiswoode, the director of the 18th official 007 escapade and follow-up to the hugely successful *Goldeneye.* "Replace the

EON PRODUCTIONS LTD.
"TOMORROW NEVER DIES"
Eon Studios, 29-33 Frogmore, Park Street, St. Albans, Herts. AL2 2UA   Tel: 01727 876   Fax: 01727 876
Mobile on set: Paul Taylor (2nd A.D.): 0374 257

<u>1st UNIT</u>

PRODUCERS:	Michael Wilson	**Callsheet No:**	60
	Barbara Broccoli		
		Date:	Thursday 19 June '97
DIRECTOR:	Roger Spottiswoode		
		UNIT CALL:	07.30
		Breakfast avail. from:	07.00

<u>LOCATION:</u>   A STAGE: - EON STUDIOS, 29-33 PARK STREET, ST ALBANS, HERTS.

UNIT NOTES
NO SMOKING ON THE SET. PLEASE REFER TO RISK ASSESSMENTS PREVIOUSLY ISSUED
IF FURTHER COPIES OF RISK ASSESSMENTS REQUIRED, PLEASE CONTACT PRODUCTION OFFICE

INSERTS UNIT SHOOTING TODAY

Set / Synopsis	Scene No's	D/N	Pgs	Cast
1. INT. HALLWAY & RECORDING STUDIO	122J to complete	Night	4/8	1.
(Guards take Bond into Recording Studio. They start to beat him up)				
2. INT. RECORDING STUDIO	122L-2, 122N-1 to complete	Night	1 4/8	1.
(Bond beats up four Guards)				
3. INT. RECORDING STUDIO	122S-1 to complete	Night	1/8	4.
(Stamper bursts in. Bond is gone)				

ID	Artiste	Character	D/R	P/Up	M/Up	On Set
1.	Pierce Brosnan	BOND	Translux	06.30	07.15	08.00
4.	Götz Otto	STAMPER	66	11.00	12.00	As req.

Stunt Co-ordinator
Dickey Beer   07.30

Stunts				
Rocky Tailor	GUARD 1		07.00	08.00
Terry Richards	GUARD 2		"	"
Terry Plummer	GUARD 3		"	"
Neil Finnighan	GUARD 4		"	"

Stunt Double
Wayne Michaels   BOND   07.00   08.00

Stand-ins
Dean Taylor   Bond   07.30

Extras
1 x MAN   Goon   10.00

REQUIREMENTS

Art / Props   As per script to incl.all artiste personal props - mixing console, monitors, tape machines, breakaway musical instruments - piano, drum set (x 2), electric guitar, cello (+ 3 repeats), sound mikes, walkie talkies for guards.

Camera/Grip   As per Robert Elswit to include addt'l camera crew: Tony Jackson (Operator), Brad Larner (Focus), Chris Bain (Loader), Jimmy Waters (Grip).

Computer FX   As per Mara Bryan & Justin Owen. Video footage required for playback of Carver's Party onto monitor for scenes 122J, 122L-2, 122N-1

Construction   As per Ray Barrett

Original cast and crew call sheets from the 1997 production of Tomorrow Never Dies.

1st Unit No.60 Thursday 19/6/97

Costume	As per Lindy Hemming.
Electrical	As per John Higgins.
M/Up / Hair	As per Norma Webb and Eithne Fennell.
Medical	Unit Nurse s/by on set from 07.30 + paramedics + ambulance (+ separate paramedics & ambulance for stunts)
Production	Air conditioning engineer (Pat Cullenane via Air Trembath) on set from 07.30.
Publicity	VIP set visit by 20 European Exhibitors plus David Giamarco
Sound	As per Chris Munro. Addt'l Boom Op. (Keith Batten - replacement for Colin Wood)
S/ Fx	As per Chris Corbould. Recording booth glass window to shatter + repeats
Stunts	Stunt rehearsals (motorbike) taking place on the backlot today (see risk assessment previously issued plus addt'l page attached). Plus: Tom Lucy / Gary Kane / Robert Patton / Matt Price rehearsing fight Int. Carver's Office, Saigon. Plus: Tak Ngai Yung (Jackie) / Chi Wah Ling (Tony), Philip Kwok and Vincent Wang from 09.00 to rehearse re. Market Scenes.
Video	As per Don Brown.
Catering	Breakfast avail at 07.30. Lunch available from 13.00 in the canteen. PM break @ 16.30 for 100 people
Rushes	Picture for delivery to Rank Labs; sound for delivery to Editors at Eon Studios. Please note following times for rushes screenings: Lunchtime: mute film rushes of previous day (main and 2nd Unit). 2.30pm onwards: sync rushes of previous day on tape followed by film rushes of Model Unit.

ADVANCE SCHEDULE

Friday 20 June '97

INT. CARGO HELICOPTER	287	Day	6/8	1, 3, 4
INT. CORRIDOR, CMGN BUILDING	289A, 289B	Day	3/8	1, 3, 4

Saturday 21 June '97
Sunday 22 June '97
REST DAYS

Monday 23 June '97
Tuesday 24 June '97

INT. CARVER'S OFFICE - SAIGON	289Apt, 294Bpt, 304, 313	Day	4 pgs	1, 3, 4

Gerry Gavigan, 1st Assistant Director

Transport

Car. 1 (Brian Brookner) (0831 241)	P/Up Mr Spottiswoode and Mr Elswit from homes as arranged.
Car 2. (Colin Morris) (0410 410)	P/Up Mr Brosnan at 06.30 from home and convey to Eon Studios for time 07.15
Car 3.	P/Up Mr Otto from hotel at 11.00 and convey to Eon Studios for 12.00
Minibus x 1 (S/Wkshps)	S/By at Eon Studios from 07.00 - as per Keith Young
1 x Coach (via S/Workshops)	P/Up Crowd at 07.45 the Chinese Community Centre, 44 Gerrard Street, London W1 and convey to Eon Studios. S/By to return after lunch - time tba
Self-Drive Minibus / Car (via BCR)	P/Up Philip Kwok and Stunt Team from Hotel at 08.15 and convey to Eon Studios for 09.00

ashtray, and let's do it again."

Take Two: The fight scene plays out flawlessly, but now when Brosnan goes for the ashtray he can't find it amid the clutter.

"Cut!!"

Take Three: The mayhem ensues as staged, but this time when Brosnan picks up the prop ashtray it immediately crumbles in his hands.

"Cutttt!!" groans Spottiswoode. "We only have one ashtray left now."

As the actors and props are reset to original positions, an exasperated Brosnan quips, "Smoking won't kill me, but this damn *ashtray* will!"

Take Four: Brosnan pulls all his punches, locates the ashtray, and successfully smashes it over the bad guy's head.

"Cut! Good. Nice work," breathes Spottiswoode with a sigh of relief.

"Yeah, nice work if you can get it," smiles Brosnan as he comes over to say hello. As we exit to a less frenetic area of the soundstage, Brosnan unknots his bow tie and unbuttons his now sweat-soaked tux shirt to talk about the daunting demands of *Tomorrow Never Dies*. Not only is he 10 weeks into what would become a physically punishing, hurried, and sometimes stormy five-and-a-half-month shoot, but also his 007 debut in *Goldeneye* became the highest-grossing installment in the 35-year history of the franchise, raking in well over $350 million — nearly twice the total of any previous Bond. Topping that success had everyone feeling a little stirred, shaken, and in dire need of more than just a few vodka martinis.

"I was so pleased, proud, and relieved that *Goldeneye* did so well, because the stakes were just so high, and there was a lot of pressure on me to deliver," admitted Brosnan, easing into a director's chair. He was noticeably more confident with his portrayal compared to two years previous when we spoke on the set of *Goldeneye*. "I feel the part is mine now, and when it was all over I had a quiet satisfaction that I did James Bond finally, and I didn't fall down or embarrass myself. . . .

"But in many respects," he continued, "there's more pressure this time around because, having now brought the franchise back up to speed, you have further to fall should anything go amiss. The expectations are just so high to make this even bigger and better than the last one."

With the Soviet Union in tatters, Bond's expertise is transferred from the Cold War to a media war of sorts in *Tomorrow Never Dies*. Bond is dispatched to the Far East, where the Rupert Murdochesque media giant Elliot Carver (Jonathan Pryce) is instigating a war between England and China in order to boost ratings for his worldwide satellite TV network and newspaper chain. Teri Hatcher plays Carver's wife, Paris, who shares a secret past with Bond. And Michelle Yeoh, famed for her Hong Kong action films, plays China's 007 equivalent, who teams up with Bond to prevent World War III. The budget for *Tomorrow Never Dies* was doubled to $100 million from *Goldeneye*'s $50 million, and the film shot on locations as varied as Thailand, Mexico, Hamburg, Florida, England, and the French Pyrenees, with as many as five separate crews shooting simultaneously. And with virtually no postproduction time due to the rushed release date, director Spottiswoode was forced to edit the film while shooting. It would become the most complicated Bond production in recent memory.

Though 007 had tangled with the world's worst villains and megalomaniacal madmen over the decades, for *Tomorrow Never Dies* Bond's greatest nemesis proved to be the press. SMERSH, SPECTRE, Dr. No, and Blofeld were all paper tigers compared to the Fleet Street tabloids. For when the start date for *Tomorrow Never Dies* was pushed from January to April 1997 due to location problems in Vietnam ("at the last minute, the old guards behind the prime minister got cold feet, and we lost 10 weeks [of production time] and a million dollars," explained Spottiswoode) as well as frantic script revisions, reports immediately started surfacing that *Tomorrow Never Dies* was in trouble. And no sooner had filming commenced on April Fool's Day when the U.K. tabloids — followed quickly by the U.S. press — began publishing rumors of an out-of-control budget in addition to heated on-set fights among, in various combinations, Brosnan, Hatcher, Spottiswoode, screenwriter Bruce Feirstein, and Pryce.

"If it wasn't a Bond film, the press would never be writing this stuff," explained Jonathan Pryce between takes of his gruesome death scene. "I mean, we'd laugh about the stuff we were reading in the papers. I would then come on set and jokingly curse Roger [Spottiswoode] as 'the worst director I'd ever worked with,' and sure enough the next day it would be in the papers. It's annoying, really, but it's part of a film that is of this magnitude

— there's a lot of journalists out there with a lot of pages to fill.

"Then this stuff gets picked up by the wire services and goes around the world," added Pryce with a wry grin. "Stuff like Teri Hatcher smashed Pierce in the face because they didn't get along is so completely untrue. You have to really wonder where this stuff comes from."

Flash back to October 1996, and the original script for *Tomorrow Never Dies* centered on the Hong Kong changeover from British to Chinese rule, "but the film would've had to open in May to have any immediacy, and there was no way we could've made the picture in that short space of time," explained Spottiswoode, sipping a cup of coffee during a break in shooting. "So they had to radically alter the whole concept, start a new script, plan huge action sequences that required months of preparation, and tackle logistics no one had attempted before. The villain stayed from the original story, but that was all. . . ."

"I mean, there *were* tensions," he pointed out, "but not *impossible* ones." But when a finished script still wasn't ready by start date, *Tomorrow Never Dies* went into production anyway.

"The studio [MGM/UA] badly needed this film; they wanted it yesterday, so we went out of the gates with it not exactly in the finest of shape," noted Brosnan. "The story was there . . . but making it has been a bit like pulling teeth. However, the misrepresentation in the British press was kind of a gross inflation of what's been happening here on set. There's been no disharmony, or backbiting, or arguments, but there has been some heated discussions about what should happen within the story. And as it is my second Bond, I've had more of a voice and more of an opinion and more of a take on it."

But Brosnan says he was determined this time out to rectify certain mistakes he felt were made in *Goldeneye*. "First, I wanted a story line you could follow," he laughed. "The story line should be as lean as possible, because in *Goldeneye* you never knew what the hell was going on. At least I didn't anyway. It was so elliptical. I wanted to give this one a real edge and make it more personal for me."

That included deeper shadings for the characters, especially between Bond and his former flame Paris. Those quieter, subtler moments of

Brosnan's Bond evoked some of the best character development of earlier Connery films such as *From Russia with Love* and *Dr. No*. "I wanted Paris to mean something to Bond, as opposed to some big-breasted broad," offered Brosnan. "Because this is a woman he loved, and there's no reason you can't go there with these kinds of emotions — it makes him more colorful. It just heightens everything else he does. And they listened to me in that department. When you see the reality of what gets to him and how much he conceals. . . .

"When you read the books, Bond conceals so much fear," he added. "This guy is shit-scared the whole time. He's got to be. But also, he's the ultimate hero. But to see that crack, to see the flaw, and to let the audience in for that brief moment — that's what I find exciting about doing it."

Director Roger Spottiswoode and author David Giammarco on set of Tomorrow Never Dies.

For Canadian-born and U.K.-raised Spottiswoode — whose father, Raymond, was one of the founders of the National Film Board of Canada — helming a Bond film offered a chance to get the series "back to basics" as he saw it. "I'd always loved the first few Bonds, but frankly I stopped watching them until Pierce came along," confessed Spottiswoode. "The first movies had an edge to them which became more ludicrously fantasy-oriented as they went along. I wanted to bring back that edge the movies had lost but were starting to get back thanks to [director] Martin Campbell and *Goldeneye*. Suddenly, the whole premise worked when it clearly didn't do so before.

"Obviously, the Bonds are fantasy-oriented to begin with, but I felt they'd become silly. And they can be terrific and smart thrillers. So I figured there was a way of bringing the whole concept back into an area that, quite frankly, other people had begun taking over — like James Cameron and his *True Lies*. Other people had moved into the genre Bond had created. They were doing them moodier and better while Bond had got lost. It was time for 007 to take his rightful place in the heightened reality world of recent action adventures rather than being so resolutely retro-'60s."

Spottiswoode began his feature career as film editor for Sam Peckinpah, cutting such classics as *Straw Dogs, The Wild Bunch*, and *The Getaway*, later turning to direct such films as *The Pursuit of D.B. Cooper, Under Fire, Turner & Hooch, Air America, And the Band Played On*, and *Hiroshima*. Spottiswoode said that in retrospect he was glad the *Tomorrow Never Dies* script was in flux, "because it meant I could bring in lots of my own ideas, so I wouldn't be completely absorbed by this 'Bond Machine.'" Spottiswoode hired his team of Canadian film editors from *Hiroshima* (Dominique Fortin and Michael Arcand), as well as production designer Allan Cameron (*Air America, Starship Troopers*) and director of photography Robert Elswit (*Boogie Nights*). (Incidentally, Allan Cameron replaced longtime Bond production designer Peter Lamont, who was tied up with his duties on James Cameron's *Titanic* at the time but would return for *The World Is Not Enough*.) "Left to their own devices, I think the producers would be happy making the same kind of Bond film they've always made," said Spottiswoode. "I think it's up to you as the director to make sure that doesn't happen."

Brosnan expressed his desire to shake up the Bond films too, at the time mentioning directors like John Woo, Danny Boyle, and Quentin Tarantino for future 007 outings. "You try it, and if it doesn't work so what? You do another one. They have done 18 of them already," shrugged Brosnan. "I said to [producers] Barbara Broccoli and Michael Wilson last night at dinner, 'Next time, we should really go out there and mix things up.' I remember, even at the premiere of *Goldeneye*, Martin Scorsese told me he would love to direct a Bond film. And he said he would love to be in one as an actor too. I think he would make a great villain. Guys like him and [Brian] De Palma — look at their work. They're incredible talents. . . . Let's see what they can bring to Bond.

"But you have a family organization here that has done things over a period of years, and old habits die hard," he continued. "I mean, I love them dearly, but they like to have control over their productions and they feel that, if you bring in someone like that, they will not have control. But to bring in any one of those guys to direct would be a great kick in the pants for the series."

Brosnan also tossed out some new scenarios he had in mind for Bond: "I'd like to see him hang it all up. I'd like to see him go see M and say, 'I'm outta here!' What would happen if Bond wants to get out of the business? There's so many story lines to come up with for this character. I mean, what would happen if he suddenly gets a kid? Or I guess he'd have a few *thousand* by now," he chuckled. "But you know, I suppose you can only mess with the formula so much. You have to pay attention to the form that has been established over 18 movies."

At that point, Brosnan unintentionally pulled a very Bondian maneuver. He quickly and deftly knotted his bow tie without looking in a mirror or missing a beat in the conversation. Acknowledging my amazement, Brosnan just smiled and said, "Ahhh . . . years of practice." And with a wink added, "I am *James Bond*, after all!"

Indeed, the role had become second nature for Brosnan. Box office was at an all-time high, and critics were virtually unanimous in their praise for Brosnan's portrayal. Yet the actor was circumspect when it came to acknowledging the adulation as *Tomorrow Never Dies* hit movie screens in November 1997 and proved that *Goldeneye* was no fluke. "I've tried not to read any of the reviews," admitted Brosnan. "I just find it too painful if they're bad. And the good ones only last a certain amount of time.

"I mean, you can read them over and over again and carry them around with you and hang them up on the wall for only so long," he quipped with a hearty laugh.

"No, the response of the people everywhere has just been so warm and positive," Brosnan added. "Having people thanking me for bringing Bond back, and putting it back on the map, is very gratifying. And being able to enjoy all this with my family and them enjoying it for me . . . it just doesn't get any better than that."

TOMORROW NEVER DIES: CRAFTING THE ACTION

Maestro Of Mayhem: Action Unit Director Vic Armstrong.

To conceive and design the action sequences that are the hallmark of every Bond film, director Roger Spottiswoode enlisted Vic Armstrong, a veteran of some of the greatest action blockbusters, including *Terminator 2: Judgment Day* and *Raiders of the Lost Ark*, to be second unit director and oversee the substantial stunt load, including a riveting motorcycle chase across the rickety rooftops of Saigon, a radar-eluding, high-altitude, low-opening parachute plunge from 30,000 feet at minus 54° centigrade, five-mile free fall, ending at 200 feet, and hitting the ocean at 30 miles an hour, and an explosive final showdown in the intricate confines of Elliot Carver's stealth ship.

Realizing action sequences of true Bondian scope and size requires extraordinary planning and coordination between the various technical teams. Led by stunt supervisor Dickey Beer — who earned his stripes as a stuntman in films like *Return of the Jedi, Superman III, Never Say Never Again, Indiana Jones and the Temple of Doom, Rambo III*, and *Indiana Jones and the Last Crusade*, as well as coordinating the snow-ski stunt unit for the pretitle sequence of *A View to a Kill* — the stunt team varied in numbers throughout *Tomorrow Never Dies*, depending on which action sequences were being filmed, totaling 85 British stunt persons, 10 Germans, 15 Thais, and 12 more from Hong Kong, including Philip Kwok's team of martial arts experts, who go blow-to-blow with Michelle Yeoh. And special effects supervisor Chris Corbould utilized a team of 70 effects technicians, sometimes with four different units filming in varying locales around the globe at the same time and in three workshops in three different studios — Frogmore, Pinewood, and Elstree.

Thai Shtick: Bond and Wai Lin's acrobatic bike chase in Bangkok.

Principal photography began on Tuesday, April 1, 1997, at Eon Production's new studio facility at Frogmore, northwest of London, and at Pinewood Studios. The film's trademark pretitle sequence had been previously completed in the snowfields of the French Pyrenees, centered on a high-altitude airfield. But perhaps the most intricate action sequence occurred at street level — the motorcycle chase through the congested and tangled snarl of Saigon's downtown core. "We had to try and come up with something better than the tank chase was in *Goldeneye*," explained Spottiswoode. "I didn't know how to put Bond in a bigger vehicle, so I thought I'd better do the opposite and put him in the most vulnerable, fragile position — on a motorcycle. And to add to 007's troubles, he's handcuffed to Wai Lin. Then to have a helicopter trying to kill them would certainly shake things up a bit."

Added Armstrong: "The motorcycle chase is horrendous because Bond and Wai Lin are handcuffed together, with her riding with one hand operating the clutch, and he's riding with one hand on the throttle. That's a monster in itself. They have to leap the bike from one roof, across the street over a hovering helicopter, and onto another roof. That was real drama." And it was all done for real — no

CGI help whatsoever.

Production designer Allan Cameron had just completed work on the sci-fi thriller *Starship Troopers* when Spottiswoode invited him to design the look of *Tomorrow Never Dies*. One of the early challenges facing Cameron was having to re-create the Saigon streets and marketplace on the back lot at Frogmore. "The setting was Saigon, although we actually shot it in Bangkok, and we were able to move from Thailand to the streets of Frogmore with a seamless join," explained Cameron. "The spectacular motorcycle chase we filmed on this set was equal in excitement to the tank chase in *Goldeneye*. Unlike the St. Petersburg street set in *Goldeneye*, the Saigon street is full of stalls selling trinkets and food, with 500 Asian extras, most of whom were riding bicycles. Whereas the St. Petersburg street was very formal, almost like symmetrical facades all the way down the street, the Saigon street is a jumble of different buildings, which matched what we filmed in Bangkok."

Amazingly detailed storyboards were created to choreograph each moment of the sequence and allow Spottiswoode and Armstrong to forecast how much of the stunt work could be accomplished by Yeoh and Brosnan. "Then Vic went in and started shooting the wide shots and some of the action shots that we wouldn't be able to get with the principals, and then we went and did the entire thing with the principals, using various rigs and so forth," added Spottiswoode.

Dickey Beer elaborated: "We started the sequence in Bangkok with the motorcycle being driven over the rooftops pursued by bad guys in a helicopter. It turned out to be a real big deal with cannons firing and bullet hits, much like *Apocalypse Now*. We had about 100 yards of rooftops with bullet hits at three or four foot intervals. It was very loud and gave an eerie feeling as you could hear them approaching from 100 yards away as they came towards you.

"Then we continued the sequence on the studio back lot, where a composite of a Saigon street had been constructed. At one stage, the bike rode along a high balcony with sections of the balcony collapsing behind it. All the balcony sections were dropped by levers, which were triggered by the bike so, in theory, the balcony couldn't drop until the bike had passed over the triggers, which would collapse the balcony."

Another sequence in the chase had the helicopter swooping in and flying near ground level through the marketplace, its whirling blades slicing and dicing up the stalls and scattering the crowd until Bond heaves a heavy metal spike into the rear rotors, causing them to disintegrate. The pilot quickly loses control and careens into the side of a building, and the 'copter explodes into a giant fireball.

The next challenging sequence — which immediately precedes the motorcycle chase — involved Bond and Wai Lin leaping from the 44-story high-rise headquarters of Elliot Carver in Saigon and ripping down the giant banner bearing the likeness of Carver. "We filmed that on the studio back lot with Pierce and Michelle 70 feet in the air," said Armstrong. "We got computerized winches in, and we built a rig to the side of the building that could lower a camera at the same speed as the falling actors. Both Pierce and Michelle were in harnesses and were as comfortable as you can get, but harnesses are not really meant for spending a long time in — they are a safety aspect that you rely on to hold you there if something goes wrong."

"Working with Pierce Brosnan has been a real joy," added Beer with a smile. "He's absolutely wonderful, one of the greatest ones. He's in the same league as Harrison Ford and a very few like that. Working with Pierce and Harrison makes your job so much easier, and therefore you can make them look so much better. It's wonderful."

Then there are the vehicles. Bond's business car in *Tomorrow Never Dies* is a BMW 750 IL. Special effects supervisor Corbould journeyed to Munich several times to meet with the BMW engineers to discuss the logistics of what they could and couldn't do with the vehicle with regards to the gadgets. "We spent the first day in the research and development looking into the way in which we could show the car being driven by remote control," said Corbould, who first joined the Bond team on *The Spy Who Loved Me* building action props and mechanical rigs, with *Tomorrow Never Dies* marking his eighth 007 outing.

Insurance Waiver: Bond drops his BMW off at Avis.

"BMW helped us out to a certain extent before we went ahead and refined it a little. The gadgets were all important. My department came up with lots of drawings of what, potentially, we could supply. Initially, it was suggested that we had rockets coming from the headlights, but that had been done in previous Bonds. It suddenly dawned on me that we could have a row of little multirocket launchers concealed behind the sun-roof which came into view as the sun-roof tilts up. We had a powerful cable cutter which came out of the BMW emblem on the bonnet hood, we had an emission of gas from under the car, metal tire spikes behind the rear bumper, self-inflating tires, and a hidden glove box which opens automatically. All of these gadgets are operated by Bond in the back of the car from a mobile phone display during a very thrilling car chase in a multistory car-parking garage."

In this highly inventive sequence, Bond escapes Carver's henchmen by crouching in the back seat and operating his custom BMW using a remote-control touch pad with a small LCD viewing screen. "Bond is not able to sit in the driver's seat because the steering wheel is shot out, and the front seat goes, and the windows go," said Spottiswoode. "He's sliding around in the back of the car, and he can't see where he's going except on this little screen. It's quite an unusual chase."

For this elaborately staged stunt, Spottiswoode enlisted the aid of ex-world-motocross-champion Dave Bickers. "Dave came up with the perfect vehicle and drives the camera car himself," explained Armstrong. "If you watch him, you can see the professionalism of a guy like that. We decided to go with a new sort of camera vehicle. I asked them to build me the fastest camera car possible. And they did. It's like a car but has loads of suspension so you can have a stabilizer in it to eliminate the vibration, and you just drive as fast as you can. Put two bucket seats in it and harness so people can sit there like dragster drivers and operate the camera. They are all caged, so if the vehicle turns over it is safe. We just have a very fast camera vehicle."

So when Bond's BMW comes racing down the circular ramp and accelerates onto the particular floor, the camera car was waiting for it. "We roar up with it in a straight line, but as we accelerate the BMW slows down, cuts round behind us, and goes away from us," continued Armstrong. "The camera car is going over 60 mph in a multistory car park — and that's traveling. We shot this sequence in the enclosed car park at the Brent Cross Shopping Centre, one of Europe's biggest undercover shopping malls. You can see why Dave Bickers used to win all his races."

The final — and no less daunting — major action sequence involved two seafaring vessels: the British naval frigate *Devonshire*, which is sunk using a metal-grinding sea-drill, and Carver's state-of-the-art stealth ship. "We had the sea-drill bursting through the side of the Royal Navy frigate followed by huge amounts of water," elaborated Corbould. "The three specifically designed sets have allowed us to accomplish this, including the exterior tank at Pinewood Studios. The sea-drill was designed to cut its way through the side of a ship and, once the vessel was sunk, to carry off specific naval weapons. The art department did conceptual drawings, and we pretty much took over from there and made it work using the steering mechanisms, driving the wheels, all those sorts of things."

The full-size interior of the stealth ship was constructed on the 007 stage at Pinewood. And as there weren't any available stealth ships to use as a guideline, it all had to be original design. "The U.S. Navy has one stealth ship at the moment, which has not really been photographed, but of course there's a do-it-yourself model of it in the toy and model shops," laughed Spottiswoode. "We improved on that and used some other sources to build Carver's stealth ship."

"It was great fun to conceive," said Cameron. "The stealth ship was supposed to be at sea, so we built it over water. It was sort of an amalgamation of those. But it didn't look very interesting from a film point of view, so I used elements from the American stealth bomber/fighter and welded them all together with a large chunk of imagination. We built the underside of the ship, with the full-size pontoons, on Pinewood's exterior tank. We also designed a model of the stealth ship which [miniature effects supervisor] John Richardson shot on the tank in Mexico. This was about one-tenth scale but still very big."

The set had to be counterlevered to allow its giant doors to slide into the set, which is built over three stories. There are the doors in the hull, then a gallery, and then another gallery. "It's quite a high set and was made difficult from a construction point of view because it all had to be suspended with a scaffold frame," he explained. "The interior profile of the ship is metal sheeting siding, within which we plant all the detail — such as rockets and other weaponry, a cruise missile in its launcher, and the all-important sea-drill, which plays such an important role in the story."

In its entirety, the set was roughly 150 feet long, 50 feet high, and 60 feet across, on three different levels. It took over 22 weeks to build with a crew of 60 men working continuously, "and then model makers, props, drapes, and everyone else on top of that, so probably about 80 people involved in total," figured Corbould.

The ship comes under shell fire from a British naval frigate, and it is subsequently destroyed by explosions and direct hits that cause several fires to erupt on the three levels of the ship. "We have many explosions in this film. . . . I think we have done about double the amount of pyrotechnics that we did for *Goldeneye*," noted Corbould. "All the way through the film there have been lots and lots of pyrotechnics, whether it be bullet hits or explosions or fires from missile launchers. It has all gone very smoothly, and nobody was hurt, which is always the main consideration no matter how good the effect looks. And all the explosions are real – we don't use CGI – which, as you know, is unusual in this day and age. I just don't think you can beat a real explosion; you get a spontaneity which you certainly don't get from CGI explosions. The reactions from the actors are better if it is all real, as was proved by Pierce, Michelle, and Jonathan when they were right there with the first big explosion on the stealth ship."

✿

TOMORROW NEVER DIES – THE LOCALES

France

The all-important pretitle snow sequences were shot high in the mountains of the French Pyrenees, under the supervision of second unit director Vic Armstrong, making extensive use of one of the few operational high-altitude airfields in Europe. Filming took place in January–February of 1997 to make best use of the snow and ice. Four Czech L39 jet fighters were showcased in this sequence — two on the ground and two in the air.

Bond shoots his way out of trouble in the opening teaser.

The airport location, in the ski resort of Peyresourde, was situated on an exposed ridge and completely surrounded by snow-covered peaks at an altitude of over 5,000 feet. The unit was based in the town of Luchon, nine miles down the mountain, an old thermal bath center which is now a seasonal tourist resort.

The road to the remote mountain location was opened each morning with the help of snowplows and gritters, and a final patrol was back at base by eight o'clock in the evening. When heavy snowfalls were encountered, a convoy procedure had to be adopted, and no single vehicle was permitted access to the location in the dangerously adverse conditions.

A Bang-Up Job: Bond makes his getaway in a L39 jet fighter.

Special effects supervisor Chris Corbould explained the logistics: "We only had six weeks to get that all on the road. We were still importing weapons and explosives from the U.K. and America into France after we started shooting. We had some French pyrotechnics to keep us going in the meantime, but that was how tight it was. There were a lot of explosions and bullet hits during this sequence, which terminated in a massive cruise missile explosion which involved a lot of petrol and dynamite — 300 to 400 gallons of gasoline and several pounds of dynamite."

Thailand

Bond returned to Thailand for the first time since 1974, when *The Man with the Golden Gun* was filmed in Bangkok, Phuket, and on a small remote island off Phang Gna Bay called Ko Phing Kan — which housed

Scaramanga's lair in the 1974 film — and is now internationally known as "James Bond Island," having become a fixture on Thailand's tourist map.

Michelle Yeoh, Pierce Brosnan, and director Roger Spottiswoode on loaction in Thailand.

"We actually prepared to shoot and set the film in Saigon and Hanoi and also found locations on the Vietnamese border with China," explained Spottiswoode. "They were all wonderful and remarkable places, and we spent a week flying up and down Vietnam in a helicopter. That was the most interesting and, finally, the most frustrating, because after giving us permission to shoot in Vietnam they withdrew it. They got scared that there was too much Western influence too quickly. To have so many foreigners come in on such a high-profile enterprise, they lost heart for a while and felt that it was going too fast. So, just three weeks before shooting, we have to find a whole new set of locations . . . which we did in Thailand."

But because Bangkok doubles as Saigon, none of that city's exotic landmarks could be featured in *Tomorrow Never Dies*. The locations eventually selected represented more general but scenic views of Southeast Asia and concentrated more on a Vietnamese look. It was through these dingy streets and across cluttered rooftops that the spectacular motorcycle chase was filmed, with Bond and Wai Lin handcuffed together and astride a BMW R 1200 C motorcycle.

During the four days of filming off the island of Phuket, the cast and crew were based at Nai Yang beach, in the northwest of the island just south of the airport. Most of the filming took place about an hour's journey by speedboat from the Phuket base in the vicinity of "James

Bond Island," which has undergone a remarkable transformation since *The Man with the Golden Gun* filmed there. The narrow sandy beach in front of the rock face is now a mass of market stalls surrounded by tourists seeking bargains and Bond memorabilia.

Germany

The headquarters of Elliot Carver's global media network are based in Hamburg, and many key scenes were filmed in the German city. The most notable scenes were shot at Hamburg International Airport, where Bond is met by Q and given an Avis rental car — a BMW — containing several hidden gadgets, in a nearby street where the car eventually ends up nose first in the Avis outlet window, and around a swanky hotel where Bond revives a past romance with Paris (Teri Hatcher), which proves fatal for his former flame.

Mexico

The Bond model unit, under the supervision of John Richardson, started its seven-week shoot on May 26 at Fox Baja Studios at Rosarito, where 20th Century Fox had built the 40-acre studio facility for James Cameron's *Titanic*. The ocean-front tank is the largest in the world, with an area over 360,000 square feet, and is located three hours from Los Angeles and 20 minutes from the U.S.–Mexican border. A number of key miniature action scenes were staged here for *Tomorrow Never Dies*, including the sinking of the British frigate *H.M.S. Devonshire* and the final battle sequence between Carver's stealth boat and the *H.M.S. Bedford*. Since the cooperation from the Royal Navy back in Britain did not extend to the sinking of a fully equipped missile-bearing frigate, the miniature option was adopted.

U.S.A.

Bond's spectacular HALO jump (high altitude low opening) was performed near Key Largo off the coast of south Florida by longtime

Bond stunt coordinator B.J. Worth and his highly skilled aerial unit. The scene required 007 to jump from a plane above the limit of ground radar and to free-fall for five miles before releasing his parachute below radar detection and hitting the water at 30 miles per hour.

U.K.

Tomorrow Never Dies filmed on several locations in the U.K. — as per usual — with principal locales being Brent Cross in north London (where the car chase was shot in the multilevel parking garage of the Brent Cross Shopping Centre); Portsmouth, where the Royal Navy frigate and the simulated high-tech ship's bridge were featured; and at the USAF bases at Mildenhall and Lakenheath — 70 miles northeast of London, where key scenes were shot with CIA agent Jack Wade and James Bond planning the dangerous mission behind enemy lines.

Mildenhall's hangar 711 was outfitted with a Combat Talon II, MC130 H Hercules to film a parachute jump, and Lakenheath's flight line was transformed into an American air base in Okinawa, where Wade has a secret meeting with Bond, who arrives in an MH-53J Pave Low III helicopter gunship.

Designed for Special Forces use, both the Hercules and the helicopter are the most technically advanced combat infiltration/search-and-rescue and resupply aircraft in the world. The Hercules, built in 1988 and operational since 1992, has seen action in Bosnia, Saudi Arabia, and Afghanistan and is an all-weather-capable plane. The helicopter was the only aircraft capable of inserting Admiral Leighton Smith into fog-shrouded Sarajevo during turnover of Bosnia to IFOR in December 1995. Two MH-53s helicopters were also involved in the rescue attempt of two downed French airmen in Bosnia, and both aircraft sustained combat damage in firefights. The helicopter also saw service in Monrovia, Liberia, and in Albania during the 1997 civil war.

HEIR TO THE BOND LEGACY: MICHAEL WILSON

*Assuming The Reins: Producer
Michael Wilson.*

Deconstructing Bond

Look closely at the past 20 years of Bond films, and you'll see more than just the behind-the-scenes presence of longtime Bond producer Michael Wilson.

In one of the series' long-running in-jokes — à la Alfred Hitchcock — Wilson has popped up in cameo roles in every 007 film since *The Spy Who Loved Me* and even made an appearance in *Goldfinger*, where, as a 21-year old student about to start law school, his stepfather and Bond series creator "Cubby" Broccoli invited him to the Fort Knox location to help as a production assistant. Wilson wound up buying and supplying cases of beer for the nonactor American GIs recruited for the scenes where Pussy Galore's Flying Circus nerve gases the Fort Knox troops into an immediate slumber.

Sitting in his Eon Production office at Pinewood Studios, Wilson laughed recounting his brief moments of on-screen glory. "In *Moonraker*, I'm in the control room looking at the radar screen, and I say, 'It looks like it's 150 meters in diameter!' In *For Your Eyes Only*, I was a Greek Orthodox priest marrying a couple. And in *Goldeneye*, I'm sitting at the Kremlin roundtable as one of the advisers."

His cameo in the 20th 007 outing was still TBD, and Wilson could only say with a smile that "I have to fight for my part every time because the directors are always very reluctant, saying, 'Oh, God! We can't have a *nonactor* in the film.'"

Of course, when you're the film's producer and the driving force behind the Bond legacy, you can pretty much demand as many cameos as you want. Heck, he could even insist on playing Bond himself if he wanted to. "Well, I promise I won't take it that far," he laughed.

The son of Lew Wilson — who played the first film Batman in 1923 — Michael Wilson became part of the Broccoli family when his mother, Dana, married Albert "Cubby" Broccoli in 1960. A native New Yorker, Wilson graduated from college as an electrical engineer with a keen interest in scuba diving and photography. But after his *Goldfinger* sojourn, Wilson went on to study law at Stanford University, later becoming a partner in a prestigious Washington and New York law firm specializing in international taxation.

Wilson ended up joining Eon Productions in a legal-administrative capacity in 1972. But after Broccoli's producing partner, Harry Saltzman, had called it quits after the ninth 007, *The Man with the Golden Gun* in 1974, Broccoli decided he needed someone to help share the producing chores and turned to Wilson for aid in the increasingly complex productions. Wilson became assistant to the producer on *The Spy Who Loved Me* — it became the highest-grossing 007 adventure at the time — and then earned his producing stripes as executive producer on *Moonraker*. He continued in that capacity on the next two Bonds, *For Your Eyes Only* and *Octopussy*, and then served as coproducer with his stepfather on *A View to a Kill*, *The Living Daylights*, and *Licence to Kill*. At the same time, Wilson was taking an increasingly active part in the creative direction of the series as co-screenwriter of the films, starting with *For Your Eyes Only*.

After a six-year absence of Bond, Wilson returned the world's most successful film franchise to the big screen in 1995 with *Goldeneye*, which at the time became the highest-grossing Bond to date, with over $350 million in global box office receipts. Wilson produced the film along with his stepsister, Barbara Broccoli. By that point, Cubby Broccoli at age 86 was in failing health and suffering from fading eyesight, and although he got to view some rushes from *Goldeneye* he didn't live long enough to see the finished film or its overwhelming response from Bond-hungry audiences.

Wilson admitted to me that his stepfather's friendship is deeply missed and his guidance on the Bond series irreplaceable. "We had been working together since 1974, on a daily basis, and in our office we sat across from each other at our desks," Wilson said softly. "He was my mentor and my dearest friend. . . .

"I really miss being able to talk to him and tell him about problems," he continued. "Over the years, he still always took a pretty active role. He came down to Mexico when we were shooting *Licence to Kill*. But what was always nice is you could always call him up and chat and laugh about stuff. Like if we were having a problem with the production, he would laugh and say, 'Oh, we had that problem before on *Thunderball* or something. It was that kind of attitude which was nice. I guess the difference is *I* have to do that now. Part of my function is just to make everyone else feel good and not worry about stuff and help solve their problems."

Wilson admitted he and Barbara Broccoli feel an obligation to carry on the Bond series, partly out of the love for the films, and partly because of their heritage, "but certainly not because of financial necessity," he added.

"I feel the responsibility mostly when I go out or when I go to the location we're shooting, and the press and the public come up, and their enthusiasm is just so overwhelming," related Wilson. "Everywhere you go, people want to know when the next film is coming out and what it's about. I was at dinner not too long ago where three of the waiters — who are always very formal and careful — couldn't contain themselves and were asking me all about Bond and the new film. . . . It's a nice feeling.

"And, you know, you realize that in different ways over 500 million people see the Bond films and have two hours where they can forget their cares and have good escapist entertainment. So that ability to bring that kind of experience to those many people – how can you not do it? I mean, when you think about it, how can you *not* do Bond? So in that sense, I don't look at the obligation as a burden but an opportunity to bring much joy and fun to people."

But Wilson agreed that it's also a duty to keep the series from falling into possible disarray at the hands of someone else. Because if Wilson and Barbara Broccoli ever stopped producing Bond, someone else inevitably would – and this is their family's legacy. "See, that's the thing," explained Wilson. "I don't have much faith in anyone else assuming the reins. There may be people who could do it better, but the way it would probably go there's more opportunity for it to be done worse. And I think all you have to do is look at some of the great writers we bring in and listen to what they pitch us. With the ideas they pitch, believe me, it would be very easy for this thing to go off the rails."

Wilson cited the recurring desire of writers in story ideas to ridicule Bond and his image. "It's almost perverse, and I don't know why," said Wilson, with an incredulous shake of his head. "They love to make him the butt of jokes or make him appear foolish. And that's not Bond. I mean, it's always good to put him at a disadvantage – it makes it more interesting – but there's a difference between being at a disadvantage and being ridiculed."

Wilson laughed, recalling that out of 10 writers – all A-List – who came in and did major pitches after *Goldeneye*, two of them had the same idea: "That Stephen Hawking was the villain, sitting in his wheelchair with his little computer – this is the guy Bond has to fight!" Wilson couldn't help but chuckle recalling those memorable story meetings. "I said, 'Well, after Bond pushes his wheelchair down the stairs, what happens in the fight?' And the other guy with the same idea said, 'Stephen Hawking is the villain *and* he's blind, because Bond blinded him in a previous encounter! So he lives underground in a dark place with no light!' So I said, 'Well, how do we photograph this

Director Roger Spottiswoode and producer Michael Wilson confer before a scene on location in Thailand for Tomorrow Never Dies.

if it takes place in the dark? I mean, these ideas used to work well in *radio*, but for the movies???'"

After so many years of involvement with the Bond films, Wilson said that at pitch meetings he can predict virtually every idea that new writers will present to him. Among the ones he usually gets are Goldfinger's son or daughter as the villain, as well as the melting of the polar ice caps. "It's always the same ideas, and after a while you've basically heard them all. So you sit there and listen and realize that you have to really do it yourself from the ground up," said Wilson. "That's why I spent four months with Bruce Feirstein (who was brought on board with *Goldeneye* and also helped script *Tomorrow Never Dies* and *The World Is Not Enough*), because you have to really invent it yourself. Most writers seem to be cliché-ridden. I mean, maybe we've done so many that it's harder to come up with new ideas. But they need to realize that you start out with a strong villain and a caper, and everything else follows.

"See, the problem is everyone remembers the things they liked best about the Bond films — so they bring back Jaws or bring in Goldfinger's daughter — and they figure, 'Well, if it worked once, it'll work again.' But we try to stay away from that because that's a trap. It's an easy way out."

The bottom line, he contends, is that "It should be fun to think up the ideas but difficult to achieve them, because otherwise," explained Wilson, "*everybody* would be doing these films."

Of course, when James Bond came onto the scene in the '60s, he was practically the only game in town. Action adventure had never been so fantastic. But these days, with big-budget actioners opening almost every week, how does 007 keep the edge over the competition? "As far as I can tell, we are still the only real action adventure films, with the sort of suave, European-style leading man," offered Wilson. "We try to paint on a big canvas — he's underwater, he's mountain climbing, he's in the jungle, he's in the snow, he's in the urban environment — it takes you to countless locales. It's a structure which keeps the picture moving and interesting. That's always been our trademark component. And Bond's a different kind of guy too — action heroes are always blue-collar guys with only one T-shirt in their closet. Bond is far more sophisticated with a real brutal side underneath."

In the six-year absence between 1989's *Licence to Kill* and 1995's *Goldeneye*, there was constant speculation about a major retooling of the Bond series for today's audiences. There were those who felt the premise had grown tired and too familiar, with a complete reinvention necessary to prevent a repeat of the lackluster performance of *Licence to Kill*. Rumors abounded of turning the next Bond adventure into a comedy or bringing Schwarzenegger or Stallone into the role, or even turning Bond into a woman, with Sharon Stone assuming the lead. But Wilson insisted all those stories were completely false; he would never mess with a proven formula and a trademark as indelible as 007.

"The thing about James Bond is he's an identifiable character on the order of Sherlock Holmes, Batman, Superman, and Tarzan. He's one of those fictitious characters who is now part of our modern mythology. And you can't make him into something else. He's an established character."

Wilson says he breathed a giant sigh of relief when the triumphant box office results for *Goldeneye* proved him correct. "It was very gratifying," he demurred. But in the days leading up to the release, Wilson says he wasn't wracked by nerves. "You're really too exhausted by that point to be nervous," he smiled. "You're always running on empty by the time the film comes out. . . . You can only hope that the audience likes it. But no, we didn't know *Goldeneye* would be so successful. . . . You can never predict that sort of thing." Though *Goldeneye* was deemed the highest-grossing Bond by that point, Wilson was quick to point out that there are too many variables to accurately compare current box office receipts with those from forty years ago. "For instance," he explained, "in 1962, the U.S. theatrical take counted for 50% of the entire gross box office in the world. But with *Goldeneye* in 1995, the U.S. box office accounted for only 10% of the gross worldwide film rentals. So how do you compare those two things? I mean, the market has changed so much."

Analyzing the box office trajectory of the Bond films, Wilson says it breaks down to peaks and valleys. "It went through a very steep increase through *Thunderball*, sort of leveled out with *You Only Live Twice*, then dipped drastically for [George] Lazenby. Then it came back with *Diamonds Are Forever*, and then the first Roger Moore films were okay but didn't really take off until *The Spy Who Loved Me* and *Moonraker*. Then it dipped again, and then it went up with *Octopussy* and then dipped again. With Timothy [Dalton], it went up a little bit but then went down. And with Pierce, it went way up again."

And from a creative standpoint, Wilson feels that, once Pierce

Brosnan assumed the role, more opportunities suddenly opened up to explore the character of Bond. "Pierce has brought a dimension of vulnerability which I think is really good," he said. "It gives us some added areas for the scriptwriting. He plays the humor well, which is good, and he plays the action stuff well. And he can be really tough when he needs to be."

But Wilson is also concerned about not revealing too much behind Bond's mystique. "We've had [questions] from certain actors, like 'Where does Bond actually live? How is his place furnished?' But Bond is a civil servant — he can't really be in a lavish country house. Do you really want to see a place with the laundry piled up in the corner? He's more a guy who lives in grand hotels on his expense account playing some kind of undercover role. It may be interesting for the actor to explore the other side of Bond's life, but the question is 'Is it interesting for the public?' You have to keep that in mind. Bond is much more interesting not shown at home with empty soup cans on the counter."

With the collapse of the Soviet Union and the Cold War defrosted, Wilson admitted it has become increasingly difficult to create formidable opponents and missions worthy of Bond's talents and legacy as the preeminent MI6 secret agent. "We wrestle with that all the time," revealed Wilson. "Every time we sit down, we start out by saying, 'We're going to make a picture like *From Russia with Love* — mystery, intrigue, the plot and structure fairly specific and confined — and we always end up with *Thunderball* by the end of the process. It just always seems that, whenever you write something, someone always says, 'Oh, that's not big enough for Bond.' So it always comes down to the lives of hundreds of thousands — if not millions — of people have to be at risk. That always seems to be the necessary ingredient for these things, and it makes it difficult to write. So, in a way, the stories have a sense of sameness because of those types of elements, but it seems to be the inevitable situation."

THE PRYCE OF EVIL: JONATHAN PRYCE INTERVIEW

Over-Pryced: Jonathan Pryce goes big as media giant Elliot Carver.

Jonathan Pryce is remarkably calm and composed for someone who's going to die in a matter of minutes. Five months into the shoot of *Tomorrow Never Dies*, Pryce is finally facing the inevitable fate that awaits every villain who dares to tangle with James Bond. Dressed in an all black, sharply tailored Kenzo suit, Pryce's megalomaniacal media mogul character Elliot Carver is about to be impaled by a giant sea-vac drill for the film's final showdown with Bond.

Pryce had long been a personal favorite of producer Barbara Broccoli, who was eager to cast the Tony and Olivier Award-winning actor in a Bond film. With an immensely diverse body of work on stage (*Miss Saigon, The Comedians, Hamlet, Accidental Death of an Anarchist*) and on screen (*Brazil, Glengarry Glen Ross, The Adventures of Baron Munchausen, Evita* [as President Juan Peron opposite Madonna in the title role], and *Carrington* [for which he won Best Actor honors at the 1995 Cannes Film Festival for his portrayal of Lytton Strachey], Pryce had distinguished himself as one of Britain's most versatile and compelling actors.

The enormous 007 soundstage — housing the hull of Carver's state-of-the-art stealth battleship — is abuzz with early morning activity in preparation for filming the explosive climax. But Pryce remains rather contemplative amidst the frenetic maneuverings around him as his grisly demise is being mapped out by director Roger Spottiswoode mere steps away. In fact, Pryce admits the lengthy and often strenuous shoot hasn't been daunting in the least for him. "Depending on traffic, I'm only about a half hour from home, so it's been very comfortable for me," smiled Pryce. "My scenes have been spaced out, so I've had periods where I've been off for a couple weeks. It's a rather relaxed way of working, actually, because I keep coming back to the role refreshed and ready to have fun with it all again. I suppose if I had been living and breathing Elliot Carver every day for five months it might have been a little wearing."

So what has the whole Bond experience been like for you?
"It's been very good indeed. I've really enjoyed it. It's been quite extraordinary, really. You could make a lot of money just giving guided tours around this set. My children normally never visit me on sets, but they've visited these sets more times than I can count. My kids absolutely adored *Goldeneye*, and their response to that probably had a lot to do with my accepting the role."

After having done so much acclaimed theater work, what's the difference in portraying such a larger-than-life villain in a larger-than-life film franchise?
"You get a lot more money, that's for sure! And I think partly why I'm enjoying it is a chance to give a performance which is the kind of size of character you would normally only do in the theater. You know, coming from the Macbeths and the Richard IIIs, to be this kind of charming yet evil man is a lot of fun to do. It's not often you can play something with that kind of range in a character. That very theatrical element. And, at times, it can be very theatrical, and I've personally worried that maybe I've gone over the top a bit, but it's the kind of character who has very intense private thoughts and private moments. He has a public face that is very charming and, hopefully, very believable to the public in that what he's doing with his satellite

communications are not to make money but for the benefit of mankind. And then there's another side of him which is this gleeful villain, alone in large rooms, talking to people on banks of video screens. So I'm having a ball, really."

Some of your speeches in the film are pretty lengthy in terms of dialogue.
"Yes, well, I think they'll chop them up with a bit of fighting in between. But the words are very important to this character. He's someone who is in the communications business — both satellite broadcasting and print — so words are important. I mean, I've noticed that, if you look at the old Bond villains, there was a lot of dialogue. In *Goldfinger*, there was a 12-minute scene on the golf course. So we have tried to introduce that again. A richness in Carver's language and the way he says things, and I think Bruce [Feirstein] has done a very good job in that."

What did you bring to the character of Elliot Carver that wasn't necessarily apparent in the script?
"When the character is written as large and richly as this is written, in many ways it seemed fairly obvious what sort of guy he was. And we had a few months evolving the character. . . . It's very important how he looks, because in a film like this you need a single image that is very telling. And we went through a number of changes with Lindy Hemming, the costume designer. Starting off in kind of these lounge suits, and . . . if you look at Rupert Murdoch — although the character isn't based on him per se — he's fairly ordinary looking. He's probably got a hundred versions of the same business suit. And you could go that way, but for a Bond film that's a fairly intellectual approach to a character. So we've evolved a fairly vivid, or a fairly exciting, look for him — it's quite out of the ordinary in a way. It's a shame when I have to take the wig off before I go home, actually."

There are the obvious comparisons between Elliot Carver and Rupert Murdoch or Ted Turner. Have you heard any similar remarks about this film?

"No, but one would hope they would have a sense of humor, and it would amuse them. But what attracted me to the part was that it's based in a great deal of truth, not necessarily about Murdoch or Turner, but the truth of what their potential is or people like them. That potential to control the information. And, as we all know historically, if you control information, you control the people. That's what Carver is interested in. And the reality it's based in are the dangers of potentially putting the sources of information in the hands of one man."

What was the original pitch when they approached you for this film?

"It was very straightforward, actually. There was initial interest, and so I asked to read the script. I did that and said yes almost right away. It wasn't a long process. You kind of know what kind of film you're going into. You're not saying, 'Well, what kind of film are you going to make?' You already know the kind of film you're going to make, and you hope they're going to make a very good version of a Bond film. And why wouldn't they want to? Coming from *Goldeneye*, they made great advances with that film in presenting Bond in a very up-to-date, modern way so it would continue to find a new audience. If you look at those advances, and then with this film, they are building on the strides they've already made with *Goldeneye*."

Were you a fan of the Bond films?

"I wouldn't say I was a fan, but I enjoyed them. But I suppose I would've been a fan when I was much younger. I especially liked Connery, and I think Pierce is closer to that kind of thing that Connery did. I think Pierce does a great job."

Pressing The Flesh: Michelle Yeoh, Jonathan Pryce, and Götz Otto.

Does being on the set of a Bond film make you feel like a little kid all over again?
"Oh, absolutely! I've watched people who have visited, and it's exactly as you describe it. You see these serious, mature businessmen suddenly turn into children. It's very amusing. I would guess it would be like on the Universal Studios tour for a lot of people. And it's greatly enhanced by the fact that it's James Bond. And I have to say, it's great to be the villain, just to be able to utter the line '*So, Mister Bond. . . .*' The villains do say '*Mister Bond*' a lot in the films. You actually get so hooked on saying it that I kept finding myself wanting to add it to the beginning of every sentence!"

Is there a trepidation in accepting the role of a Bond villain?
"I suppose there's a slight fear that you can't be as good as the last villain or any of the previous ones. Lots of people have their favorite Bond villains, and you're judged by previous villains. I suppose I assessed this character as a character within its own right and tried not to compare it to past villains and whether it stood up as a character in itself. And I think it does."

Do you have a favorite Bond villain? One that always intrigued you?
"I liked Goldfinger. And I've just watched it again on tape, and he had some really good lines. Like when Bond says, 'You expect me to talk?' and Goldfinger says, 'No, Mister Bond, I expect you to *die*!' Stuff like

that is very good. Of course, it shouldn't be surprising, but it's like a cat and mouse: the villains always allow Bond to live just one too many times to play with him, and then he always wins in the end."

What scene was the most fun to shoot?
"I felt like a kid in a toy shop for the scene where I address all the video screens of my heads of departments around the world. That was a lot of fun to do. And just being part of all the technology is fun."

What changes struck you about these new Bonds compared to 10 or 15 years ago?
"They seem much more sophisticated. If you look at the older ones, there's still a sense that it's a bit kitsch. It's difficult to say because I think they belonged in their time. Nobody thought they were a bit odd at the time, but when you look back at them some of them look rather dated. And it's just the look of it. I haven't seen very much finished footage, but I see quite a lot on the playback monitors on set, and the look of it is very exciting, and it doesn't look like the '70s. And I think some of the ones before *Goldeneye* were showing their age a bit. But now the special effects are quite extraordinary, and the technology is up there with the best of it."

After you signed on, the script went through a number of changes, and the Elliot Carver character started evolving into something else.
"Yes, well, what happened is, if you don't stay with the original writer who has conceived that character — which happens a lot on Holly-wood films — then you get new writers on who don't know what the original impulse was to create the character of Carver. And you don't have Bruce's experience working within a large news organization and don't realize how pertinent the way Carver says things is. And then you get new writers in, and it develops and changes, and he suddenly becomes an *all-purpose* villain. He can say anything and do anything.

But what was good about the original is he says or does things because he's a press baron. He speaks in a particular way and reacts to people in a particular way. And that's what had disappeared, but fortunately they ended up going back to the original script, and it's all back in. I was very happy about that. And it was worrying to me at the time because you think the public perception is that it's a difficult film, or 'I hear it's not very good,' and that's absolutely not the case."

What is the key to playing a good villain, particularly in a Bond film?
"The key is in the writing, plain and simple. I don't feel as if I'm doing anything special other than — and I'm not trying to sound too pompous about it — but other than being as truthful as possible to the character."

Does Elliot Carver know he's evil?
"Oh, yeah. And he enjoys it. What is wonderful about a character like this, unlike say Lytton Strachey in *Carrington*, where I was playing a real character based on research, there were constraints. They were very creative constraints, but you would always have to examine how straight you would react in this situation, what the truth of the situation was. But you come to somebody like Elliot Carver, this all-mighty, all-powerful being who creates his own logic. There are no rules. He creates his own rules. Everyone who surrounds him will say yes to him. And as an actor, you can indulge it. And as a character, he indulges it as well. He knows no one is going to cross him, and when they do cross him, like Teri Hatcher's character — my wife, Paris — when there is a hint that she has betrayed me, she's gone. She's dead."

How tricky is it when you're playing the villain in a Bond film to not go too far over the top but also not underplay it either?
"I think the beauty of this character is that there are moments when you can underplay it and be fairly subtle. But when I shot the scenes

where I address my heads of departments on the screens, I think I did get pretty extravagant. I mean, this set is just so huge — it covers the entire soundstage with all these hundreds of monitors — and there's just me reacting to hundreds of video images. And it could get very theatrical and over the top. I did worry about that. We spent a day shooting it, and I got home, and the first thing I said to my wife, Kate, was 'I think I overdid it today.' And I went in to see Roger [Spottiswoode] the next day and said, 'I'm a bit worried about yesterday,' and he said, 'No, no, no — it's wonderful! Something that has the size of a Bond film will absorb large performances.'"

What is your take on Pierce as Bond?
"I think he's very good. It must be a very strange position to be in, to be James Bond. But I think he handles that side of it very well. And I enjoy being with him. He's good company, and he's good to work with. I'm really enjoying it. I mean, he's not as good a kisser as Madonna, but apart from that. . . ."

⊘

THE ONE-TWO PUNCH: MICHELLE YEOH

When Roger Spottiswoode's young nephews first heard he was going to direct the latest Bond film, "they immediately called me and said, 'Go out and see some Hong Kong movies. There's this extraordinary woman who has done some films with Jackie Chan, and she should be in it,'" recalled Spottiswoode.

That woman was Michelle Yeoh, and her physical prowess was indeed extraordinary. Legendary. In Asia, Yeoh was the highest-paid and most popular female star in Hong Kong's almost exclusively male-dominated action cinema. With her dazzling dexterity, fists of fury, and gravity-defying leaps, Yeoh transformed the image of the female action star from accessory to avenger, from sidekick to ass-kicker.

Fists Of Fury: Michelle Yeoh as Wai Lin.

From her first starring role as a Hong Kong cop in 1985's *Yes, Madam,* to such cult classics as *Heroic Trio, T'ai Chi Master, Police Story III: Supercop*, to 2000's Oscar-nominated and internationally acclaimed *Crouching Tiger, Hidden Dragon*, Yeoh has brought a stellar elegance and grace to her lethal martial arts mastery. And it's no wonder, since Yeoh's roots are not as a fighter but as a ballerina.

Raised in Malaysia by her ethnic Chinese, English-speaking parents, Yeoh pursued a career in dance from an early age, eventually earning an advanced-level degree in ballet from London's Royal Academy of Dance and a B.A. in creative arts. Upon her return home in 1983, Yeoh was crowned Miss Malaysia and a year later was invited to Hong Kong to shoot a commercial with Jackie Chan. An instant hit, Yeoh quickly became the most-sought-after new star in the industry, making her film debut in 1985's action comedy *Owls V. Dumbo.* But it would be her next film, *Yes, Madam,* that firmly established the five-foot-four powerhouse as Hong Kong's highest-kicking heroine, earning her the nickname of "the female Bruce Lee." And as Wai Lin, a spy from the Peoples External Security Force – China's MI6 – in *Tomorrow Never Dies*, Yeoh happily embraced her new moniker as "the female James Bond."

It's now the end of August, and you've been shooting since April — this must be the longest film shoot you've been involved with.
"Oh, yes! You know, in Hong Kong, the average film shoot only lasts three weeks. So this has been quite an experience. And it's not over yet. I still have another month left. But it's been fabulous, I must say.

The crew has been amazing, and Pierce is an absolute delight to work with. Everyone in the cast has been a joy to work with, from Jonathan Pryce to Götz Otto. And luckily Pierce is such a sweet guy, because we've been handcuffed together for so much of the film. And whenever we're not working, we go out and go for a meal and party. And because I'm so far away from home, Barbara [Broccoli] and Michael [Wilson] always make sure I'm okay. So it's been a warm feeling with everyone. It's just been a little long."

The helicopter sequence through the streets of Bangkok must have been quite difficult to shoot.
"Oh, yes. We've finished most of it, and it looks quite amazing so far. When they first told us how the sequence was going to play out, we were like, 'Yeah, sure!' I thought they would just CGI everything or do it all blue screen. But I was very surprised to find out we were going to be doing it all for real. It was pretty awesome. But I do think [stunt director] Vic Armstrong is completely mad!"

How much has Roger's directing style influenced the mood and look of this film?
"Oh, totally. If you think about it, the director is like the soul of the film. You sometimes have a lousy script, but if you have a great director something will come out of it or vice versa. So the director definitely affects the mood of the crew, of the people. He's always trying to bring the best out of the artists, and Roger has certainly done wonders for me. He's really helped me tremendously, because I'm very used to doing action movies. And because of that, you're always thinking 'Okay, I have to get my energy going,' and sometimes you forget about the beats or the dynamic between the characters. Roger has been very good in bringing that out in me. He's not an aggressive director; he doesn't shout or scream on set. He's very quiet. So it's good to work with someone like that."

Roger has also brought a more moody, darker look to this Bond film.
"Yes, very much so. I think the ambience and the whole feel of the movie is more realistic with Roger. Like the specific lighting and the way the shadows create the characters. And if you think about it, it's the first time in a Bond movie where the woman plays such a strong role in that way. So Roger has brought a big difference to the Bond movies."

How did they originally propose this film to you?
"Well, it's funny, but about two years ago, around the time that *Goldeneye* was such a big hit, I started going over to the States because of my manager, Terrence Chang, and Chris Godsick, who is John Woo's producer, said to me, 'You know, I think it's a good time for you to come out to the States. John [Woo] is doing exceedingly well, and you speak English, so it's time you should broaden your horizons and not just stay in Hong Kong.' So when I came out to L.A., we set up meetings with producers and directors so that people would start to get to know my work and things like that. One of the people I met was Jeff Cleeman, a producer from L.A., and he was one of the producers on *Goldeneye* as well as this movie. So he was the one who brought me in, who suggested me in the first place. Two years ago, he said to me, 'You know, you would be perfect in a Bond movie,' and at that time my managers and myself were saying 'Wouldn't it be great to be in a Bond movie — I could just see myself doing all those things in a Bond movie!' And then last year, I think it was August when they first started planning and working on this movie, Jeff called up and said, 'I think it could be happening — we've started working on the script, and we have a director who is very much for a woman of the '90s, who will play a part on par with Bond. And not just in looks but in the action sequences and all that.' So he mentioned my name at a meeting, and one of the writers said they knew my work as well and how I did all this great action stuff. So it sort of happened from there. And then in October, I met up with Michael [Wilson] and the casting director,

and then two days later I met with Barbara [Broccoli] and Roger Spottiswoode, and I think the character sort of grew from there."

Then how soon after did they actually say, 'You're hired'?
"Oh, God, I think that is what took the longest! That was something I was completely not used to, because in Hong Kong we work very, very quickly. I would be talking to a director, and in two weeks we would be shooting already. And in Hong Kong, there's no such thing as screen testing and all these kinds of things, because everybody knows everybody. But when I first met Michael and the casting director and then everybody else in Milan, we were still talking about the project and the script. Because at that point, the script hadn't been completely done yet, and you can't really say you're going to do a movie until you see the script — it could be something completely different from what they had verbally. So I think it was only by Christmas when my agent started talking to the producers, and finally they said, 'We know you're the one.' And then I had to do a screen test with Pierce. And Pierce, fortunately, I met the night before, and he was such a sweetheart. Even though they told me not to think of it as a screen test, you know a lot is riding on this. The studio didn't know who I was, and they wanted to see what Pierce and I looked like together on the screen. And he really helped me through that, so I was very lucky. And then I think it wasn't until the end of January before they actually said, 'Yes — you're coming out in April.' It was a very long process. The period of waiting for a yes or no was the most harrowing part. But I'm glad it was a yes, and I'm glad I'm here."

How much did the script change from when you first signed on?
"It changed quite a bit. But the general outline is there. Now, we're sort of changing lines to make them better for the character. Because as characters start to develop and the whole movie starts evolving, things have to change to make it better, and that's what's going on right now. It's a little strange."

How would you describe your character Wai Lin?

"She's exactly the equivalent of Bond, only she's Asian. She's a spy from China, basically. England sends 007, and China sends me. She's very much like Bond. When they first meet, she's like, 'I work alone, and I really don't need you around,' and he's like 'I work alone too — what are you doing here?' And we grow to respect each other's work and decide to work together. But not by choice at first."

What do you think you've brought to the character that wasn't in the script?

"That's a good question. I think I brought a chemistry between Pierce and myself! Actually, I brought a great Hong Kong team. I brought action sequences that normally you would not see in a Bond movie. We brought in a Hong Kong stunt coordinator named Philip Kwok. He's worked extensively with John Woo and was in fact in *Hardboiled*, playing the assassin. In fact, a lot of John Woo's action sequences were done by Philip. He's a very well-known and well-respected stunt coordinator and actor in Hong Kong. Because of the kind of action I do, the studio understood that you needed the right people to do that. And who would understand that better than to have the team from Hong Kong come here? And it worked out fabulously. So there's a real surprise for Bond fans."

Most actors in Hollywood will claim that they do their own stunts for a film. But in your case, it's actually true.

"Yeah, I would say almost everything was done by me. All the fight sequences, everything. There were just a couple stunts on the bike, though, that Barbara and Michael just would not let us do, and I can understand that. Because if anything happens to you, then the movie will stall. I had a very bad accident in one of my previous movies, so it's something I understand and know that I can't afford to be injured like that. But apart from that, I did everything else.

Walk This Way: Michelle Yeoh defies gravity.

But you know what? It's really not good for actors who don't know what they're doing, and not properly trained, to do their own stunts. Even fight scenes should be done by professionals."

What was your worst injury?
"It was in *The Story of the Sun Woman*. We were shooting a sequence where I jumped off this highway bridge onto a moving truck going underneath the bridge about 50 feet below. And we'd done the long shot, which went fine. But when we came to do the medium shot, I think I lost my focus or something. Because when I was pushed off, I went forward and I basically did a nosedive onto the boxes on the truck. The first thing I heard was my neck crack and my head going back. And because of the angle I was coming down, my legs came from behind me and sort of hit my head. I heard my back just snap! It felt like two planks of wood just smacking together. I immediately thought, 'This is it, Michelle! You've had your last dive!'

I ended up being in the hospital for two weeks, but I was so lucky because, when I was wheeled into the hospital, the doctors were amazed that I didn't break any of my vertebrae or discs. I'm so thankful I didn't end up permanently damaged in any way. It was a nightmare for months afterwards. That was not a very happy time."

Did that make you reconsider what you would attempt in future films?
"When I was taking that ride into the hospital, all I could think was 'If

they tell me I'll never walk again, what am I going to do?' We were only about three weeks into shooting and still had another month left, and there I was in the hospital. All I could think was 'How are we going to complete this movie?' But the good thing is you learn to be very calm in these kinds of moments.

However, the worst part was I had to go back and reshoot that sequence all over again because it wasn't finished. I tried to look at it like riding a horse, that if you fall off you have to get back on again and get it out of your system. I'm glad I faced that again.

It's funny, because now in Hong Kong, if the insurers see my name or Jackie Chan's attached to a film, they won't insure us!"

What was the most dangerous stunt for Tomorrow Never Dies*?*
"The level of safety precautions is so good here, they would never let you go near anything that's remotely dangerous. Everything around you is well taken care of when you get up to do it. The hardest work I had to do would have been the action sequences that I did with my Hong Kong stunt team, because it was really intense hand-to-hand combat fighting. The bicycle shop sequence was probably the hardest. Normally, in Hong Kong, we break up our sequences — because, if you don't, you're going to be dead before you reach the end. Here, I'm fighting like five different guys, and you're trying to remember all these moves and get the same intensity with every single punch that you take. It's very, very tiring. That was probably the hardest work that I had to do. But being on the bike, and doing all these stunts, it's been a good learning experience.

I have to say, though, the one action sequence that was really tough on Pierce and me was where we jump out of Carver's head-quarters and slide down the banner on the side of the building, which is 30 stories high. Those were some rough moments."

It is a pretty spectacular stunt.

"Oh, yeah. I definitely think Pierce's shoulder is two inches longer now as a result! I mean, we were on cables, and you really have to work with the stunt coordinator, because once you go up on those cables you're on your own basically. So, you know, you have to find ways to make it look like you're just hanging there by yourself, without trying to really yank your hand off. And there is just that fine line of depending on that cable and making it look like you're hanging by the cable. Because if you change your position, however slightly, you would know we're not really hanging there. So you really have to let it go and let your shoulder support your weight. And the first time, I have to admit, I was really scared. You're coming down at such a fast speed, but then after a few times both of us got used to it. And we ended up having to do it at least 30 times. But with these types of stunts, practice does make perfect. The first time you do it, you're not quite sure, but by the 10th take we were dancing and singing up there!"

How was shooting on location in Thailand?

"Very, *very* hot! And when you're out on rooftops and riding around on bikes and on the streets, it gets very exhausting. Especially in Bangkok, there's so much traffic and congestion. But we had a great time, and we had a really nice boat when we were out in the ocean shooting. And every day on the way back to shore, we would party up a storm. When you're location shooting, all of you are thrown together as a group, so you all hang out together and get to know each other a lot better. You really bond . . . so to speak."

If Wai Lin got into a real fight with James Bond, who would win?

"Oh, definitely Bond would win . . . actually, I'd *let* him win!"

Were you a big fan of the Bond films growing up?

"You know, I don't know anybody who hasn't seen a Bond movie. It's

Slow Boat To China: Wai Lin and Bond go low-tech to evade radar detection in enemy waters.

something that is always a part of your life, and every time a new one comes out you have to see it, because it's the thing people will be talking about for the next two months. I'm a big fan of Sean Connery's. He was a dashing Bond."

So he's your favorite Bond?
"Well, apart from Pierce, of course!"

Do you have a favorite Bond film?
"*For Your Eyes Only* is one of them. *Dr. No* is one of them, and so is *Goldeneye*. But, of course, *Tomorrow Never Dies* will probably be the best!"

What were you expecting when you first started working with Pierce?
"I really didn't know what to expect. I was already so nervous about the fact that I had to be doing this screen test thing. But it was good because Barbara [Broccoli] organized this dinner before the shoot the next day, so we had met under very relaxed conditions. Pierce is such a very sweet guy, very down-to-earth. He had no airs about him and he's not full of himself. He's joking with you, he's laughing with you, and he makes you feel like 'Let's just go out there and have a good time.' And I love people like that. It gives you a great feeling that you're with a good guy, and you feel safe."

You have to admit Pierce personifies Bond, even when the cameras aren't rolling.
"Oh, yeah. But that's really him. He's very charismatic, he's suave . . . and then suddenly he can turn into this nutty Irishman, which is great fun to watch."

And what's Jonathan Pryce been like to work with?
"He's different. He's quieter, but he's got a wicked sense of humor too.

It's nice to have those differences on a set, because everyone can then bounce off each other. Half the time we feel like we're in a party scene. And just to watch Jonathan work as an actor is breathtaking. He has these amazing speeches, which, when you read the script, are such mouthfuls. But when he says them, you're completely mesmerized. Even when I wasn't in a scene, I'd still go to the set, just to watch him do his stuff. And you learn a lot from these people who have worked so hard to be where they are today and yet still be so human. It's fabulous."

Usually, the really strong women in the Bond films turn out to be the villains, but you are the exception to that.
"You don't have to be a bitch just because you're strong. But I think also the producers recognize that the audience is changing, and they're much more sophisticated, and they want to deal with women who are strong. Every day around you in working life is like that, so why not on the big screen, where we are dealing with issues of society today and characters that surround us? And also I think it makes Bond a man of the '90s, going into the next millennium. I loved it that M is now played by Dame Judi Dench. It's about time! And now this fully endorses Bond as a man of the '90s who is strong and confident about who he is, and he doesn't have worries about working with a woman."

What's been the reaction back home to your new role? Have you been able to gauge that yet?
"The reaction has been tremendous. First of all, to have a local girl in an international movie — a *Bond movie* — that's been a tradition and everybody knows of and loved for so many years, it's a big accomplishment. It's like, '*Yessss!*' We should have that effort where both sides work together a lot more often. And the women back home are also very proud and very excited too, because Asian women still do

have this stereotype of what Asian women should be like. They should be demure and stay at home. But there are a lot of Asian women who are not like that, who are entrepreneurs and successful business-women. So this is a good opportunity for them to see themselves recognized, and you can't top being on par with James Bond!"

Have you kept any souvenirs from Tomorrow Never Dies*?*
"We kept the handcuffs! Pierce and I both have a set of our own hand-cuffs. It's a nice reminder of all the time we spent chained together."

The World Is Not Enough

Retreating to his dressing room on the Pinewood Studios set of *The World Is Not Enough*, Pierce Brosnan is still trying to catch his breath after just completing a *harrowing* morning of love scenes with costar Denise Richards.

"It's a tough job, but *somebody's* gotta do it," quips Brosnan with a devilish smile as he towels down, exchanging his crisply tailored wardrobe for a more comfortable pair of jeans and black T-shirt. He stretches back on the sofa, fires up a Marlboro Light, and exhales an audible sigh of satisfaction on this, his third outing as the supersmooth superspy. But even with Denise Richards and French beauty Sophie Marceau, Brosnan admitted that bedding a Bond babe isn't always as easy as it looks. "It's been a load of fun with Denise," explained Brosnan, "but then a few weeks ago I was in bed with Sophie, and it was all so excruciatingly technical. We couldn't show any nipples, but that's *all* that kept showing. And it was on the same day that the Columbine school massacre took place. So here are all these kids buying guns and killing their schoolmates, and here we are on the Bond movie worrying about a *nipple* showing. So, 18 takes later, you're still trying to do this love scene and make it look spontaneous because of censorship

EON PRODUCTIONS LTD.
"THE WORLD IS NOT ENOUGH"
Location, Pinewood Road, Iver Heath, Bucks. SL0 0NH   Tel: 01753 70   Fax: 01753 70
Mobile on set: Paul Taylor (2nd A.D.): 0374 25

1st UNIT

PRODUCERS:	Michael Wilson	CALLSHEET NO.	68
	Barbara Broccoli		
		DATE:	Monday 26 April 1999
DIRECTOR:	Michael Apted	UNIT CALL:	08.00
		Breakfast avail.from:	07.30

LOCATIONS: 1) A Stage   2) Backlot behind 007 Stage Pinewood Studios, Pinewood Rd, Iver, Bucks, England
Weather: Sunny spells with showers in the afternoon. Light SW winds (10 mph). Max.temp. 16 deg.C

UNIT NOTES
PLEASE REFER TO RISK ASSESSMENTS PREVIOUSLY ISSUED

**KEITH HAMSHERE WILL BE SHOOTING STILLS ON ELEKTRA'S VILLA SETS ON C STAGE -
PLEASE RE-DRESS AND CLEAR EQUIPMENT**

**PLEASE NOTE REVISED SCRIPT PAGES ISSUED FRIDAY 23.4.99
IF YOU HAVE NOT RECEIVED YOUR COPIES, PLEASE CONTACT PRODUCTION OFFICE**

Set / Synopsis	Sc. No's	D/N	Pgs	Cast
Location 1				
1) EXT./INT. BALCONY / PENTHOUSE	326, 328	Night	5/8	1. 6.
(Bond & Christmas cuddling / satellite watching them)				
2) INT. SNOW HOLE	99pt	Day	2/8	1. 3.
(Bond digs a way out)				
Location 2				
3) EXT. MOUNTAINS	100pt	Day	1/8	1. 3.
(They escape into the light)				

ID Artiste	Character	D/R	P/Up	M/Up	On Set
1. Pierce Brosnan	Bond	F.71	07.00	08.00	As req.
6. Denise Richards	Christmas	F.74.	06.45	07.30	As req.
3. Sophie Marceau	Elektra	F.68	10.00	11.00	As req.

Stand-ins			
Dean Taylor	Bond		08.00
Emma Stokes	Christmas / Elektra		08.00

REQUIREMENTS

Art / Props   As per script to incl. all artiste personal props: bed / couch etc., candles etc., caviar, champagne and glasses, net curtains, Bond's knife in sheath, Bond's & Elektra's ski's, poles etc.

Camera / Grip   As per Adrian Biddle.

Costume   As per Lindy Hemming.

Dialogue Coach   Sandra Frieze to s/by on set from 11.00

Electrical   As per Kevin Day.

Fire / Safety   As per David Deane.

Original cast and crew call sheets from The World Is Not Enough.

Make-Up / Hair — As per Linda DeVetta and Colin Jamison and Bron Roylance and Rick Provenzano.

Medical — Unit Nurse (Lesley Quinn) to s/by on set from 08.00

Sound — As per Chris Munro

Special FX — As per Chris Corbould

Stills — As per Keith Hamshere. Stills shooting on C stage on Elektra's Villa sets

Video — As per Stephen Lee

Visual FX — As per Mara Bryan. Green screen req'd for scenes 326, 328

Catering — Via Busters. Breakfast avail. from 07.30. Lunch at 13.00. PM break at 16.30 for 140 people, please.

Facilities — 1 x Trailer for Mr Brosnan on Backlot by 007 Stage ready from 10.30
1 x Prowler for Ms Marceau on Backlot by 007 Stage ready from 10.30

Rushes — Rushes (picture) to Timekeepers Gate for collection by Deluxe Labs. Sound to Cutting Rooms via Sound Dept. Rushes viewing in Theatre 7 at lunchtime today. Note: Rushes of Maiden's Tower - Istanbul shots to be shown please for matching re. Tuesday's shooting

ADVANCE SCHEDULE - Subject to Artistes' availability.....

Tuesday 27 April 1999 - Late Call for Dusk Shots
BLACK PARK LOC. - a.m.

EXT./INT. BOND'S BMW	66B, 66C, 66D, 67	Day	4/8	1.

PINEWOOD - p.m. - F Stage / Backlot

EXT. MAIDEN'S TOWER / BALCONY	234pt	Night	1/8	2.
"	279pt, 279A	Night	1/8	1.
INT. H/C	77pt, 209	Day	1/8	11. 12., 1. 6. 36

Wednesday 28 April 1999

INT. ELEKTRA'S HALL / STAIRS	102, 110A
INT. ZUKOVSKY'S LAIR	105F

Thursday 29 April 1999

INT. ZUKOVSKY'S LAIR	105F

Friday 30 April 1999

INT. TORTURE ROOM	270

Saturday 1 & Sunday 2 May 1999 / Monday 3 May 1999
REST DAYS / MAY DAY HOLIDAY

Tuesday 4 May 1999
INT. TORTURE ROOM
EXT. LANDING SITE

Gerry Gavigan, 1ˢᵗ Assistant Director

TRANSPORT

Car 1. (0831 24   )
Brian Brookner — P/Up Michael Apted from home as per instructions and convey to Pinewood

Car 2. (0410 41   )
Colin Morris — P/Up Mr Brosnan from home at 07.00 and convey to Pinewood for 08.00

Car 3. (0973 55'   )
Mike Smith — P/Up Ms Richards at 06.45 from home and convey to Pinewood for 07.30

Car 4. (0956 24   )
Len Furssedonn — P/Up Ms Marceau from home at 10.00 and convey to Pinewood for 11.00

for a nipple, which really infuriated me.

"I mean, what's wrong with showing a little nipple?" added Brosnan. "It's tasteful and innocent. I definitely want to do it for the next Bond film, because this is ridiculous. I mean, we are entering a new *millennium!*"

Playing Doctor: Bond gets a clean bill of health from Dr. Warmflash (Serena Scott-Thomas).

But the Bond films are steeped in tradition, and the formula has always pushed the limits of sexuality and violence as far as possible while still adhering to the confines of the more "family-friendly" PG rating of cinema censors. Brosnan, however, hopes to change all that. "The censorship is pathetic," he fumed. "I mean, you're dealing with sex and violence in a fantasy package of spies; that underlying sexuality of the character and how it's executed has always been the appeal of these films. That, and, of course, action, locales, and mystique . . . but I say *sex, sex, and more sex*. It's about turning the audience on."

Which is something Brosnan definitely did with *Goldeneye* and *Tomorrow Never Dies*, which became the highest-grossing Bonds to date. But going into *The World Is Not Enough*, Brosnan insisted on some necessary changes. "Pierce didn't want to spend five months just blasting guns and dodging explosions," explained director Michael Apted between camera setups of Bond's bedroom scene with Denise Richards later that afternoon. "He wanted to do real scenes and have real relationships." What Brosnan desired was a throwback to the earlier Bond films, where the story unfolded through character and intrigue, not pyrotechnics. "*Tomorrow Never Dies* was just wall-to-wall action," conceded Brosnan, "but there wasn't enough story to kind of hang your hat on. It was kind of just set

Manning The Guns: With Renard (Robert Carlyle) in hand, Bond faces a Catch-22 escape.

piece, set piece, set piece, and a little bit of nonsense in between. The film worked well in the end, and I thought it was a good old ride of a movie. But I think, when they get it right, it has the action but also the character and the story. And in this one, we have these lovely nuances to play. We have a story you can sustain throughout the action sequences — you have a goal, you have an emotional subtext to it within the Bond universe."

But with a budget at over $110 million at stake — the highest of any previous Bond — *The World Is Not Enough* couldn't stray too far from the tried-and-true 007 formula. So the elements involved in Bond's last assignment of the 20th century turned out to be not that different from his first: greed, revenge, and world domination. With the title coming from the Bond family coat of arms described in Ian Fleming's novel *On Her Majesty's Secret Service* and glimpsed briefly in the 1969 film, *The World Is Not Enough* pits Bond against megalomaniac villain Renard (played by *Trainspotting* and *Full Monty* star Robert Carlyle), who, with a bullet lodged in his brain, has been rendered impervious to pain. "The twist is that Renard is already dying, so that makes it particularly difficult to kill him," noted Carlyle. "He doesn't fear death, he doesn't feel any pain."

Renard hungers after the world's oil supply and the affections of Elektra King, the seductive heiress of murdered oil tycoon Sir Robert King. Bond must protect Elektra while trying to avert a nuclear strike that will sabotage the planet's major oil pipeline. With nuclear weapons expert Dr. Christmas Jones (Richards) by his side, Bond hopscotches across Europe, from England and Spain to Turkey, the French Alps, and finally Baku — the capital of Azerbaijan — where the oil pipelines, situated in a strategically dangerous military position, are Renard's key to terrorist control. The ripped-from-the-headlines battle over Caspian Sea oil was what intrigued Apted about this Bond adventure.

"We are the first film to be dealing with the whole issue, and it's great to be doing a Bond that's ahead of the game for a change, rather than dealing with old-hat intrigues about Russians," remarked Apted. "I didn't

Director Michael Apted: "I wondered what the hell they wanted me for."

want to recycle what others have done before, although it's kind of a high-wire act delivering what the audience expects while not keeping it in a rut. Bond must imperceptibly keep changing to move along."

Better known for directing more dramatic, female-centric films like *Coal Miner's Daughter*, *Nell*, and *Gorillas in the Mist*, as well as the BBC documentary series *14 Up, 21 Up, 28 Up, 35 Up*, and *42 Up* (the acclaimed British Academy Award-winning series that revisited the same group of British citizens every seven years beginning in 1963), Apted admitted he was perplexed when he was approached to direct a James Bond film. "Quite frankly, I thought it was a big joke," laughed Apted, recalling the phone call he received from his agent. "I wondered what the hell they wanted *me* for, 'cause I had never done anything like this before. Never done an action film per se, never done a big-budget film, and, quite honestly, the last films I'd done hadn't really been that commercially successful."

Nevertheless, Apted's curiosity was piqued, and he agreed to meet with the Broccolis and Brosnan in the summer of '98. "I said 'sure,' not believing it would ever happen," he shrugged. "But then when I realized Michael Wilson and Barbara Broccoli were deadly serious, I then understood why they asked me. It wasn't going to be 120 minutes of wall-to-wall pounding action — I got the feeling they wanted more emphasis on the story, on the characters, stuff like that. So once I figured out that I had something to offer, I was very taken with the idea."

Apted's previous collaborations with actresses like Sissy Spacek, Sigourney Weaver, and Jodie Foster proved to be his greatest asset. "The fact that this is clearly a story with women at the center of it, and some of my most successful films have been with women, was obviously a major selling point on me," said Apted. "I guess they thought that, if they are going to do a film where the women are much more central to it, they wanted to kind of change the slight dinosaur reputation that Bond has with women. They wanted to do a much better job with the women than they have before."

But Apted saw clear advantages for himself as well. "At my age, to come into something so totally new was a fantastic opportunity," admitted Apted, who relocated to Los Angeles from London in 1980. "To learn about doing an action blockbuster of this scope and size, and handling all these enormous stunts and action scenes, was a way of doing my career some good, I suppose. If I could pull it off, I could have a 'blockbuster' under my belt — which would make life a little easier for all the other things that I want to do. And for me to come back here to England to do a Bond film and be part of the franchise that I grew up with was a real added bonus."

When I spoke again with Apted later that year in Los Angeles, however, he confessed to moments of second-guessing his decision to tackle Bond. "There were days when I wondered if I could ever get through it," he said.

"It was very intimidating at times, with such a huge crew and four other units shooting simultaneously, with everybody needing decisions constantly. The hardest thing was having to pay attention to what everyone else was doing as well. Because normally, I'd only have to pay attention to what I was doing, but I had to watch everyone else's dailies to make sure it was all making sense and they were doing what I wanted. There are about 500,000 different shots in this movie, and the hardest thing was keeping the 'big picture' in mind and making sure that it didn't get eroded away or change course in a way that's irretrievable.

"Because on a film," continued Apted, "everyone has great ideas, and someone will say, 'Well, why don't we change this scene?' or 'Why don't we try this?' and suddenly you find nothing makes sense anymore. That is a difficult part of any movie, but suddenly on a Bond movie it's a hundred times harder because there is so much going on."

Brosnan, though, was confident in Apted's skills and knew he would develop *The World Is Not Enough* on a much deeper level. "I don't think Michael was the obvious choice for this kind of film, but he's an A-1 director in my books, and he's somebody who has great integrity when it comes to storytelling and character, and that was very much desired," offered Brosnan. "I was much more involved this time, and Michael and I had many, many meetings beforehand. I think we have more of a character in Bond. There's more of an understanding between him and M, in the respect they have for each other. And also what does the woman who he will encounter in the film mean to Bond? What if she gets close to his heart? And I think Bond does fall in love with Elektra King — he's very seduced by her."

That relationship, said Michael Wilson, was pivotal to the success of *The World Is Not Enough*. "Because if that doesn't work, it will be a disaster," admitted Wilson during production. "Barbara and I fought very hard for Sophie Marceau; we didn't want to have somebody who was well known to the American public. Because if you cast someone who is a famous actress who plays 'good roles,' say like Sandra Bullock or somebody, the audience is going to *hate* you when she turns out to be the villain. You'll lose the audience. And, conversely, if you cast someone like Sharon Stone, who's played nasty parts, everyone will say, 'Bond, *wake up!* You can't trust her.' So you have to cast someone who is a great actress but doesn't come with any baggage."

Apted described Sophie's task as "fantastically difficult" on a number of levels. "Firstly, you have to believe you can fall in love with her — just as Bond does — and then you have to believe that she's so villainous that you want Bond to kill her — all in the space of about 70 minutes of screen time," explained Apted. "And with Sophie, she is so incredibly adorable that, when you sit with her, you fall in love with her in *life*, let alone in a *movie*. She's very beautiful. But she also had something else, which is kind of weird: she has this kind of child-woman thing. You can see that she is a very elegant woman, but she has this kind of childish spitefulness. She can be a woman one minute and a child the next. And suddenly I realized, 'That's the key to Elektra!' And when I met her, I knew she was the one. Because, for Elektra, you couldn't have a woman who was just sophisticated — there had to be a certain immaturity at work so you could believe that she could be childlike and crazy."

Conversely, Apted cast Denise Richards for her rough-and-tumble American bravado. "Denise has a real sassiness about her that I liked immediately," he smiled. "In a conventional way, she is sort of the 'Bond babe,' but we tried to give her some extra weight. It's perfectly believable someone like that who does that kind of job . . . I just knew she wouldn't be passive. Denise has very appealing spunk."

Apted said he resisted indulging in the stunt-casting effort by the studio to place big-name American actors in the film. "These are very European stories," said Apted. "Probably the only European-centered films left. They have always had mostly European actors. And the franchise doesn't really need huge movie stars in them. *Bond* is at the center, but the studio would love a great marquee of posh names. But I think the Broccolis are very clever at protecting that; Bond doesn't need a big marquee, Bond *is* the marquee. Which means you don't have to stuff a lot of American movie stars in it. The Broccolis have never done that, and they've always resisted that."

The same approach applies to the tradition of using British directors

(New Zealand-born *Goldeneye* director Martin is the lone exception). "There is an English sense of irony that's very much at the heart of Fleming's work," related Apted. "It's a British sense of humor that is kind of understated and isn't wacky. The humor in Bond is cool and witty and light on its feet. And I think it would be very difficult for an American to do that, because it's nothing you can learn. You can't learn an English sense of humor, just as you can't learn an American sensibility."

Before he began filming, Apted read a number of Fleming's novels and rewatched some of Connery's early Bonds. What Apted gleaned was "the realism of it all," he marveled. "It all seemed very well researched, with a real truth to it. The books are actually very seriously told. And you have to take it seriously as a filmmaker and not allow the actors to wink at it. Roger's were going that way more and more. But you can't do that. You've got to take it seriously. Because if *you* don't take it seriously, the audience won't.

"And there's a humanity in Bond as well," continued Apted, "that Pierce has really nailed. And, actually, I think in some ways Pierce is nearer the Bond of the books than even Sean Connery was. Sean brought a rather ruthless machismo to it, which I didn't really think was what Fleming was talking about. But Pierce has a nice balance between being very vulnerable and very mean. Plain and simple, Bond is a killer. He has no compunction about offing people, like Elektra, in this film. And yet he doesn't treat women in that kind of dinosaur way of Connery."

But Brosnan was quick to point out that his portrayal by no means represented a softening of the character. "I don't think he's a gentler Bond at all," he reasoned. "He's a man who has been doing this job a long time and has seen a lot of killing. His life has always been under threat of death, so he is maybe a bit more *philosophical.* You know, so much of when I do it, I don't even think about it anymore. It's just instincts that lead you down certain directions, and you just follow them."

After viewing the final cut of *The World Is Not Enough*, Brosnan expressed his satisfaction that he had made the right choices. "I think we've captured some of what happened in the days of Sean Connery in terms of character and mood," Brosnan told me later that year in Los Angeles. "We came out of the gate with *Goldeneye*, and now, looking back, it seems like I

Slippery Slope: While shooting the parahawk attack in the French Alps, the Bond crew narrowly escaped a lethal avalanche.

French beauty Sophie Marceau, Pierce Brosnan, and director Michael Apted on the Azerbaijan set of The World Is Not Enough.

was just a baby then. My assuredness within the role and my confidence has grown a lot. And, quite frankly, I wouldn't have expected anything less of myself. And I think the same could be said of Connery: if you look at him in *Dr. No* in 1962 and then his third time in *Goldfinger*, there was this whole mystique about the third Bond, where suddenly the actor really gets into his stride."

As Apted put it rather succinctly, "Without question, Pierce is leaving an indelible mark on the role."

But even though *The World Is Not Enough* was a much smoother process than *Tomorrow Never Dies*, it was still fraught with production problems during the six-month shoot. "We had the absolute worst luck with weather on location all the way through," sighed Apted. While shooting the para-hawk attack on Bond and Elektra on the snowy slopes near Chamonix in the French Alps, the remote area was hit by major avalanches that put everyone in real-life danger. "The worst of the avalanches happened on the other side of the mountain," related Apted. "We shut down production and gave them all our helicopters to help with the rescue efforts. It was another month before we could go back to finish all the scenes."

Shooting at the Guggenheim Museum in Bilbao, Spain, for part of the film's pretitle sequence further tested Apted's patience. "I chose to shoot at the Guggenheim because of the stunning architecture, but it rained the whole bloody time we were there. It was very frustrating, because you could never see the magic of the building. In the sunshine, the beauty of the place is absolutely staggering." But the freak weather in Spain was a problem that paled in comparison to the violent civil unrest they faced in Turkey for many of the film's key sequences. "Turkey was a complete horror story," Apted explained. "We were supposed to do a huge amount of filming there, but just as we were due to arrive the PKK (a Kurdish terrorist group) announced that their agenda was to destroy the Turkish tourist industry, which they have completely succeeded in doing. And, suddenly, we had to make a split-second decision at the eleventh hour. If we went in there for five weeks with two units, we would assuredly be sitting ducks for terrorism. So I ended up quietly going in for a week with a very small crew to shoot the absolute essentials, because we had to have some stuff in Istanbul

Frequent Flyer: A perilous pursuit leaves Bond hangin' tough above the Millennium Dome in the film's thrilling teaser chase.

— it was the center of the story. I ended up using doubles of the actors to shoot a lot of the stuff, and then we eventually had to relocate all the Istanbul stuff to Spain."

Back safely in the cozy confines of Pinewood Studios for week 16 of the shoot, the cast and crew were in much better spirits. They had just completed one of the most spectacular stunt sequences ever designed for a Bond film, and it had been pulled off without a hitch. At a reported cost of $5 million, the mere five-minute pretitle sequence took an entire month to shoot. Reacting to an explosive attack on the London headquarters of MI6 by Vauxhall Bridge, Bond commandeers a prototype speedboat from Q Branch and sails out of the crippled building onto the River Thames, where he engages in a high-speed pursuit that climaxes in a spectacular showdown at the newly constructed Millennium Dome. The day after finishing the elaborate boat chase, Brosnan was still on a high from the adrenaline rush. The souped-up Bentz jetboat reached speeds in excess of 80 miles an hour, and, yes, that was Brosnan behind the wheel. The only time a stuntman stepped in was for the memorable midriver barrel roll. "They didn't realize I was as good with the boat as I was, and it kind of blew everyone away," enthused Brosnan with a giant Cheshire cat grin. "It was absolutely amazing! The boat has a V-8

MI6 Headquarters at Vauxhall Bridge. Bond's Bentz jetboat bursts through the 6th floor on the east side of the building.

engine in it — it was like a bat out of hell. And there's only one way to drive a craft like that, and that's full-out. 'Cause if you took your foot off the gas, you couldn't steer it. So it's like you're sitting in this bath-tub — the boat wraps around you, and you gas it, and, 'zoooom,' you are truly flying. It's been the most fun I've had on this film. It was so spectacular."

In order to capture all the angles of the sequence, Apted and second unit director Vic Armstrong utilized a flotilla of 35 camera boats as well as a specially designed flying camera rig from Belgium to swoop under the Thames River bridges in pursuit of the action. "It was pretty harrowing stuff to do, but that's why a Bond film takes so long to shoot," said Apted. The chase careens past such British landmarks as the Houses of Parliament, Tower Bridge, and Docklands before ending in the high-altitude confrontation between Bond and the mysterious "Cigar Girl" (played by Italian *Il Postino* star Maria Grazia Cucinotta) at the Millennium Dome. Though technically daunting in its execution, Apted was surprised by the ease with which they could command miles-long stretches of the Thames. "What was most shocking to me about the Thames is that no one uses it," said Apted with obvious disbelief. "In the film, it looks like we cleared the whole place off, but in reality we didn't have to do anything. It's only busy during the tourist season, so it was virtually empty. The Thames is a fantastic resource in the middle of a city which you cannot drive through because it's so congested. It's a shame that such a breathtaking resource is not used."

Though the entire sequence could have been faked with digital trickery, Apted maintained the rich tradition of the Bond films to make all the stunts

real. "It's very difficult and very dangerous and time-consuming, but that's what sets Bond apart from other films. The audience expects that realism." And that goes for Brosnan too, who insists on performing a lot of his own stunts. "What you mostly see is me up there," explained Brosnan. "With a character like this, you have to give it your all." However, that dedication backfired — so to speak — on Brosnan while

"I was on fire about 600 yards through the tunnel," says Brosnan about this stunt that backfired.

shooting the escape from the nuclear test facility. Dangling by chains as he slid down a 200-foot tunnel being engulfed by a massive fireball, Brosnan suddenly realized "I was on fire about 600 yards through the tunnel with all these huge plastic sacks of gasoline going off around me," he grinned. "And then for another stunt, a big explosion went off behind me, and I dove into the bag, and the next thing I know they're yelling 'Lie down! Lie down!' and they're spraying me with the fire extinguisher. . . . It turned out my trousers and feet had caught on fire."

Just another day at the office for Brosnan, who said being beaten, burned, and bruised is part of the job. "The hard part really is just trying to keep your stamina going for 25 weeks of shooting," said Brosnan. "I worked out much more strenuously on this one than the other two. I've lost a few pounds from *Tomorrow Never Dies*, and I've got much more of a leaner, fighting weight. With all these action sequences, you have to stay constantly alert and be at the top of your game and remain quick and light on your feet. But it's such a physical role that by the end you can be pretty hammered and bone-weary."

That's partly why Brosnan wanted a three-year break before tackling "Die Another Day" in January 2002. "We've been shooting the last three films every two years, and it's all gone by in a flash for me," reflected Brosnan. "I mean, I still can sort of smell and see Leavesden from five years ago. It's been the most exhilarating time of my life, but, between all the time filming and then months of traveling around the world promoting it, you wind up starting the next one almost immediately. And the rest of your life kind of falls away, and you end up basically running on empty.

"There's a part of me that says, 'Let's just get it out of the way, and let's go straight into production on the next one,'" continued Brosnan. "But then there's another part of me that says, 'I've got to give myself a break here.' It became very claustrophobic living with the character so close to you the whole time. I'm an actor, and hopefully I've got other performances and other characters in me. And I've reached the point now where I have to start shaking it up a little bit and paying attention to some more dramatic roles."

Brosnan also hoped that a three-year hiatus could only improve the storytelling process for the 20th James Bond adventure. "I think we've set kind of a good benchmark with *The World Is Not Enough* for a fourth film."

And the stellar box office results (over $400 million worldwide) for *The World Is Not Enough* proved that James Bond — a fictional creation born of the Cold War paranoia during the 1950s — was still a vital screen hero at the dawn of a new millennium. "We just faced it head on in *Goldeneye*: was Bond a dinosaur, or was he still useful and relevant?" surmised Michael Wilson after the release of *The World Is Not Enough.* "And the audience who votes with their admissions seems to think he's extremely relevant all around the world. That's an enormous satisfaction for all of us and for the legacy."

THE WORLD IS NOT ENOUGH:
DENISE RICHARDS AND SOPHIE MARCEAU

Nuclear Reaction: Denise Richards heats things up as Dr. Christmas Jones.

Denise Richards

She may have bared her breasts and locked lips with Neve Campbell as a bisexual vixen in 1998's *Wild Things*, but Denise Richards is mighty modest when it comes to the video playback of her early morning love scene with Pierce Brosnan.

"I had no idea people were watching the monitor," Richards exclaimed rather bashfully. "I'm so embarrassed now."

Richards has slipped back into jeans and white T-shirt while taking a break in her dressing room on the set of *The World Is Not Enough*. She may be needed again later in the afternoon for love scene close-ups, and Richards is fretting away the time. "People don't understand about love scenes," she insists. "They are very technical, especially in a Bond film, because nothing is supposed to show. So you have to always be very careful with how you move your body. It can be quite awkward. It's not as romantic as it seems."

Richards has certainly come a long way since her first break on TV's *Doogie Howser, M.D.* The then-27-year-old Illinois native and former model had been steadily losing her girl-next-door persona for more adult, sexually charged roles. She played Loni Anderson's saucy daughter in *Melrose Place* and helped crush an army of vicious alien bugs as a feisty fighter pilot in *Starship Troopers*. Richards was next seen as a spoiled beauty queen brat bumping off her pageant competitors in *Drop Dead Gorgeous* and then made the big leap to helping the world's most famous spy save the world.

"It's all been so thrilling," smiled Richards. "Even just being here in London is amazing. I've never spent much time in Europe, so it's been a really good experience." She described her character — Dr. Christmas Jones — as "very intelligent and completely fearless. She becomes Bond's ally, really, and helps accomplish his mission, which I like. She's not afraid to do anything that he does. She's very strong, very sassy, and loves danger."

And apparently also loves being barely dressed. Christmas Jones is certainly not your average nuclear scientist. "I think I spend the whole movie in shorts and a tank top," Richards laughed, rolling her eyes. "Although I do wear my boiler suit as I'm taking the plutonium out. But then I, of course, strip down once again to my shorts and tank top. . . .

"It is *Bond*, after all," she added with a grin.

And though she reluctantly admitted she'd never really seen a Bond film before getting the role, she quickly immersed herself in a 007 crash course, courtesy of a nearby video outlet. "I'm still in the process of watching them all," she said. "So far, my favorites are *Goldfinger* and *Tomorrow Never Dies. . . .*

"I knew Bond was huge," she continued, "but I didn't realize what a big deal it was until I got the role, and, suddenly, it was all over the news that I was the new Bond Girl. It was pretty overwhelming. I had never experienced anything like that. But I think my mom was even more excited than me, because she's a big James Bond fan. She'd seen *Goldfinger* two dozen times. She's been so thrilled with all of this."

Despite her whirlwind success, Richards said she was taking it all in stride. "It's nice, but believe me my family keeps me pretty grounded. To me, everything that's happened the last couple years is like a stepping stone. I'm just trying to get through this movie and do a good job and then figure out what I'm going to do next. . . .

"It's flattering that people want you on the cover of magazines and all the interviews, but I don't think of it as real life," she adds.

The same could probably be said of Richards's sizzling sex symbol status, according to the brown-haired, blue-eyed beauty. "I was raised to be a nice Catholic girl," she said coyly. "But I'll admit it's fun sometimes to go the other way and get away with stuff. But when I see myself up on screen doing these wild things, it really feels like it's someone else, not me at all. It's a weird feeling.

"Still," she said, "I have a four-month-old nephew, and I hope someday I'll make a film that he'll actually be able to see!"

Sophie Marceau

Elektra King (Sophie Marceau) tries to screw with Bond.

World domination through the power of petroleum and high-tech terrorism . . . just three of the ingredients of *The World Is Not Enough*, which takes Bond from England and Spain to Turkey, Azerbaijan, and the French Alps. Exotic locales call for an equally exotic beauty, and 32-year-old Sophie Marceau filled that order quite nicely.

"A Bond Girl should have very kissable lips," offered Brosnan on his ideal Bond beauty. "She's got to have kind of curvy hips, a great pair of . . . hands, shoulders. Intelligence helps."

French actress Marceau supplied all that in spades. Her hallmark curvy hips and kissable lips are Marceau's claim to fame as one of France's most popular actresses. And her long black hair, bewitching eyes, and cheekbones as high as skyscrapers make Marceau a definite throwback to the sultry European Bond Girls of the '60s.

Tall, confident, and with catlike poise, Marceau was eating a Twix bar and savoring every morsel. "Chocolate is my only weakness . . . well, one of them," purred Marceau, reclining on her dressing room sofa after lunch.

Unlike her American counterparts, Marceau admitted she never had any qualms about baring her body on screen and admitted very matter-of-factly that she rather enjoyed doing love scenes. "They're not difficult at all," she smiled. "They can be quite fun. I have no problem with nudity. In France, it's an everyday part of filmmaking. But for Bond, they can't even show a *nipple!* Which is crazy, because they kill millions of people in the films. But if it's beautiful, I don't have any problems with nudity at all."

Marceau was cast in her first movie, *La Boum*, at age 12, after she answered a talent search ad. At 16, she won a César, the prestigious French film award. At 29, after 15 French films, came her first English-speaking movie, the Oscar-winning *Braveheart*, which led to her landing the title role in 1997's *Anna Karenina*. In 1999, she was seen as the object of David Spade's obsession in the romantic comedy *Lost and Found*, but she admitted Hollywood film offers had grown tiresome.

"The scripts I receive from America I'm just not very interested in," she sighed. "The stories are not very appealing."

But what appealed to her about *The World Is Not Enough* was the Bond legacy she grew up with in her Parisian household. "I've been watching the Bond films since I was a teenager. My mother and I went to the cinema every time there was a new one. They've always been very popular in France. I was very excited when they asked me to be in this one. Coming into Bond's world is pretty amazing. . . .

"I remember, when I got to the set of *Braveheart*, I couldn't believe how huge it was. But Bond is definitely bigger. There are 300 carpenters and 200 electricians alone on this film. It's like an army. But there's a great family feeling here. They've all worked on the Bond films together, so they all know each other. They've made me feel part of the family."

Marceau played the deliciously evil femme fatale Elektra King, both lethal and lovely, whom she described as "eccentric and mad. She's a woman in her 30s, living in a wealthy family, and a mixture of two different cultures — Turkish and English. I'm a villain, but it doesn't mean you have to play the villain.

"A lot of the scenes are unreal and — how you say — *over the top*? Clichéd? But it works like a charm in the Bond films. It's a total fantasy. You believe. I like being a part of this — James Bond is a part of history."

❧

THANK Q FOR THE GADGETS: DESMOND LLEWELYN

Desmond Llewelyn: "I can't even fix my toaster."

You may not have known his name, but you certainly knew his letter: "Q," a.k.a. Major Boothroyd. As head of MI6's "Q" Branch — the British Secret Service department responsible for supplying James Bond with his dazzling array of uniquely lethal gadgets and wildly modified sports cars — 86-year-old Desmond Llewelyn remained the longest-running thread throughout the Bond series up until his final appearance in *The World Is Not Enough*.

"Bond is the most famous fictional character in the world, and I suppose I'm the most famous small-part actor," laughed Llewelyn on the Pinewood Studios set of *The World Is Not Enough*. "I've only had tiny parts in the films, and yet I'm known all over

Q introduces his assistant "R" (John Cleese) to Bond. "Now someone else can share in the grief Bond has given Q," chuckled Llewelyn. (right) Cast Off: rocket launching leg cast.

the world."

Llewelyn, the distinguished, silver-haired Welsh actor, marked his 17th and — sadly — last appearance in the 007 series with *The World Is Not Enough*, having acted in every official Bond film but *Dr. No* and *Live and Let Die*. For 36 years, the long-suffering and crotchety Q had to endure 007's cavalier treatment of his technological wonders. Q remained the series' most endearing and enduring character, constantly admonishing "Pay attention, 007!" and futilely pleading with him to "Bring it back in one piece!" Of course, Bond never did. Llewelyn admitted those ever-frustrating lectures to Bond were always enjoyable, despite the mouthful of technical jargon he was constantly required to spout.

"Any acting is always fun to me," smiled Llewelyn, who made his film debut in 1939 in the Will Hay comedy *Ask a Policeman* and had roles in 1963's *Cleopatra* alongside Elizabeth Taylor and Richard Burton, as well as the 1968 cult classic *Chitty Chitty Bang Bang* (not, coincidentally, since Ian Fleming wrote the children's story and Albert Broccoli produced the film). "Unfortunately, I don't get much of an opportunity to do it these days because I've been so typecast as Q. But when I get a chance to play Q again, I just love it. And I was lucky, because I've managed to get three days' worth of work on this one."

And for *The World Is Not Enough*, Llewelyn received a new assistant named "R." To the rest of the world, R was perhaps better known under his civilian name — John Cleese. The Monty Python funnyman made the first of what will be regular Bond appearances as the new Q Branch wizard. "John Cleese is *extremely* good," said Llewelyn. "He's very funny, and it's been quite enjoyable working with him. . . .

"Now someone else can share in the grief Bond has given Q," he added with a chuckle.

Even though he played cinema's most brilliant inventor, Llewelyn not only lamented that he was technologically illiterate in real life but also admitted that he was absolutely hopeless. "I can't even fix the toaster," he sighed. "I know nothing about gadgets. I've had to learn all my lines over the years like a parrot! If I'm in the London underground and my train ticket doesn't work going through the turnstile, somebody will inevitably say, 'You're Q — I thought you ought to be able to at least do *that!*'"

He noted people were always surprised to see him traveling London's public transit system from his home in East Sussex, "but I'm a pensioner, and to travel up to London by car or taxi is too expensive," he explained. "So even though I've been a small-part actor — only a couple days on each film — my face is so well known all over the world via the Bond films, and it throws people. They don't expect to meet well-known actors in ordinary life."

Llewelyn said his favorite Bond film always remained 1963's *From Russia with Love*, where he took over the Boothroyd character from actor Peter Burton, who played Major Boothroyd in *Dr. No* but couldn't return for the follow-up. That's when Llewelyn got to show his stuff as the gizmo guru and introduce the now infamous trick briefcase, complete with balanced throwing knife, tear-gas disguised as a talcum powder canister, infrared telescope sight, 40 rounds of ammunition, and an AR-7 folding-stock survival rifle.

"I just think it was an extraordinarily good film," Llewelyn reflected.

Q-Tips: Desmond Llewelyn with author David Giammarco in London (1997)

"I think Sean [Connery] was at his best. Terence Young directed it absolutely brilliantly. And to be honest, I think a lot of the success that the Bonds have had should be attributed to Terence. He was sort of a Bond character himself. I think those first four Bond films are absolute classics, because they were Fleming's stories, you see. And brilliantly adapted by Richard Maibaum. I think they showed Bond at his best.

"But I think the others are extremely good too," added Llewelyn, who met Ian Fleming for the first time on the set of 1964's *Goldfinger*. "They've all kept the same essence of Fleming. But, of course, the last one [*Tomorrow Never Dies*] was more adapted for young people. There was terrific action, action, action. And I think, with any luck, this new one doesn't have quite so much action — it's more going back to what it should be."

For his final appearance as Q in *The World Is Not Enough*, Llewelyn delivered a new array of high-tech toys to his least favorite secret agent, including a souped-up speedboat, new sports car with all the bells and whistles, and even an inflatable coat. "You know, the usual stuff," said Llewelyn matter-of-factly. However, after 36 years of every gadget imaginable, Llewelyn said his favorite still remained the Aston Martin DB-5 from *Goldfinger*.

The fact that Llewelyn was still acting up until the end was a feat in itself — one that well-meaning relatives, the call of the cloth, and a world war could not derail. Born in South Wales in 1913, he was the son of a coal-mining engineer and seemed destined for a career in that field. When he failed the eye exam to become a policeman, he contemplated becoming a minister and went on a week-long retreat. "But I knew right away that was definitely not for me." What was left was acting, Llewelyn decided. "I was accepted to the Royal Academy for the Dramatic Arts," he said, feigning a bit of pomposity before chuckling and adding, "They had about 50 men and 200 women at the academy. . . . I think they were only too glad to take any man who happened to come along."

But World War II put an end to his plans. In September 1939, Llewelyn went to Sandhurst and was later commissioned as a second lieutenant in the British Army. He was assigned to the Royal Welsh Fusiliers and was sent to France in early 1940. In a short time, his regiment was fighting the Germans, and Llewelyn's company was captured during the British evacuation at Dunkirk on May 27, 1940. For the next five years, until his Easter release in 1945, he was a prisoner of war at several camps in Germany, including Lauten, Warburg, and Rotenberg, and was eventually confined to solitary after his captors discovered him working in an escape tunnel dug by his fellow prisoners.

"There were a lot of bloody awful things to recall," he admitted about his years as a POW, "but as I get older I find that I only remember the good times. I think I left a good bit of my youth in Germany, though. But I didn't have a bad war, I guess, compared to some. None of us liked the confinement and the inadequate food, which got worse as the war wore on, but life in the prison camps was bearable. As long as we behaved, the Germans treated us properly most of the time. But there was none of that romantic nonsense about escaping that you see in war films. *No one* escaped from any of the camps where I was imprisoned — we found that out the hard way."

After the war, Llewelyn returned to London and revived his acting career, appearing in numerous stage roles and World War II action films, including *They Were Not Divided*, a British adventure about the Irish Guards. The director of the film was a youthful Terence Young, who remembered Llewelyn years later when it came time to recast the role of Major Boothroyd. "My agent called me one day out of the blue and said he had a role for me in the new James Bond movie," recalled Llewelyn.

That was spring 1963, and producers Albert Broccoli and Harry Saltzman were gearing up for production on their second 007 adventure, *From Russia with Love*, following up on the character's debut in *Dr. No* the previous year. The popularity was building steadily, but Llewelyn never imagined he would end up becoming part of a worldwide pop culture phenomenon for 37 years. "Oh, good God, no! I don't think *anybody* did," he exclaimed, shaking his head in disbelief. "I thought it would just be a onetime thing, really. And then I was thrilled when I was asked back to do *Goldfinger*, but every time I did another one I figured it would be the last."

So what did Llewelyn think was the secret to the enduring success of the James Bond films? "I think it's because, as Ian Fleming said, Bond is what every man would like to be and knows damn well he can't be," Llewelyn mused. "The films are pure fantasy, you see. Everything is bigger and larger than life. And Cubby Broccoli, who was responsible really for the whole setup, followed Fleming's dictum, which was to any thriller add all the advantages of expensive living.

Give Bond the right clothes, the right background, and the right girls, set your story in the most beautiful place, describe everything in minute detail, and take your story along so fast that nobody notices the idiosyncrasies in it.

"And Cubby did that wonderfully," Llewelyn added, "and he also added Hitchcock's thing, which was, when you come to a climax, you then have another one and another one. If you think of the films, they should end when Bond saves the world, but there's generally another flip to it, and it goes on a bit more. The fascinating thing, I think, is that, when you go to see a film for the first time, you know damn well that he's going to defuse the bomb, because if he didn't there wouldn't be another Bond film. But yet, even when you've seen it for the fourth or fifth time, you're still held."

I decided to ask Llewelyn to break ranks, after loyally serving Her Majesty's Secret Service for close to four decades and suffering through five different 007s, and hand over his dossier on working with the actors who were Bond . . . *James* Bond.

SEAN CONNERY: "It was very difficult because then I was in a small part, which I still am. But Sean had this enormous part, and I had to speak lines where I didn't really know what I was talking about. And Sean used to fiddle a lot in the scenes, which used to distract me from remembering my lines. He would never be looking at the gadget in an interested way. And so it was much more of a strain, in a way, to work with Sean than anybody. After Sean, the character of Q had been established, and it makes life much easier to act once you've become an established character. And, of course, one didn't want to hold up people by flubbing lines and everything like that. So there was much more tension, as far as I was concerned. Now I'm an old man, and as much as I flub I don't really mind. One can always say, 'Oh, poor old Desmond. He's so old he can't remember his lines.' Which is really quite true."

GEORGE LAZENBY: "An amateur. You cannot put a man who has had no experience in the theater or in films into a part like that. He was a car salesman, and he really didn't know anything about acting. For what he did, he was extremely good, but he got bad press because of his own stupidity. Unfortunately, some idiot told him to behave like a star, and he didn't realize that stars are highly competent actors and didn't argue with the director. He rather made a fool of himself."

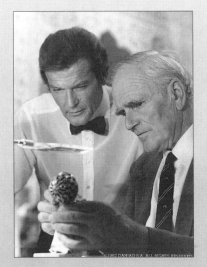

Giving some helpful pointers on the Fabergé egg transmitter in Octopussy.

ROGER MOORE: "Roger is an extremely good actor, and he obviously couldn't imitate Sean and wouldn't want to imitate Sean, so he made Bond much lighter, more jokier. But I know Roger very well. We were great friends. And so, being so bad at learning lines, Roger used to play jokes on me as much as he could by changing my lines and giving me a 'revised' script just before we were to shoot our scenes. He gave me a lot of headaches. But it was always great fun working with Roger. He's an incredibly relaxed character. And again, I was more established in the role, and he was now the second real Bond. I think a lot of people underestimated Roger, because he had such a fantastically difficult job to do following Sean Connery. But he did it brilliantly. A lot of people prefer Roger to Sean and say that's who Bond should be."

TIMOTHY DALTON: "Timothy made him a rather serious Bond, and to the Bond aficionados he is the nearest to Fleming's Bond. Timothy was a classical stage actor and had done much more stage work than film work. Timothy went back to the Bond of Fleming's books. He took the part very seriously — perhaps too seriously, some say. The public didn't like it because they dropped all fantasy from the films. They made them *real*. The villain in *Licence to Kill* wasn't a member of SMERSH or SPECTRE; he was a really nasty piece from South America, which everyone could identify. But I think Timothy was a much more real Bond than the others."

PIERCE BROSNAN: "Pierce is extremely easy to work with and very, very nice. He has this fantastic Irish blarney charm. He's actually a very good mix of Sean, Roger, and Timothy. He's gone back, I think, more to the original type of Bond. He's made him a bit more serious. And I think he's definitely much more comfortable in the role now. I really enjoy working with Pierce, and I think, perhaps as I'm getting older and rather stupider at learning lines, I find it easier to work with him than anybody. Pierce makes a sensational Bond — the role fits him like a glove."

"Pierce has this fantastic Irish blarney charm," said Llewelyn on working with Brosnan.

My last conversation with Desmond Llewelyn took place in Los Angeles in late November 1999, where he summarily dismissed the impression that *The World Is Not Enough* would be his last appearance as Q. "No, it's not my farewell to Bond at all," he chuckled. "I'm going to be there as long as the producers want me and the Almighty *doesn't*."

"One of the sweetest men I've ever known," said Brosnan of the late Desmond Llewelyn.

At 86, Llewelyn was still full of spunk and spark, and his enthusiasm for the Bond films had never waned over the course of our many chats throughout the years. A very kind and gentle man, Llewelyn's sudden and tragic death on Sunday, December 19, 1999, came as a complete shock to everyone. Llewelyn had been at a book signing for *Q: The Biography of Desmond Llewelyn* in Drusillas Park and was driving back to his home in Bexhill, East Sussex, when his car was struck head-on by another vehicle on the A27 motorway. Llewelyn had just completed work on his first non-Bond movie in 20 years — called *Error 2000* — where he finally got to save the world himself, and was due to sign copies of his book the next day at an event on New Oxford Street in Central London when he was killed. Much like Q's dogged devotion to his craft, Llewelyn loved working and preferred to always keep active. And he stayed that way right up until the end. Llewelyn's indelible contributions to the Bond legacy and his mark on pop culture will, like Bond, always be remembered.

♡

THE SCREEN HISTORY OF Q'S GADGETS

Dr. No (1962)

Major Boothroyd was the official armorer for 007's first screen outing (played by Peter Burton for this one film) and was responsible for persuading Bond to change his Berretta .22-caliber pistol for the Walther PPK 7.65 mm.

From Russia With Love (1963)

Boothroyd becomes head of the division that supplies Bond with the life-saving — and life-threatening — gadgets in the field. Desmond Llewelyn makes his debut and introduces the famous leather briefcase concealing an AR-7 folding sniper's rifle equipped with infrared tele-scopic sight, 20 rounds of .25-caliber ammunition hidden in two metal rods fitted into the spine of the case, 50 gold sovereigns hidden in the back, a flat-bladed balanced throwing knife spring loaded under one of the latches, and a metal canister of talcum powder that was actu-ally a tear-gas dispenser magnetically attached to the inside wall of the case and would be triggered if someone opened the briefcase incorrectly.

Goldfinger (1964)

Now known as "Q," Llewelyn introduced the mother of all Bond gadg-ets: the Aston Martin DB-5 loaded with Q Branch modifications: revolving license plates (BMT 216A [valid in the U.K.], LU-6789 [Switzerland], and 4711-EA-62 [France]), bulletproof front and rear windshields, left and right front-wing .30-caliber Browning machine guns, rear oil slick, smoke screen and road-spike dispensers, retractable tire shredders built into the wheel hubs, radar screen for monitoring Homer tracking device (with a range of 150 miles), and last but not least a front passenger ejector seat activated by a red button under the flip-up top of the gear shift. "You must be joking!" was Bond's response when learning of the ejector seat. Snapped a steely-eyed Q: "I never joke about my work, 007."

Also fake seagull attached to underwater swimming snorkel, bulletproof vest, machine gun in dummy P.O. van, smoke screen from parking meter, and a timing device with plastic explosive.

Thunderball (1965)

Same DB-5 as *Goldfinger* but with rear dispensers that shoot powerful jets of water, glimpsed briefly in *Thunderball*'s opening teaser. Bell jet pack and miniaturized underwater breathing cylinder. Underwater high speed propulsion unit strapped to oxygen tanks and armed with high-velocity spearguns, searchlight, and dye dispenser.

Underwater camera with Geiger counter. Rolex watch.

> *Q:* "Here's something I want you to use with special care. With *special* care . . ."
> *Bond:* "Everything you give me . . ."
> *Q:* "is treated with equal *contempt*, yes, I know . . ."

You Only Live Twice (1967)

Auto-gyro nicknamed "Little Nellie." Packaged in four suitcases, the minihelicopter featured heat-seeking air-to-air missiles, rocket launchers, aerial mines, machine guns, a flamethrower, and smoke ejectors.

Also a cigarette that fires a small rocket, accurate up to 30 yards — provided in Tokyo. Special breathing shroud for sea burial.

On Her Majesty's Secret Service (1969)

New Aston Martin — DB6. Additional feature: sniper's rifle with telescopic sight housed in the glove compartment. Minox miniature camera. Computerized safe opener. Portable copying machine. Radioactive lint contained in small box.

Diamonds Are Forever (1971)

Synthesizer box for altering voice. Transparent fake fingerprints. One-man self-propelled inflatable ball. Spring-loaded clamp in Bond's jacket pocket. Electronic device for manipulating slot machine sensors.

Live and Let Die (1973)
Rolex wrist watch featuring high-powered magnetic field and circular buzz saw. Shark gun firing compressed-air bullets. Bug-detecting device hidden in toiletries kit.

The Man with the Golden Gun (1974)
Nikon camera that explodes when aimed. Homing device and detector. Plastic third nipple used for impersonating Scaramanga.

The Spy Who Loved Me (1977)
Lotus Esprit fully loaded submarine car — equipped with surface-to-air missiles, underwater heat-seeking missiles, harpoon, limpet mine launcher, bulletproof Plexiglas windows, louvers, and rear ink jet dispensers to blind pursuing craft. For land use, the Lotus also featured a liquid cement jet dispenser concealed beneath the rear license plate.

Also a Wetbike amphibious motorcycle, wrist watch with telex communication function, linear induction tray, cigarette case with microfilm viewer, bullet-firing ski poles, and hidden parachute rig.

> *Q:* "Now pay attention, 007. I want you to take care of this equipment."
> *Bond:* "Have I ever let you down?"
> *Q:* "Frequently."

Moonraker (1979)
Hypodermic needle concealed in pen. Cigarette lighter camera, cigarette case X-ray apparatus, dart gun concealed in Seiko wrist watch, high-speed gondola that converts to a Hovercraft, fully loaded speedboat that fires torpedoes and lays mines and also houses a hang glider in its roof. Also exploding bolas, fake sleeping hombre housing machine gun, and a prototype laser gun demonstrated by Q Branch in Rio.

For Your Eyes Only (1981)

Self-destruct mechanism in new Lotus (engaged), Seiko wrist watch with audio communication capability, binocular camera, underwater minisub, advanced climbing gear.

Octopussy (1983)

Vijay (Vijay Amritraj) and Bond make a pit stop at the Indian Q-Branch.

Acrostar minijet with fold-up wings, horse trailer with fake rear end of plastic horse housing the Acrostar aircraft, pen that dispenses a mix of nitric and hydrochloric acid capable of dissolving all metals, as well as a radio receiver located in pen top that is compatible with a direction finder in wrist watch. Tiny radio transmitter placed in fake Fabergé egg. Crocodile-disguised one-man submarine. Hot-air balloon with closed-circuit TV screen and camera in basket. Q's workshop (India): LCD screen watch and video camera, rising Indian rope trick, spiked door opening with lethal force.

A View to a Kill (1985)

Snooper: small robot surveillance roamer. Wrist watch with garrote cord. Bug-detecting device under the head of a Philishave razor. Fountain pen with burning ink. Minisub disguised as small iceberg. Compact photocopier/X-ray device.

The Living Daylights (1987)

Aston Martin Volante V8 with windscreen heads-up visual display, scanning digital radio, bulletproof glass, fireproof body, jet engine booster rocket, weapons control panel concealed on driver's side, heat-seeking guided missiles, retractable snow skids hidden in door sills, convertible ice tires with spikes, laser tire slasher in front wheel hubs, and self-destruct mechanism.

Also a key ring that emits a stun gas activated by whistling a few bars of "Rule Britannia," as well as a skeleton key that can open 90% of the world's locks, and a highly concentrated plastic explosive housed in the key ring which is activated by a wolf whistle. Boom box that fires a minirocket. Pen that can duplicate what another pen writes by means of a radio receiver. A couch that swallows its victim.

Licence to Kill (1989)

Travel alarm clock packed with explosives. Standard British passport that detonates upon opening. Hasselblad camera that can be taken apart and reconstructed as a gun. Polaroid camera that shoots out a laser beam and takes X-ray photographs. Explosive disguised as toothpaste.

Goldeneye (1995)

Mightier Than the Sword: Q gives Bond a grenade pen in Goldeneye.

Omega Seamaster wristwatch that emits a laser beam and also serves as an arming device. Ballpoint grenade pen activated (or disarmed) by clicking quickly three times. Silver tray that doubles as an X-ray document scanner. Leather belt with 75-foot rappeling cord built into buckle. A piton gun which fires a blade, followed by a high-tension steel cable designed to support body weight and a motorized winch. Leg cast which becomes a missile launcher. Parachute that deploys from the back of Bond's BMW.

Tomorrow Never Dies (1997)

Q masquerades as an Avis agent to deliver Bond's new BMW in Germany.

Dunhill cigarette lighter that becomes a grenade at the flick of a switch. Ericsson cellular phone — scans fingerprints, has laser beam cutter, lock pick, remote control for BMW, 20,000-volt security system/defensive weapon. An updated model of Bond's famous Walther PPK pistol — the P 99. A detonator concealed in Omega watch with ignition system in rotary face. BMW 750iL sedan with voice-assisted navigation system, GPS tracking, fire-resistant and bulletproof body, self-inflating tires, side jets that emit tear gas, rack of 12 heat-seeking rockets concealed in sunroof, metal spike dispenser behind rear bumper, chain cutter hidden under front BMW emblem. The body of the BMW produces a debilitating electric shock to unauthorized personnel trying to gain entry.

Snaps an exasperated Q after Bond navigates the remote-controlled BMW into a high-speed screeching halt mere inches from their feet: "*Grow up, 007.*"

The World Is Not Enough (1999)

Reading glasses that can fire handgun via remote control. Second pair with X-ray capability for detecting concealed weapons. Credit card that conceals a lock-picking device. Bagpipes that fire bullets and double as a flamethrower. Wrist watch with dual lasers and miniature grappling hook with 50 feet of high-tensile microfilament wire, able to support 800 pounds. Protective airbag concealed in ski jacket. Jetpropelled hydroboat that can operate in three inches of water, armed with .30-caliber machine guns, torpedoes, grenade launchers, GPS satellite tracking and radar display, ejector seat, and can dive underwater and function as a submarine for short intervals.

Also brand-new BMW Z8 car — the latest in intercepts, surveillance, and countermeasures. Titanium plating and armor, radar-guided Stinger missiles concealed behind side air vents, and a multitasking heads-up display that includes a thin beam to pick up conversation at a distance and an infrared tracking system. The vehicle is also equipped with a remote control hidden inside the car's ignition key.

Die
Another Day

Monday, January 14th, 2002. 9:05 a.m.

As the slate clapped on Scene 135, Take One, *Die Another Day* officially kicked off production on B Stage at Pinewood Studios. Though that first scene inside Miss Moneypenny's office wasn't terribly elaborate, its significance was quite profound: James Bond had reached a milestone. Not only was *Die Another Day* the 20th James Bond installment for Eon Productions, but 2002 also marked the 40th anniversary of the most successful film franchise in motion picture history. A new century of James Bond had begun.

The occasion prompted former 007 Roger Moore to wax philosophical on the enduring cinema phenomenon. "People always try to analyze the success of the Bond series and what has made them so unique. They're doing the 20th one, and it just keeps going and going. How come? I think audiences go because it's rather like telling a child a good-night fairy tale: he doesn't mind you telling the same story every night, but God help you if you change a word," chuckled Moore at his home in Switzerland. "So audiences are rather like children, in the sense that they don't necessarily want to be surprised; they want to have the formula that they're used to.

Production Office		
Pinewood Studios		
Pinewood Road		
Iver Heath,		

007 🔫

Bucks SLO ONH.

Tel: 01753 659

Fax: 01753 659

"DIE ANOTHER DAY"

EON PRODUCTIONS LTD.

CALL SHEET 85

Mob. on set 2nd AD.Paul Taylor 07774

Loc. Man: Simon Marsden 07831

PRODUCER:	MICHAEL WILSON.	**DATE: TUESDAY 14TH MAY, 2002**
PRODUCER:	BARBARA BROCCOLI.	
DIRECTOR:	LEE TAMAHORI.	**CREW CALL: 08:00am ON SET**
WRITERS:	NEAL PURVIS & ROBERT WADE.	
		Breakfast at.07:30 on "B" Stage
LOCATION:	1. " B " Stage Pinewood Studios	

UNIT NOTE:
NO MOBILE PHONES ON SET PLEASE.
REMINDER TO CREW & EXTRAS. NO PERSONAL PHOTOGRAPHS ARE ALLOWED TO BE TAKEN ON SET!

SC.	·SET / DESCRIPTION	D/N	PGS.	CAST	LOCATION
455A.	INT. GYMNASIUM, ANTONOV KOREA.	N	2/8	3.7.	"B" STAGE
	The girls fight,				
458A.	INT. GYMNASIUM, ANTONOV	N	3/8	3.7.	"B" STAGE
S/BY	*The girls continue to fight with a sword & knife Miranda is Killed.*				

CAST#	CAST & DAY PLAYERS	CHARACTER	D/R	P/UP	M/UP/H/W	ON SET
1.	PIERCE BROSNAN	BOND	F71	08:00	Fencing rehs.	09:00
2.	TOBY STEPHENS	GRAVES	F74	08:00	Fencing rehs.	09:00
3.	HALLE BERRY	JINX	Tr2	06:45	07:30	08:30
7.	ROSAMUND PIKE	MIRANDA	F69	06:15	07:00	08:30

STUNTS		CHARACTER	D/R	P/UP	M/UP/H/W	ON SET
GEORGE AGUILAR		STUNT Co ORDINATOR				08:00
BOB ANDERSON		SWORDSMAN				08:00
AMANDA FOSTER		JINX	F76		07:30	08:30
NIKKI BERWICK		MIRANDA	F76		07:30	08:30
JAMIE BLAKE		JINX GYMNAST	F75		07:30	08:30

STAND-INS/DOUBLES	CHARACTER	M/UP/H/W	ON SET
MONIQUE JOHNSON	JINX	07:30	08:00
PHILLIPA SEXTON	MIRANDA	07:30	08:00

EXTRAS	CHARACTER	M/UP/HAIR	ON SET
2. X MEN	KOREAN GUARDS	07:30	08:30

SPECIAL REQUIREMENTS & INSTRUCTIONS:

ART/PROPS:	As per script to include. All artiste personal props. Jinx' knife, Miranda's sword. Graves brassard & case, Ancient swords, Korean rugs, Gym equipment, Papers to blow around.
BAPTYS:	As per Joss Skottowe: Jinx' pistol, Swords.Guards rubber weapons.
CAMERA / GRIPS:	As per David Tattersall..
COSTUME:	As per Lindy Hemming.
ELECTRICAL:	As per Eddie Knight:
M/UP&HAIR:	As per Paul Engelen & Colin Jamison.

Production call sheets from Die Another Day.

SPECIAL EFFECTS: As per Chris Corbould. Flames/Wind, Book & knife.

SOUND: As per Chris Munro:

STILLS: As per Keith Hamshere.

PUBLICITY: As per Anne Bennett.

PRODUCTION/LOC:

RUSHES VIEWING: Rushes at 13:00 in Theatre 7.

RUSHES: On wrap to production office.

MEDICAL/ADVISOR: Unit nurse Nicky Gregory (on channel 1.) +Paramedics with ambulance req on set at 08:00

FIRE DEPT: As per David Deane. Fire crew req on set 08:00

HEALTH/SAFETY: As per David Deane.

VISUAL EFFECTS: As per Mara Bryan:

CATERING: **CREW**
Breakfast req from 07:30 on "B" Stage
Lunch available from 13:00
Pm Braekat 16:00 for 90 people please

FACILITIES: 1 x 5th wheeler trailer req for Mr. Brosnan on "C" Stage ready by 07:00
1 x Director's trailer req on "C" Stage ready by 07:00
1 x 5th wheeler trailer req for Ms. Berry on "C" Stage ready by 07.00

RADIO CHANNELS:

1. AD's	**(ACTION UNIT CHANNELS FROM 10-16)**
2. AD's Repeater channel	10. AD'S
3. SFX.	11. ART/PROPS
4. SPARE	12. CAMERA/GRIP/CONSTRUCTION
5. STUNTS	13. ELECTRICIANS
6. ART/PROPS	14. SFX
7. LOCATIONS	15. STUNTS
8. ELECTRICIANS	16. REPEATER / SPARE
9. CAMERA/GRIP/S/BYS	

ASSISTANT DIRECTOR
GERRY GAVIGAN.

FENCING REHEARSALS :

For Pierce Brosnan & Toby Stephens with Bob Anderson & Stunt D/bles at 09:00 in Band room time.

ADVANCE SCHEDULE:
WEDNESDAY 15TH MAY, 2002.

SC.	SET / DESCRIPTION	D/N	PGS.	CAST	LOCATION
455A.	INT. GYMNASIUM, ANTONOV	N	2/8	3.7.	"B" STAGE
To comp.	*The girls fight,*				
458A.	INT. GYMNASIUM, ANTONOV	N	3/8	3.7.	"B" STAGE
To comp.	*The girls continue to fight with a sword & knife Miranda is Killed.*				

"And when they stop liking that formula," added Moore, "I guess that's when Bond will die."

Another day, perhaps, but not any time soon. The 007 experience is a tradition firmly embedded in the collective cinema consciousness, a cross-generational fixture that audiences just automatically expect — presume — will be there every two years. So deeply rooted is the assumption that, when the normal two-year period stretched to three between *The World Is Not Enough* and *Die Another Day*, Eon Productions and MGM were inundated with letters, e-mails, and phone calls wondering about Bond's status. But having firmly established 007 as iconic hero for Generation Y (aided in part by the hugely popular James Bond video games), Pierce Brosnan, as well as producers Michael Wilson and Barbara Broccoli, agreed that an extra year could only better serve *Die Another Day*. The naysayers who'd questioned the relevance of a decades-old creature of the Cold War had been proven wrong with the over $1 billion worldwide gross of Brosnan's three Bonds. A much-deserved respite was in order.

"I think this extra time has given us a good little pause," surmised Michael Wilson on the set of *Die Another Day*. "It's been a nice breather for everyone involved." There's no denying the enormous creative and physical demands of mounting a production as mammoth as Bond. Slowing down that merry-go-round after back-to-back-to-back Bonds *Goldeneye*, *Tomorrow Never Dies*, and *The World Is Not Enough* also afforded Brosnan some much-needed time to replenish his personal life. "Oh, it's worked very well for me," smiled Brosnan, who has been nicknamed by Eon as its "Billion-Dollar Bond." "Putting a bit of space between this one has allowed me to take some time off to be with my family. Keely and I got married last year, and I've been able to put my life in order. It's given me time to be with my children, and really, for the first time since all this started, I've had the luxury of allowing myself to do such a thing."

And, by all accounts, *Die Another Day* was worth the wait. The extra 12-month production time allowed them to pull out all the stops in celebration of the 40th-anniversary Bond adventure. "This film has everything that everyone loves about Bond but even more so. . . . I think they've thrown everything but the kitchen sink at it," laughed Brosnan. "But in a good way,"

"Bond is betrayed and gets ousted by his own people," says Brosnan about Die Another Day's many twists. "He has to find his way back and reclaim who he is."

he was quick to add. "I mean, the set pieces in this thing are just *enormous.*"

Under the direction of New Zealand-born filmmaker Lee Tamahori, *Die Another Day* has indeed upped the ante on all the cherished Bond elements. Though the script — penned by *World Is Not Enough* scribes Neal Purvis and Robert Wade — was being kept under especially tight wraps, suffice it to say that *Die Another Day* qualifies as one of the most ambitious Bonds to date. The story kicks off with 007 infiltrating enemy lines by surfing a monstrous wave directly into North Korea, capping that with a spectacular high-speed hovercraft chase through the demilitarized zone between North and South Korea. And that's just the pretitle sequence. The action continues to Hong Kong, then Cuba, and then London, where Bond encounters the mysterious Jinx (played by Halle Berry) and MI6 agent Miranda Frost (Rosamund Pike) — the two women who will play such pivotal yet duplicitous roles in Bond's quest to literally unmask a traitor and prevent a war of catastrophic proportions. Blazing a trail in hot pursuit of principal plotters Gustav Graves (Toby Stephens) and Colonel Moon (Will Yun Lee), Bond treks to the frigid glaciers of Iceland, where he experiences firsthand the power of an ingenious new weapon called Icarus. Barely escaping alive, a bruised, battered, and betrayed Bond must return to Korea for a climactic showdown with his ruthless adversary.

The $100 million-plus production is further distinguished by its tip of the hat to the 40th anniversary, inserting numerous nods and sly in-jokes that link back to previous films and Fleming novels. "I think the connoisseurs of Bond will really enjoy the references to the past," enthused Brosnan. "Whether it's him unzipping out of an outfit and revealing another one — so to speak — or picking up a copy of *Birds of the West Indies*, there are all these great little echoes that fans will love."

"There are a number of winks that have been placed in the film for people who can spot them," offered co-screenwriter Robert Wade. "The fact that at one point in the film Bond assumes the cover of an ornithologist is probably something only few will connect back to Bond's literary origins. Also, the fact that we've incorporated elements of the novel *Moonraker* is there for those who are true aficionados."

But not all the Bond cues are as oblique. For example, the beloved Aston Martin returns in *Die Another Day* as Bond's mode of transportation. The new, top-of-the-line V12 Vanquish — fully loaded by Q Branch, of course — also features an ejector seat, which gets deployed by Bond in a clever twist on its *Goldfinger* debut in the DB5. Also designed to get a rise from audiences is Halle Berry's bikini-clad introduction to James Bond, recalling the breathtaking emergence of Ursula Andress from the sea in *Dr. No*.

"That was pretty daunting," confessed Berry, who braved unusually frigid temperatures to film the sexy sequence in the waters of Cadiz, Spain, which doubles for Cuba in the film. "To think that I'm trying to re-create a cinematic moment that is so beloved — one of the most famous moments not only in all the Bond movies but in cinema history — was a little nerve-wracking. I really tried to put out of my mind the fact we were redoing something that is so indelible in people's minds. I had to just keep telling myself that we were doing something completely new."

"I'm definitely keeping the bikini and the hunting knife as my mementos from Die Another Day," says Halle Berry about her Ursula Andress-inspired swim scene.

Halle Berry with author David Giammarco on set of Die Another Day.

But even for a more seasoned Bond veteran like Brosnan, the 40th-anniversary legacy — which would culminate with the royal premiere of *Die Another Day* on November 18, 2002 — was admittedly weighing heavily during production. "I certainly do feel the heat of the expectations," affirmed Brosnan. "It's my fourth, it's their 20th, it's the anniversary, the royal premiere with Queen Elizabeth. . . . You can just feel this massive, massive machine gearing up. I suppose, if this were my first, it would be absolutely terrifying for any man coming into it. But I've already done three, and they've all been very successful, so you kind of have to take some strength in that. . . . I'm trying not to think about it too much and just have a good time with it all."

Certainly, Toby Stephens relished his chance at cinema history. The acclaimed British stage actor, who hails from the rich theater pedigree of parents Dame Maggie Smith and the late Sir Robert Stephens, was elated by the opportunity to join the distinguished rogues gallery of Bond villains. "I kind of knew I would never get to play James Bond, but being the villain is definitely second best," smiled the 33-year-old Stephens. "There have been times I've found myself reeling after doing a scene with Pierce, because suddenly you think, 'Jesus, I'm actually doing a scene with *James Bond*!'

"When I found out that I got the part, it was just such an enormous buzz, and of course all my friends immediately loathed me — they were intensely jealous," added Stephens with a laugh. "But then one suddenly realizes you're becoming part of this huge franchise, and the responsibility of playing a Bond villain can be quite intimidating. Especially here in

England, where James Bond is part of the national fabric; there are such enormous expectations. Because inevitably the Bond villain is the catalyst for the movie, the engine of the entire thing. And if you don't deliver, then it's really not a satisfying experience for the Bond aficionado. If you don't have a good villain, you don't have a film, really."

Playing the Richard Branson-esque industrialist Gustav Graves, whom Stephens described as "extremely confident, arrogant, incredibly wealthy and full of poise," presented some juicy scenery-chewing as Graves's true identity is slowly revealed. "There are certain plot devices I'm sworn to keep secret, but I can go so far as to say I play an almost schizophrenic character, in that I'm two people in one," added Stephens rather cryptically. "I present this one person — a sort of eco-friendly industrialist who's trying to give back to the world — but I'm also the villain, so there's a whole other agenda there. I present one thing, and I'm actually being another. There's a lot more notes to play with this character, which is not only quite fun for me but equally intriguing for the audience to figure out what's going on."

On day 85 of the *Die Another Day* shoot, Stephens and Brosnan are engaged in extensive fencing rehearsals in preparation for an elaborate duel. "My character is a fencer of Olympic caliber, and he and Bond fight with a whole series of different weapons," explained Stephens, who, though proficient at stage fighting, had been training alongside Brosnan the previous two months in the more specialized skill of épée fencing. "In stage fighting, you sort of aim to miss people, and you make these very flat, buoyant moves because people are sitting way back in theater. But for epée, you've got to make these very small, precise moves that are the real deal. You're actually aiming to hit somebody. So it's been quite a strange leap for me." Stephens jokingly added that the scene was purposely left to the very end of the shoot, "because if one of us gets hurt or dies it's fine 'cause they've already got the film in the can."

Toweling off after the five-hour session, Brosnan expressed satisfaction at his own progress. "I finally felt today that for the first time I wasn't a blundering idiot," he proudly proclaimed, "which can be especially dangerous when you're dealing with foils, sabers, broadswords, and daggers. I've done swordfighting before but nothing to this extent. This is very, very big."

Die Another Day certainly wasn't without production problems. Early on in the shoot, Brosnan and Berry were both injured within weeks of each other, although both actors insisted the media blew the accidents way out of proportion. Headlines proclaimed that shrapnel from an explosion had pierced Halle Berry's cornea, necessitating emergency eye surgery. Berry had to laugh at the reports, explaining simply that some dust had irritated her eye, and, after being given eye drops by the local medic, she was back at work the same day. Though Brosnan's mishap was a little more serious, it didn't warrant the volume of media coverage it received. "I think everybody and his dog heard about my knee injury," he lamented. "What happened was I was running after a hovercraft and slipped when I jumped onto the hovercraft for a fight sequence. It was pretty wet. I had busted the knee while mountain climbing years ago, so when I looked at these X-rays I immediately knew what had happened. I just thought, 'Oh, shit!' But what could I do? It feels horrible stalling a production as big as this, but you couldn't dwell on it, otherwise it will just trip you up. But I ended up only being down for a week, and then I was back at work."

In other words, just another day at the office when you're working on a Bond film, which, by week 16 of the 23-week shoot, director Lee Tamahori was comparing to an exercise in combat survival. "I'm still alive, so it's going very well indeed," he quipped, taking a breather from shooting the explosive end battle sequence aboard a plummeting Russian Antonov cargo plane on Pinewood's B Stage.

Tamahori climbs down the narrow steps from the full-scale mock-up of the interior hull, which is perched atop a massive hydraulic system to jostle the careening aircraft. The colossal wind machines slowly wind down, the pyrotechnics are snuffed out, and the wall of fire is extinguished as the action breaks for 30 minutes between camera setups. The temperature of the entire soundstage has increased by a stifling 30° during the fiery bombardment, and, as Tamahori plops down in his director's chair, he wipes the sweat from his brow and gulps down some bottled water. He admitted this was the only break he's had all day.

"We're still kind of vaguely on schedule, and the end is in sight, which on a Bond movie means is still about seven weeks away," said Tamahori with a wry grin. "I can't help think that I shot my first film in *less* than seven weeks, and we've already been at this for almost six months now. So I'm sure all the other directors, like Michael Apted and Roger Spottiswoode, would agree that Bond is all about being able to go the distance. It really does wring you out like a dishrag. You sort of know that going in, but you don't really fathom how grueling it is until you're in the middle of it."

Since his powerful 1994 directorial debut *Once Were Warriors*, Tamahori has indulged in big-studio films like *The Edge* and *Along Came a Spider* but admitted that Bond presented a "once-in-a-lifetime opportunity" to prove his worth as a filmmaker. "When my agent approached me about it, it literally took me less than five seconds to say 'Yes,'" explained Tamahori, "because I grew up with the Bonds, and it was a much-beloved genre for me. But I never ever thought I'd ever be making one. So when I met with Michael and Barbara, I was very enthusiastic about doing it for several reasons, one of which was the chance to be part of this enormous legacy. But secondly, it would give me the opportunity to show that I could do something outside of the filmmaking pigeonhole that people tend to put you in, which is that of a violent R-18 Kiwi director. You get put into a box. And I knew I could do this just as well as anybody, but nobody knows that 'till you actually do one. Of course, this is a risk to the extreme because there's so much more money at stake. The Bonds are definitely the high end of the game, and this one in particular is probably the biggest and most expensive."

Michael Wilson said he entrusted Tamahori to the 40th-anniversary Bond after viewing *Once Were Warriors*, "which showed he had strong storytelling ability and unique visual sense." Distinguishing his vision is "a lot of edginess and vitality," continued Wilson. "He had done three Hollywood pictures, so we knew he could cope with big actors and a big set. And he works very well with our team. Works very well with the actors. I know Pierce likes Lee a lot, and that helps. There's a good relationship there, and he trusts him. We're very pleased."

Brosnan was perhaps more blunt in describing Tamahori: "He's mad. He's a mad hare . . . absolutely bloody barking *mad*!" Brosnan chuckled. "But I'm very fond of him indeed. We've never had a schedule, we've never known where we're going, so you always feel like you've been behind the

"My contract is up with Die Another Day. But if they ask me, yes. I'd love to do another one,"
says Pierce Brosnan about Bond 21.

eight-ball. And that's a scary place to be when you have a leviathan like this to get through. But everybody's settled down, and you realize he definitely has his own style of doing it. And I have to say, it's coming in as a very muscular, different film from the others."

Tamahori elaborated on his mandate for *Die Another Day*: "There's a frivolous nature to Bond movies, but I've always felt that they needed to be treated as thrillers," he explained. "They started off as spy thrillers, but then through the Roger Moore years they stopped being thrillers and became kind of these campy classics of special effects and big stunts. When they swung around in the '90s and Pierce came on board, I think Martin [Campbell] did an exceptional job with *Goldeneye* in bringing it back to that kind of smart thriller Bond. Martin certainly set the benchmark for smartening the series up, which everybody's followed. So coming into this, I was determined to bring back that hard-edged reality to kind of a frivolous genre in a way.

"We've still got the double entendres, we've still got the girls, the gadgets, the cars — we've still got to deal with all that. But at the same time, this is a psychological thriller to me. I want to keep everything sharp. I can't stand it in movies when the logic of the plot doesn't work. So I've spent the last year on this, reworking every logical point of the story so that there aren't these giant holes you can drive a truck through. And I think audiences always appreciate that — that there's a sense of logic to what's going on, no matter how absurd the villain is. I mean, there's always someone trying to take over the world in a Bond movie — it becomes virtually unassailable on that level. And I dare say that people will still find some of this film highly amusing in parts because of some of the action and some of the outrageous situations. But at other times, we go into some pretty tough stuff in this, which you haven't seen Bond do for quite a while."

Exploring the darker recesses of Bond's psyche proved especially appealing to Brosnan, who had been pushing since *Goldeneye* for a deeper examination of the character that Fleming had so skillfully dissected on the printed page. "I think you see a more desperate character this time out," revealed Brosnan. "You see Bond as this renegade, this man who's suddenly completely out of his environment. You've never seen him so vulnerable and broken, as it were, because he's captured and tortured in the beginning of the movie. He's outside of all encampments, so to speak, and he's trying to get his identity back."

Screenwriters Neal Purvis and Robert Wade acknowledged that *Die Another Day* presents notable growth in the character, "because not only from the audience's point of view, but also from the actor's point of view, it's got to be interesting," remarked Purvis during midafternoon punch-ups of the film's last scene. "Pierce doesn't just want to be running around shooting guns the whole film. . . . It would have been quite unthinkable doing a story line like this say seven movies into the series, but we're at the 20th now, and I think you need to push it further to make it feel like it's evolving. . . ."

"But also you can't break the barriers of Bond's world too much," added Wade, "because then you enter into another genre altogether, and suddenly it's not a Bond film anymore."

Brosnan agreed. "It still has to have all the ingredients that you love, all the signposts, all the emblems that make Bond *Bond*. You can't take them away. But I think we've nailed a nice balance here. We have John Cleese in top form, Judi Dench, who is brilliant, and then you have Toby Stephens, who's got such a complex character to play; it's such a delicious role for him."

When talk turned to Halle Berry, Brosnan couldn't help wax rapturous about his Oscar-winning costar. "What an absolutely wonderful person. She's just such a cool lady and lovely girl," he smiled. "And I have to say she's been great to do the love scenes with because she's so loose; she's got a great sense of herself and her whole body, so it makes it easy and fun, most of all. But what a phenomenal actress. Watching her win the Academy Award, I think every man and woman on this set was completely behind her, and we all stood with her that night."

That Berry was actually *standing* that night at the Oscar podium was a feat in itself. When the *Monster's Ball* promotional campaign started heating up, 33-year-old Berry suddenly found herself having to jet back and forth between London and Los Angeles every week for appearances and awards as *Monster's Ball* was steadily gaining momentum in the critical community. The first two months of shooting *Die Another Day* turned into one long sleep-deprived blur for Berry, which all culminated in her tearful acceptance speech at the Academy Awards. "Luckily, the Bond people here worked very hard to let me out for everything," explained Berry. "They said, 'If you want to do it, we'll work it out.' So I did it, but it was really tough on me. Most days it was literally flying back from L.A. and going straight from the airport to the set because it was just that tight to get back to do all the things I had to shoot. I was spent. Two days after the Oscars, I was right back here working, so I really didn't even get a chance for it to soak in or enjoy it. But in a way, that was probably good for me, because it didn't get too heady or trippy. . . . I was right back to what I do for a living."

Reflecting back on that momentous March evening, a smile slowly spreads across Berry's face. "How cool is it getting an Oscar and being in a

Bond film at the same time?" she beams. "It all still feels a little surreal." Relaxing in her trailer between filming scenes aboard the crashing cargo plane, Berry admitted she was never a fan of action films growing up but was always drawn towards the 007 films. "I always loved the women in the Bond movies — they were images of such beauty to me and so sexy," she said. "And over the years, they've evolved, and it feels really good to be part of this new era. They're a lot more intelligent and better matches for Bond. Both intellectually and physically, they've really started to change." Though she couldn't reveal too much about her character — "because I've been sworn to secrecy" — Berry did describe the mysterious Jinx as being "very much the female Bond. She kind of does what he does — differently of course — but she's very smart and really tough. She can go toe-to-toe with man or woman." And with a rather coy smile, Berry added that "Jinx has a lot of skills that you discover as the movie goes along. . . . They're great surprises for the audience."

But Tamahori readily admits that surprising today's CGI and video-game-weaned audiences has become a tall order. "You have to work that much harder because in some respects this is a very old genre . . . the oldest genre of all," he conceded. "It's been around a long time, like a bunch of good leather-bound books sitting on a book case. So you have to go that extra mile to convince a much younger audience — who's been growing up on the Austin Powers parodies and computer-designed comic book films — to actually see Bond as an acceptable action picture for their peer group. It's not a problem for my age group or your age group, because we grew up on this stuff, and we'll always go and see Bond. But it's a trickier thing for the younger kids today."

As a result, Michael Wilson has had to face numerous attempts to shake up the Bond formula, from de-aging the character to turning 007 into an American. But Wilson has always stood his ground. "I think this particular regime at the studio understands the importance of Bond being British and understanding how huge the international audience is," Wilson explained. "But there's always this desire in Hollywood to make things that appeal very strongly to Americans. We try to appeal to everyone, but as far as Bond we believe very strongly in the integrity of the character, and we have to maintain that. Barbara and I will always continue to produce the Bond films in the same way and, hopefully, repeat the success of *Goldeneye*, *Tomorrow Never Dies*, and *The World Is Not Enough* as the series continues."

Pierce Brosnan with author David Giammarco on set of Die Another Day in summer 2002.

On the eve of his 49th birthday, Brosnan was ruminating about his future as James Bond on the set of *Die Another Day*. He confirmed that, if asked, he would definitely return for a fifth time to the role that's played such a pivotal part in his life. But whether he would match Roger Moore's record of seven Bond films was another story. "Roger didn't have to jump around as much as I do," Brosnan chuckled. "Roger had his own style of Bond."

Still, Brosnan doesn't rule anything out when it comes to James Bond. He learned that lesson a long time ago. "I'm very proud of what I've accomplished. Ownership of the character is difficult because of the talented men who have gone before me. But I feel like the character is mine now. You're not looking over your shoulder anymore; it feels very comfortable to me. It's not like *Goldeneye*. I've done it three times now, and they've all been successful. We'll see what happens with the fourth one.

"But you hear the off-noises, the digs, the swipes, and you just have to ignore that and look to the positive and to the people that love this," continued Brosnan. "You have to think about the audience that is going to sit there at Leicester Square, and you're going to sit there with your family, so you better pay attention to every second of the film to make sure it's the absolute best it can be. I have this real kind of inner consciousness, which is fiercely protective of myself, the work, and the legacy."

12

Ice Spy: Crafting The Chilling Thrills of Die Another Day

The weather is unusually balmy on this May afternoon at Pinewood Studios, but inside the 007 soundstage temperatures are downright frigid. Or at least they appear that way.

The largest stage in Europe seems to have been frozen into the colossal Ice Palace set, which in *Die Another Day* serves as Icelandic headquarters of villain Gustav Graves. Designed by 007 veteran Peter Lamont, the Ice Palace is a breathtaking sight to behold. The majestic edifice — shimmering in brilliant shades of blues and turquoise under the studio lights — is a frosty fortress carved out of solid ice. Glistening diamond chandeliers tower over it, and ornate columns and imposing icicles loom overhead. Circular crystalline ramps wind around the perimeter of the multileveled monolith, which also boasts (of course) an elevator. The Ice Palace is an obvious throwback to the fantastical and futuristic set designs of longtime Bond visionary Ken Adam — a fitting homage in a film commemorating 40 years of cinematic Bonds. "Graves has built this enormous ice palace to, in effect, announce to the world his second son Icarus," explained production designer Peter Lamont. "But, of course, Bond gets involved as usual and comes into the Ice Palace to mess up his plans."

But this being a movie set, the icy gleam is nothing more than a remarkable facade. "The Ice Palace was a very massive undertaking and also my most difficult," acknowledged Lamont, who earned an Oscar for his involvement with another rather large chunk of ice in James Cameron's 1997 *Titanic*. "Believe it or not, the biggest challenge has been getting the Ice Palace to look like real ice. You can't use real ice because you'd have to have a refrigerated studio. Even then, once you turn all the studio lights on, the temperature will rise above the freezing point, and it will immediately melt. So we had to construct it all in clear plastics, with structural steel under everything holding it all up. For the walls and ceiling, we utilized a glazing process over a special plastic that we use for breakaway glass. To get the desired fractured look of the ice, we crunched up clear plastic and then heated it in small sections, finishing it all off with a distinctive icy glitter. It's a very time-consuming process.

"And of course this has been more than simply designing a set that looks good on film," added the soft-spoken Lamont. "Everything had to be examined by structural engineers because the upper levels of the set have to be strong enough to support the weight of several tons of cars chasing each other at high speed. It's quite a demanding set, but I'm pretty happy with the realism we've created."

Handy instructions for building your own ice palace, but if you want to *destroy* one the man you should call is Vic Armstrong. The action unit director, who began his association with the Bond films as stuntman in 1967 on *You Only Live Twice*, has distinguished himself as cinema's preeminent choreographer of organized chaos. Today, Armstrong is in the midst of shooting the weeks-long process of demolishing the stately Ice Palace as Bond's Aston Martin is chased by Graves's henchman Zao in his Jaguar XKR. Heightening the perilous pursuit is the furious meltdown of the Ice Palace which threatens to engulf the careening vehicles.

As the countdown to the next shot begins, Armstrong warns that things may get a little wet as we take our places on the second level overlooking the action. The Aston Martin and the Jag are revving on their marks. A hush falls over the crew. The cameras turn over. Audio cues are exchanged and

Partial interior of the Peter Lamont-designed Ice Palace set. 007 will eventually destroy it, thanks mostly to Action Director Vic Armstrong.

Swan Dive: Bond and Miranda Frost (Rosamund Pike). "It isn't easy doing love scenes," says Pike, "but Pierce really put me at ease by telling me about some of his first experiences doing love scenes in other movies . . . kind of someone's history of bad sex."

switches are flicked. Suddenly, a furious tidal wave of water is unleashed, and hundreds of thousands of gallons thunder past us, raging down the ramps and smashing onto the ground floor. Armstrong yells "Action!" and the cars roar off. Within seconds, the Jaguar fires a pyrotechnic rocket that blazes past us and detonates in a fiery shower on the far side of the Ice Palace. Armstrong yells "Cut!" and immediately the deluge starts dissipating, and the flooded set is quickly and efficiently drained through a network of pipes and tunnels hidden underneath the set. The whole sequence lasted less than a minute, and we got more than damp in the process. But experiencing firsthand spectacular high-octane Bond action like this was far more thrilling than any Disneyland ride.

As the crew prepares to repeat the entire process for the next shot, Armstrong explained the context of the stunt. "Bond's Aston Martin has crashed into the Ice Palace with the Jaguar in pursuit. They begin sliding around the interiors, whizzing around the narrow corridors and up and down the ramps, bouncing off the walls and smashing ice pillars, exchanging a few rockets and blowing down the ice overhangs." Over the next few weeks, Armstrong will finish directing the climax of the stunt. "What ends up happening is the Aston Martin broadsides across the balcony, about 30 feet up. The Jaguar comes around the corner and sees him stuck. After all the high-tech stuff, Zao decides, 'Right — we'll resort to basics.' He has two prongs on the front of his Jag — like ramming bars — and he backs up and goes full throttle into ramming mode. He really wants to delight in just nailing Bond mano-a-mano. As he races toward him, Bond fires one last gizmo, which puts out these longer and bigger spikes on his tires and he reverses back up the rubble of the ice wall. The Jaguar overshoots, smashes through the balcony, and soars about 25 feet off into the air. He hits that column in the center of the Ice Palace and crashes down through the ice and sinks into the water."

Far easier said than done. But I caught up again with Armstrong a month later, and he was enthusiastic with the progress they had made. He'd just finished shooting exteriors of the stunt on the back lot at Pinewood, which has been transformed into the barren snowcapped terrain of Iceland. The impressive outdoor set sprawls across acres of ground and features

Bond and Miranda Frost about to heat up the Ice Palace.

sculpted ice peaks and canyons, the shell of the mammoth Ice Palace, and several tons of fake snow which blanket the entire expanse. "Last week we finished the exterior shots of the Aston Martin bursting into the Ice Palace, which involved hitting two skidoos and smashing them up in the air," explained Armstrong. "And then yesterday we completed the Aston Martin escape, which involves a soaring 60-foot-long jump out of the Ice Palace, landing in a heap of snow.

"And we didn't even damage the car too badly, which I'm pretty happy about," added Armstrong with a chuckle.

But his proudest accomplishment is what Armstrong considers the *pièce de résistance* of the film's many action sequences. In his trailer just off set, Armstrong showed me a rough video assemblage of raw footage shot on location in Iceland two months previously. It's the full-bore chase between the Aston Martin and the Jaguar across the vast Joekulsarlon lagoon in southeast Iceland. The panorama of jagged icebergs and mirrored-sheen frozen lake ranks as one of the most breathtaking and dramatic backdrops for a car chase ever captured on film. Although the jaw-dropping sequence lasts only about five minutes on screen, it took months of painstaking preparation with a crew of nearly 200 in some of the harshest conditions on the planet. However, the ambitious plans nearly disintegrated when freak weather systems wreaked havoc in Iceland. The Bond crew was literally skating on thin ice.

"It was so volatile because we were essentially in the middle of the Atlantic at the end of the largest glacier in Europe," explained Armstrong.

"Every day you woke up, you never knew if it was going to be raining or snowing. We actually didn't decide to go until two weeks before, because although we had been planning to shoot there the lake just wasn't freezing over. And the cars are two tons each, plus you add in the insert car, plus your cameras, cranes, 60 or 70 people, and all the support vehicles, and you're looking at a lot of weight on the ice. So I flew up to Alaska and checked out some ice lakes there, and they were indeed frozen, but they all had snow on them, and I wanted a sort of glacial glass effect."

Then Armstrong's luck suddenly changed. "They called me from Iceland and said, 'It's starting to freeze, [and] we've got about eight or nine inches of ice now.' But we still needed at least a foot of ice to support the cars and crew." So Armstrong decided to tamper with Mother Nature. To strengthen the ice, the Bond crew erected a massive dam at the mouth of the inlet to keep out the warmer sea water. "We put up this barrier, which accelerated the icing-up progress," said Armstrong, "but you still have tidal effects. So it was very unique looking with all these icebergs floating around in this lake every which way with the winds blowing."

Armstrong was further blessed by a sudden retreat of the heavy cloud cover as an unexpected golden glow blanketed the stark desolation. "It's never been sunny for more than four days in Iceland and certainly not in the winter. But when the lake finally froze over, we suddenly got this marvelous sunshine which melted all the snow off the icebergs, revealing that vivid blue," he explained, pointing out tell-tale shots playing on the monitor. "So we decided to shoot the sequence in sunlight, because it's obviously so much more beautiful and provides greater definition. But if the weather did change, we would have been stymied. So we shot it all in sequence, just in case that happened, although we were praying the whole time that the weather would hold, and fortunately it did. And the weird thing was that the next day after we finished we wouldn't have been able to get on that lake anymore. It was all melting. There was no way we could have gotten those cars out there again. So we were quite amazingly lucky.

"And what you're seeing now is not even a true picture of the many shades of blue of those icebergs," enthused Armstrong as a dazzling helicopter shot came on screen. "To behold the sights of this magnificent

Ice Spy: Crafting the Chilling Thrills of Die Another Day

Ice, Ice, Baby: "It could've been a one-way ticket to the bottom," says Chris Corbould about shooting on this glacial lake.

snowscape was absolutely stunning. I've shot all over the world, but shooting on that glacier was unlike anything I've ever done. Once the lab finishes grading the footage, it will look absolutely phenomenal."

As the roughly edited footage continued unspooling, it was apparent that Armstrong had orchestrated the action like a maestro of mayhem. It's more balletic than ballistic, even though the two fully loaded vehicles are exchanging more gunfire than a small army. "I always do a beat sheet, which is all the moments in the chase and the length and the tempo," explained Armstrong, who also devised the action sequences for the Indiana Jones movies. "I draw up a graph very much like a piece of music, with highs, lows, and lulls in order to get the rhythm right. The most important thing in directing an action sequence is rhythm. It has to flow with impeccable timing."

Working hand in frozen glove with Armstrong was Chris Corbould, who, as special effects supervisor, faced the unique task of adapting the Aston Martin V12 Vanquish and Jaguar XKR for the precarious shooting conditions. "When the sequence first came up, it was just a car chase, and no one thought too much about it," shrugged Corbould, who marked his 10th tour of duty with Bond on *Die Another Day*. "But then they introduced this new element about it being on this ice lake, and suddenly it meant having to really rethink everything. You're now quite concerned with pinpoint accuracy because you've got these huge glaciers, with pieces falling off, and you're zigzagging in amongst these obstacles on sheer ice.

"So we made the decision to make four-wheel-drive versions, and, with the help of Aston Martin and Jaguar, they supplied us cars which had either been damaged slightly or pulled off the production line. We then proceeded to cut the front ends off and put in new engines and new systems to make them into four-wheel drives. And in the end, the cars had the choice of four-wheel drive, two-wheel drive, and all sorts of other options."

Of greater concern to Corbould was whether the ice could actually withstand the weight of his revamped two-ton (2,000 kg) cars. "It's a very deep lake — about 400 meters (1,300 ft) — so it could've been a one-way ticket to the bottom," Corbould elaborated. "It was a really nerve-wracking moment when we drove them out for the first time. If you broke through,

Working on the outside, Q (John Cleese) delivers Bond's new Aston Martin V12 Vanquish in an unconventional locale: London's Underground.

you wouldn't have to worry about drowning because you'd freeze to death before you ever reached bottom." To help minimize the danger, Corbould rigged each car with some real life-saving Bondian gadgets. "We put these huge inflation bags in each car, so that if someone did go through the ice you just pulled this lever to deploy the floatation device. And all of us also wore immersion suits at all times, so if one of us did go through you could last a bit longer. It was very safety-oriented. It wasn't all of us just going out on this glacial lake and driving around at 100 miles an hour and hoping for the best. It was a much more complicated risk. Everything had to be calculated."

But the icing on the cake for Corbould was flaunting the Aston Martin's technical flourishes he outfitted in tribute to *Goldfinger*. "We're all pretty pleased that the Aston's back," smiled Corbould, who got his start with the

"We made 16 of the hovercrafts, upgraded the engines, and then handed them over to the stunt guys . . . who proceeded to wreck them for the next month," says Chris Corbould about 007's harrowing escape across the North-South Korea border.

Bond series as a special effects technician on *The Spy Who Loved Me.* "We had a fun relationship with BMW for the last few films, and they certainly did us proud with all the resources at our disposal. But I think deep down we've all got a soft spot for the Aston Martin. There's a real tradition and heritage with Bond." Besides putting a new spin on the infamous ejector seat as well as the front-bumper machine guns, Corbould went a few steps further with "motion-detecting shotguns that come out of the grilles on the bonnet [hood] and lots of these other surprises that pop out of nowhere." Ditto for Zao's Jaguar, which features "a rack of mortar bombs with guns that come out and sort of pick out like clay pigeons." Corbould admitted that conceiving new and innovative Bond gadgets is always a feat, but the real challenge is not getting too carried away. "There's only so many gadgets you can use without it getting a bit hokey," he acknowledged.

"One of the great things about *Die Another Day* is that not only have you got Bond with his gadgets, but you've got the villain with his gadgets too," he continued. "So it's very much a cat-and-mouse thing where they've both got competing gadgets. And I can't remember that happening in any previous Bond, where they've gone match for match. In the end, it comes down to how clever Bond is with his car, rather than its sheer fire power."

Delivering those requisite crowd-pleasing gizmos to Bond is John

Cleese, who found himself promoted from R to Q in *Die Another Day* after the unexpected death of the much-beloved Desmond Llewelyn. "I had just talked to him two weeks before the accident," said Cleese, who was clearly shaken by the tragic news. "Desmond had been in such high spirits and determined to make as many more Bond films as he was able to. He was such a wonderful man. Of course, I wasn't brought in to replace Desmond but to support him. We had even struck a deal: I was 60 when I started, and Desmond was 80, so we agreed to work together until he was 100, by which point I'd have enough experience to take over."

Now that he's advanced in rank, Cleese admitted that he's secretly determined to usurp the power structure at MI6 by "working my way up the alphabet until I get to *L*, at which point I can sack Judi Dench!" he joked.

Back in the Art Department, Peter Lamont beamed with pride as he offered further glimpses into some of *Die Another Day*'s well-guarded secrets, from the elaborate designs of Graves's Eden Project-like Biodome to the nerve-shredding hovercraft chase from the film's pretitle sequence. At 72, Lamont still has a childlike enthusiasm for the world he's been playing in for 38 years running. "It's a business that keeps you young and keeps you on your toes," Lamont smiled. "It's amazing what can be accomplished with these films, and the nice thing is we can still do it in the traditional way. Bond just opens up so many doors. If you say you're with James Bond, people really bend over backwards to help you. So it's quite exciting to know how much people still love these films and trying to exceed those expectations each time out."

Fellow series stalwart Vic Armstrong echoed those sentiments. "You know, this year I had the choice of four films to work on, including *Terminator 3*. But I didn't even have to think about it: it was going to be Bond. I've got a great affinity for it. I go way back with the whole family. I love Barbara and Michael and all the people involved and have a great crew around me. I feel I've contributed to it since 1966, and I'm very proud to have become synonymous with Bond. I love the challenges we face coming up with something original and exciting that won't disappoint. I have a great affinity for my audience and don't ever want to let them down or let down the Bond legacy."

c.1

Bibliography

Bibliography

All interviews contained in this book are with the author, spanning from 1983 to 2002. Copyright © David M. Giammarco, 2002.

Other sources

Lycett, Andrew, *Ian Fleming* (Weidenfeld & Nicolson, 1995)
Pearson, John, *The Life Of Ian Fleming* (Jonathan Cape, 1966)
Rubin, Steven Jay, *The James Bond Encyclopedia* (Contemporary Books, 1995)
Rubin, Steven Jay, *The James Bond Films* (Arlington House, 1981)
Turner, Adrian, *Goldfinger* (Bloomsbury Books, 1998)

Goldeneye, screenplay, storyboards, and production breakdown (Eon Productions, 1995)
Tomorrow Never Dies, screenplay, storyboards, and production breakdown (Eon Productions, 1997)
The World Is Not Enough, screenplay, storyboards, and production breakdown (Eon Productions, 1999)
Die Another Day, screenplay, storyboards, and production breakdown (Eon Productions, 2002)

Recommended Reading

Adam, Ken. *James Bond, Berlin, Hollywood.* (Nicolai, 2002)
Glen, John, *For My Eyes Only.* (BT Batsford, 2001)

IDEC   2002

James Bond will return . . .